THE LITERATURE OF JOURNALISM
✦ ✦ ✦
Text and Context

THE LITERATURE OF JOURNALISM

❖ ❖ ❖

Text and Context

R. THOMAS BERNER

The Pennsylvania State University

STRATA PUBLISHING, INC.

State College, Pennsylvania

9 8 7 6 5 4 3 2 1

Published by:
Strata Publishing, Inc.
P.O. 1303
State College, PA 16804

telephone: 1-814-234-8545
fax: 1-814-238-7222

http://www.stratapub.com

Library of Congress Cataloging-in-Publication Data

The literature of journalism : text and context / [compiled by] R. Thomas Berner. p. cm.
Anthology of excerpts from eighteen works.
Includes bibliographical references (p.) and index.
Contents: The road to Wigan Pier / George Orwell — Let us now praise famous men / James Agee — Hiroshima / John Hersey — Reporting / Lillian Ross — The story of a shipwrecked sailor / Gabriel García Márquez — The earl of Louisiana / A.J. Liebling — The autobiography of Malcolm X / Alex Haley — A mother in history / Jean Stafford — In cold blood / Truman Capote — Hell's Angels / Hunter Thompson — Slouching towards Bethlehem / Joan Didion — The onion field / Joseph Wambaugh — A welfare mother / Susan Sheehan — Friendly fire / C.D.B. Bryan —Dispatches / Michael Herr — The right stuff / Tom Wolfe — The soul of a new machine / Tracy Kidder — The great China earthquake / Qian Gang.
ISBN 1-891136-00-3
1. Reportage literature. 2. Prose literature. I. Berner, R. Thomas.
PN3377.5.R45L58 1999
082—DC21   98-21190
                                                                              CIP

Text and cover design by Leon Bolognese & Associates, Inc.
Printed and bound in the United States by Data Reproductions Corporation.

Credits and acknowledgments appear on pages vii and viii and on this page by reference.

*This book is dedicated to my students in the
China School of Journalism who allowed me to be
part of their lives in the spring of 1994.
They are:
Chen Yu, Gu Ming, Huang Tianbo, Li Xiaohong,
Ma Zhan, Lin Zhishen, Ren Xianfang, Tao Wenge,
Tang Minchu, Tan Guoqi, Tan Xinmu, Quan Lan,
Zhu Xiaofei, Yuan Li, and Wang Xiangjiang.*

托马斯·伯纳

Credits and Acknowledgments

The origins of Chapter 14 can be traced to my essay on C. D. B. Bryan in
Thomas B. Connery, ed., *A Sourcebook of American Literary Journalism*
(Westport, Conn.: Greenwood, 1992) and to my essay in Arthur J. Kaul, ed.,
Dictionary of Literary Biography, American Literary Journalists, 1945–1995,
(Detroit, Mich.: Gale Research, 1997).

Portions of Chapter 18 were presented by the author at the Fifth Congress
and International Conference on Literature and Cultural Dialogue at
North-East Normal University, Changchun, Jilin Province, People's Republic
of China, August 1–5, 1996.

Contents

Preface

This book is intended to be used in courses that are concerned with the study of good writing, such as courses on the literature of journalism, literary journalism, non-fiction writing, feature writing, or writing analysis.

The book grew out of my efforts to show my students some of the best nonfiction of the twentieth century in its social, historical, and journalistic context. I wanted my students to understand that, while the pieces are worth reading in and of themselves, they were not written in a vacuum. I wanted them to see that important works are inspired by social conditions, shaped by historical circumstances, and influenced by other writers.

The Literature of Journalism: Text and Context is built around books that represent the evolution of journalism in the twentieth century and, coincidentally, major historical events or movements of that era, such as the Great Depression, the rise of information technology, the Vietnam war, and the drug culture. I have focused on eighteen works that characterize that evolution and have presented these works in their contexts.

The commentary that accompanies each excerpt helps set the piece in history. It describes the social or historical context that inspired the work, how it came to be published, its critical reception when it was first published, how it has come to be viewed with the passage of time, and how it influenced and was influenced by other writers. In writing the commentaries, I have drawn extensively on a variety of sources, including critical reviews and academic essays that may, in themselves, provide additional resources for anyone who wants to dig more deeply into a particular piece.

FEATURES OF THE BOOK

Several specific features of the book illustrate my general approach.

The excerpts are from works that, collectively, represent the evolution of nonfiction writing in the twentieth century. No doubt I could have included more or chosen others, but I felt these were good examples of the points I wanted to make and, collectively, would provide a starting point for teachers and students of the literature of journalism. One can read John Hersey's *Hiroshima* and see the seeds of social documentarians such as Tom Wolfe and Tracy Kidder. Similarly, the stylistic experimentation in James Agee's *Let Us Now Praise Famous Men* is also evident (albeit muted) in Michael Herr's *Dispatches*.

The specific excerpts from the works reflect major points made in the commentary. The excerpt from *The Autobiography of Malcolm X,* for example, focuses on Malcolm X talking about his mother's troubled life after the death of her husband and Malcolm X's father, and the commentary notes how Alex Haley used a question about Malcolm X's mother to get Malcolm X to talk more freely. The excerpt from *The Earl of Louisiana* shows A. J. Liebling using his trademark interview trick to get not only an interview with Earl Long, but dinner and an evening's worth of insight. The commentary provides more history on how Liebling decided to ask the question he did. Some critics noted that Truman Capote cut back and forth in *In Cold Blood* the way a film does, and the excerpt gives a flavor of that.

The commentary in each chapter also explains the social and historical context for the works studied. The background on *Hiroshima*, written for a publication in the United States about people who were essentially "the enemy" the year before, is illuminated in the commentary. The commentary also explains why George Orwell's *Road to Wigan Pier* and Gabriel García Márquez's *Story of a Shipwrecked Sailor* were acts of subversion.

The commentary also explains how each work came to be written. For example, the commentary in Chapter 10 explains how Hunter Thompson became interested in the Hell's Angels and how a magazine piece led to his book. The commentary in Chapter 18 provides background on how Qian Gang came to write *The Great China Earthquake.*

The commentary discusses how a single writer evolves. *The Right Stuff*, by Tom Wolfe, certainly stands on its own, for example, but when the book is presented in the context of his earlier New Journalism, especially *The Electric Kool-Aid Acid Test*, the modern reader can appreciate the evolution of Wolfe's style.

The commentary explains how writers influence each other. Qian Gang, for example, acknowledged a debt to John Hersey. C. D. B. Bryan and Joseph Wambaugh cited Truman Capote's influence. Truman Capote mined Lillian Ross's memory on her reportage and writing technique for *Picture*.

Finally, the commentary discusses how the work was initially reviewed and, in some cases, how it is regarded now. That information provides a greater understanding of the nonfiction world at that time. For example, when Truman Capote produced what he called a "nonfiction novel" and turned the publication of *In Cold Blood* into a media event, some reviews focused more on Capote's misnomer and his ego than on what he had accomplished. Not all reviewers reacted kindly to Capote's "new" form, but today it is a standard. I discuss why *Let Us Now Praise Famous Men* was not well received when it was first published, but became, upon republication, a classic.

Although the chapters have been written to stand alone, the commentary brings out connections among them. Readers can discover their own links and create their own knowledge about the literature of journalism. I have used twelve of the eighteen essays in this book in my literature of journalism course, asking students to read the essays before reading a particular book, and each week students would come up with yet another link or make a comparison based on their own reading lists. I hope that this book, with its combination of features, will serve as an introduction to the study of good journalism in its social, historical, and journalistic context.

Speaking of links, I'm always available to anyone to discuss the literature of journalism. I make that offer because my research on the subject is ongoing. Anyone can reach me via e-mail at bx2@psu.edu. And since I use the web to post new or updated resources for all of my courses, anyone can get a current look by going to www.psu.edu and searching for me by my name.

ACKNOWLEDGMENTS

Many people deserve my heartfelt thanks for helping me with this book. Let me first thank Jeaneen Aldridge, who as a dutiful graduate assistant in 1990 dug out numerous reviews and articles on many of the authors who formed the nucleus of my first undergraduate seminar in the literature of journalism. Five years later, another graduate student, Sun Tao, would be extremely helpful in tracking down Qian Gang, interviewing him and translating letters from him. I also got help on Qian Gang from Thomas E. Moran, who sent me a copy of his dissertation on Chinese writers. Betsy Hall, the faculty secretary in my college, converted Moran's diskette to my word-processing program, leaning on an uncle to assist her when her office software proved not up to the task. Subsequent research help came from another graduate assistant, Karen L. Schlag, who as this book was coming together would drop research she was doing for me on a course and head to the library to find yet one more article. Last-minute invaluable service also came from John Yingling, who is in charge of reprography in my college.

I got a wonderful tip on Alex Haley from Bernard Asbell, the author of several nonfiction works. Bernie directed me to Sam Vaughan, an editor at large at Random House, who set up an interview with Lisa Drew, vice president and publisher, Lisa Drew Books. Their efforts show in the chapter on Alex Haley.

Over the years I learned a lot about the literature of journalism from the late James E. Murphy, Norman Sims, Jon Franklin, Daniel W. Pfaff, Peter Parisi, Roy Peter Clark, Don Fry, Thomas B. Connery, Arthur J. Kaul, Ben Yagoda, and Barbara Lounsberry. They have written or edited their own books or moderated discussions that have informed my writing not only in this book, but in other research and writing that I've done. On the practical side, I've leaned heavily on *Book Review Digest*, *Contemporary Authors*, and related publications. Nexis (as in Lexis/Nexis) was also a great research tool.

I have yet to write a book or article that was not improved through the blind review process. So let me salute here the professors who took the time to review my prospectus, sample chapters, and finally the entire manuscript. My salute to David Abrahamson, Northwestern University; Paul G. Ashdown,

University of Tennessee; Thomas B. Connery, University of St. Thomas; Thomas H. Foote, Evergreen State College; John Gaterud, Mankato State University; Carolyn B. Matalene, University of South Carolina; Nancy Roberts, University of Minnesota; Patsy G. Watkins, University of Arkansas; and Jan Whitt, University of Colorado at Boulder.

I also want to thank Sharon Barrett, Mark Masse, Melinda Wilkins, David Hayes, Carolyn Wells Kraus, Paul Many, Cathy Mitchell, and Ed Cray. When I first discussed the idea for a book, my publisher suggested I find out what interest there was. I sent queries to various journalism lists on the Internet and the people noted here were some of the respondents. Others are credited earlier. General appreciation also to the members of WriterL whose musings inform my thinking.

I've said it before, but no writer is above the pencil and so I gladly offer my deepest appreciation to Sally A. Heffentreyer for copy editing my manuscript. Copy editors don't get credit, only blame, so let me take blanket blame for any mistakes in this book and advise all readers that Sally saved me countless times. Sadly, as this book was nearing completion, we both lost our aging golden retrievers, Buck and Bailey.

I am deeply grateful to my publisher, Kathleen Domenig. One of my editors at Holt, Rinehart and Winston nearly two decades ago, she went on to become a publisher. I can't tell you how many times a publishing representative would visit me at Penn State and ask whether I had any ideas for a book. I'd pitch this book and watch as their eyes glazed over; after all, I was not pitching a book for a mass market and they quickly lost interest. But Kathleen, because she is a niche publisher, was not only interested, she was downright imperative.

Finally, my wife, Paulette, who as she holds this book in her hands will finally believe that when I "work at home" I really do work. Much love, Dear.

THE LITERATURE OF JOURNALISM

✦ ✦ ✦

Text and Context

Introduction

T his book is about eighteen pieces of journalism that are worth reading, re-reading, and remembering. These stories show how journalists have risen to the challenge of reporting twentieth-century events and social conditions, from the Great Depression to the world of information technology. When they were written, these stories broke new ground and advanced the practice of journalism. They are bench-marks and standards to which beginning journalists can aspire. They helped elevate the field of nonfiction and demonstrate what a reporter and writer could do.

Why were these stories unique and why were they written the way they were written? What interviewing methods did some writers use to draw stories from reluctant sources? What were the reactions when these stories were published and how are the stories viewed now? How did the writers influence each other and what were the results? What models do these writers provide for journalists today? Some quick answers follow. Longer and more detailed answers are discussed in each chapter.

These stories were written differently from the way standard journalism stories are written because the conventional tools of the trade would not have permitted the writers to convey their stories as fully. James Agee knew he could not use the standard magazine format, with its requirement to be quickly readable, to report what it was like to be a sharecropper—he needed to use methods of writing not common to journalism at the time. To use a conventional format would have allowed form to override story, preventing Agee from painting a unique picture, from immersing the reader in the details necessary to become fully involved in the story he titled *Let Us Now Praise Famous Men*. He wanted the reader to experience not only what it was like to be a share-cropper, but also to participate in his own process of conveying that experience—to let the reader live each moment, make each daily decision, right along with the people in the story.

A correspondent during World War II, John Hersey also needed a different form to tell the story of the survivors of the atomic bombing of Hiroshima. The fact that he wrote about civilians of the enemy nation was striking, but he also needed a way to convey their experiences so his readers in the West would stay with his story, *Hiroshima*. He fashioned an understated narrative that told the stories of four survivors. So compelling was the book-length story that it was printed in a single edition of *The New Yorker*, the magazine's editors having recognized the significance of the work. It is a delightful coincidence that one of the survivors is quoted reading from Psalms 90.9: "We spend our years as a tale that is told . . . ," as though Hersey was intertextually explaining the form he had chosen.

Gabriel García Márquez had a great story to tell, but had he told it in conventional newspaper format his newspaper would have suffered severely because the story would have bluntly pointed out the corruption of the Colombian government. Instead, García Márquez extensively interviewed the survivor of a shipwreck and told the sailor's story in the first person of the sailor, in effect removing himself as the mediator and deflecting official censure. Thus was born *The Story of a Shipwrecked Sailor*.

Alex Haley told Malcolm X's story in the first person in *The Autobiography of Malcolm X*, but Haley's uniqueness lies more in the devices he used to get a sometimes reluctant Malcolm X to tell his story. Haley also had to protect the story from changes Malcolm X wanted to make—and contractually had the right to make, because it was *his* story, not Haley's. To get the well-rounded story, the one that showed how Malcolm X evolved from a black separatist to an integrationist, Haley had to adapt his interviewing techniques to the personality of Malcolm X.

In other words, for these writers and the others in this book, the inverted pyramid was not the best form and conventional reporting methods were not adequate. The writers did not want just to get the attention of readers and inform them, but also to make them think and feel. The task was not simply a matter of providing data, but of conveying character and feeling.

Some authors represented in this book were considered "New Journalists," whose work, according to Tom Wolfe, was more or less structured on four attributes: scene-by-scene con-struction, real dialogue, status details, and point of view. As   the techniques that characterized "New Journalism" came into more common use in the 1960s, conventional societal behaviors and beliefs were changing. John Hellmann argued that in the 1960s New Journalists were dealing with "a new set of American realities"[1]—among them, an assassinated president, an unpopular war, a generation seemingly high on drugs, and a society of changing values.

But societies are always dealing with new realities, so I would lengthen the time period and extend the national borders. Many journalists in this book, whether writing in China, Colombia, England, or the United States, had to deal with changing values and circumstances. Readers were looking at stories in new ways—seeking deeper meanings and more immediate relevance—requiring writers to find new ways to tell their stories. Hellmann noted that the New Journalists needed "to break through the prepackaged insights and perspectives which permeate the corporate fiction produced by conventional journalism."[2] Hellmann's observation can be applied to nearly every story excerpted in this book, regardless of where and when it was written.

The context, the social circumstances in which a piece was written and the way it was received, tells us something about society and the state of journalism then. More recent reactions to the work can tell us something about journalism now. For example, most critics panned Agee's *Let Us Now Praise Famous Men* when it was published, in part because Agee found fault with conventional journalism in a book that, unlike conventional journalism, was difficult to grasp for all but the most persistent reader. When the book was revived after Agee's death, however, it was seen as a literary classic. So the retrospective comments were kinder than the contemporaneous ones—even though the book had not changed.

Agee said the book was a failure. In some ways, he was right, but credit must go to him for trying what he did. Through his unconventional methods of reporting and writing, which drew different reactions depending on when the book was read, and through his attempts to give readers something more than facts, but also a sense of his characters, Agee unknowingly provided a preview of the New Journalism that was to come twenty-five years later—also accompanied by brickbats.

In Cold Blood was also not universally praised when it was published, in part because of the author's outrageous self-promotion as the creator of a new art form, the nonfiction novel. In addition, Truman Capote was trying to push the bounds of journalism, sticking to facts but still giving the reader the sense of reading a story.

C. D. B. Bryan used *In Cold Blood* as a model to structure part of *Friendly Fire*, but when he realized that the story needed closure—an explanation of how Michael Mullen died in Vietnam—Bryan changed voices and entered the story himself to report on his findings and Michael's parents' reactions. He too was criticized by some reviewers.

George Orwell was not without critics when he wrote *The Road to Wigan Pier*. Orwell not only examined the life of coal miners, he included chapters of commentary in which he disagreed with the book's sponsors, a liberal book club, about the subject. Despite his own liberal politics, Orwell examined poverty from a more disinterested view and then trashed liberal ortho-doxy on poverty. He bit the hand that fed him and got away with it. He found a way to deal with changing circumstances. Although it is not among Orwell's better known books, *Wigan Pier* is frequently quoted in late twentieth-century stories about poverty, a testament to its staying power.

The overarching point to remember about these books is that they reflect evolutionary changes in journalism and society. Studying them reveals that what was once seen as "revolutionary," even heretical, is today considered standard.

The stories in this book, to some degree, also exemplify how writers influence other writers. Qian Gang relied on John Hersey's *Hiroshima* when he organized *The Great China Earthquake*. Jean Stafford tried to imitate interviewing tech-niques A. J. Liebling used in *The Earl of Louisiana* when she wrote *A Mother in History*. Joseph Wambaugh, in *The Onion Field*, followed the lead Capote provided in *In Cold Blood*—

and Capote cheered him on. Likewise, Tom Wolfe, who acknowledged a debt to Hersey, has influenced several generations of writers with *The Right Stuff*, even though by the time the book was published, his own style had already changed. Wolfe and Michael Herr, who wrote *Dispatches*, owe a debt to Agee. Many journalists who wrote after Lillian Ross—Susan Sheehan and Tracy Kidder among them—derived much from Ross's fly-on-the-wall reporting, that method of staying unobtrusively in the background and going so unnoticed that people forget the reporter is there and behave as they normally would.

These writers influenced each other and remain today as models of good writing and reporting. Studying their reporting methods enables those new to journalism to learn from the masters. Their texts, in other words, are manifestations of their reporting and thus become a textbook.

If you want to know how effective fly-on-the-wall reporting can be, read Ross' *Reporting*. It is, as one reviewer said, a postgraduate course all by itself. Ross, for having captured Ernest Hemingway off the pedestal so many had placed him on, was excoriated—not just when her portrait of the writer was published, but again when it was reissued in 1961 as a book. Yet the piece remains truer to Hemingway than a lot of other stories do because Ross showed Hemingway, not Ross writing about Hemingway. She was one of the journalists who set the stage for the practitioners of the saturation reporting and narrative journalism that arose in the 1960s, among them, Susan Sheehan, whose *Welfare Mother* demonstrates an understated writing style buttressed by fly-on-the-wall reporting.

When it came to capturing personalities, Liebling, like Ross, was also a master worth emulating. His skill shows in several of his books, but especially in his last, *The Earl of Louisiana*. Interestingly, Liebling used Earl Long's nonstandard English the way Ross used Hemingway's, but nobody complained about Liebling because Long was not only dead, he lacked Hemingway's stature.

The reader can examine the opposite of fly-on-the-wall reporting by reading Hunter Thompson, who rode with a motorcycle gang and even went on a beer run—in other words, partied with his sources—to learn the truth about the bikers and write *Hell's Angels*. Joan Didion also "hung out" with her subjects to produce her essays, including what many consider her best, "Slouching Towards Bethlehem."

All the authors in this collection shaped their stories rather than following a formula, and the reader can sense the "shaping presence"[3] of the writer. The stories discussed here represent journalism at its best. They endure because they were good at the time they were published and remain significant decades later.

❖ ❖ ❖

ADDITIONAL READING

Anyone interested in the contemporary development of journalistic writing beyond what appears in newspapers is encouraged to read the following books. This list does not include every useful book on the subject, but should provide a starting point for further study.

R. Thomas Berner. *Literary Newswriting: The Death of an Oxymoron*, Journalism Monographs No 99. Columbia, S.C.: Association for Education in Journalism, 1986.

Thomas B. Connery, ed. *A Sourcebook of American Literary Journalism: Representative Writers In an Emerging Genre*. New York: Greenwood, 1992.

Lennard J. Davis. *Factual Fictions*. New York: Columbia University Press, 1983.

Shelley Fisher Fishkin. *From Fact to Fiction: Journalism and Imaginative Writing in America*. Baltimore, Md.: Johns Hopkins Press, 1985.

Jon Franklin. *Writing for Story: Craft Secrets of Dramatic Nonfiction by a Two-Time Pulitzer Prize Winner*. Reprint. New York: New American Library/Plume, 1986.

Walker Gibson. *Tough, Sweet & Stuffy: An Essay On Modern American Prose Styles*. Bloomington: Indiana University Press, 1966.

John Hellmann. *Fables of Fact: The New Journalism as New Fiction*. Urbana: University of Illinois Press, 1981.

Michael L. Johnson. *The New Journalism*. Lawrence: University of Kansas Press, 1971.

Arthur J. Kaul, ed. *Dictionary of Literary Biography: American Literary Journalists, 1945–1995*. Detroit: Gale Research, A Bruccoli Clark Layman Book, 1997.

Kevin Kerrane and Ben Yagoda, eds. *The Art of Fact*. New York: Scribner, 1997.

Bill Knight and Deckle McLean, eds. *The Eye of the Reporter.* Macomb: Western Illinois University Press, 1996.

James E. Murphy. *The New Journalism: A Critical Perspective*, Journalism Monographs No. 34. Lexington, Ky.: Association for Education in Journalism, 1974.

Norman Sims, ed. *The Literary Journalists.* New York: Ballantine, 1984.

Norman Sims, ed. *Literary Journalism in the Twentieth Century.* New York: Oxford University Press, 1990.

Norman Sims and Mark Kramer, eds. *Literary Journalism.* (New York: Ballantine Books, 1995.

James N. Stull. *Literary Selves: Autobiography and Contemporary American Nonfiction.* Westport, Conn.: Greenwood Press, 1993.

Gay Talese and Barbara Lounsberry, eds. *The Literature of Reality.* New York: HarperCollins, 1996.

Ronald Weber, ed. *The Reporter as Artist: A Look at the New Journalism Controversy.* New York: Hastings, 1974.

Ronald Weber. *The Literature of Fact.* Athens: Ohio University Press, 1980.

Tom Wolfe. *The New Journalism* with an anthology edited by Tom Wolfe and E. W. Johnson. New York: Harper & Row, 1973.

ENDNOTES

1. John Hellmann, *Fables of Fact: The New Journalism as New Fiction* (Urbana: University of Illinois Press, 1981), 2.
2. Ibid., 4.
3. James N. Stull, *Literary Selves: Autobiography and Contemporary American Nonfiction* (Westport, Conn.: Greenwood, 1993), 3.

Chapter 1

❖

GEORGE ORWELL

The Road to Wigan Pier

Mention George Orwell, who once wrote that "good prose is like a window pane,"[1] and the novels *1984* or *Animal Farm* come immediately to mind. Press for an example of Orwell's nonfiction or journalism, and his first book, *Down and Out in Paris and London,* or his book on the Spanish Civil War, *Homage to Catalonia,* is mentioned. Few name the book published the year before *Catalonia, The Road to Wigan Pier.* Yet as the twentieth century came to a close, writers looking for a connection with poverty would quote from *The Road to Wigan Pier,* a tribute to its staying power.[2]

Wigan Pier represents, in V. S. Pritchett's words, "extraordinary honesty."[3] It serves as yet another example of Orwell's exquisitely detailed and powerfully simple writing style, "windowpane prose," and graphic descriptions.[4] Even today, one can admire Orwell's skill as an observer and a journalist. While the politics of *Wigan Pier* may no longer be pertinent, the prose endures, "an elegy on the spirit of poverty."[5]

The politics were socialism and it was the Left Book Club, with its 38,000 members, that published the book in England in 1937. Orwell was to go to the coal town of Wigan Pier and write a documentary on the unemployed, the world being in the throes of the Great Depression. Orwell did that, although he also wrote about some people who were employed. Where he really deviated from his assignment was in the second half of the book, however, where he stated rather bluntly that socialists, who believed in a classless society, redistribution of wealth, and state ownership of most industry, did not understand poverty any better than anyone else did. As one reviewer put it, "the second part of the book constitutes the most remarkable and perceptive dissection of the socialist point of view ever written by a socialist."[6] When they could not talk Orwell into splitting *Wigan Pier* into two books,[7] his sponsors published it as he had submitted it (while he headed to Spain), but added a twelve-page foreword that includes phrases such as "autobiographical study," "devil's advocate," "highly provocative," and "conflict of two compulsions" and that is clearly aimed at undermining the second half of the book.

The following excerpt begins the book. It is followed by an excerpt from later in the book, in which Orwell describes going into a mine.

⚜ ⚜ ⚜

The first sound in the mornings was the clumping of the mill-girls' clogs down the cobbled street. Earlier than that, I suppose, there were factory whistles which I was never awake to hear.

There were generally four of us in the bedroom, and a beastly place it was, with that defiled impermanent look of rooms that are not serving their rightful purpose. Years earlier the house had been an ordinary dwelling-house, and when the Brookers had taken it and fitted it out as a tripe-shop and lodging-house, they had inherited some of the more useless pieces of furniture and had never had the energy to remove them. We were there-fore sleeping in what was still recognisably a drawing-room. Hanging from the ceiling there was a heavy glass chandelier on which the dust was so thick that it was like fur. And covering most of one wall there was a huge hideous piece of junk, something between a sideboard and a hall-stand, with lots of carving and little drawers and strips of looking-glass, and there was a once-gaudy carpet ringed by the slop-pails of years, and two gilt chairs with burst seats, and one of those old-fashioned horsehair armchairs which you slide off when you try to sit on them. The room had been turned into a bedroom by thrusting four squalid beds in among this other wreckage.

My bed was in the right-hand corner on the side nearest the door. There was another bed across the foot of it and jammed hard against it (it had to be in that position to allow the door to open) so that I had to sleep with my legs doubled up; if I straightened them out I kicked the occupant of the other bed in the small of the back. He was an elderly man named

Mr. Reilly, a mechanic of sorts and employed "on top" at one of the coal-pits. Luckily he had to go to work at five in the morning, so I could uncoil my legs and have a couple of hours' proper sleep after he was gone. In the bed opposite there was a Scotch miner who had been injured in a pit accident (a huge chunk of stone pinned him to the ground and it was a couple of hours before they could lever it off), and had received five hundred pounds compensation. He was a big handsome man of forty, with grizzled hair and a clipped moustache, more like a sergeant-major than a miner, and he would lie in bed till late in the day, smoking a short pipe. The other bed was occupied by a succession of commercial travellers, newspaper canvassers and hire-purchase touts who generally stayed for a couple of nights. It was a double bed and much the best in the room. I had slept in it myself my first night there, but had been manoeuvred out of it to make room for another lodger. I believe all newcomers spent their first night in the double bed, which was used, so to speak, as bait. All the windows were kept tight shut, with a red sandbag jammed in the bottom, and in the morning the room stank like a ferret's cage. You did not notice it when you got up, but if you went out of the room and came back, the smell hit you in the face with a smack.

I never discovered how many bedrooms the house contained, but strange to say there was a bathroom, dating from before the Brookers' time. Downstairs there was the usual kitchen living-room with its huge open range burning night and day. It was lighted only by a skylight, for on one side of it was the shop and on the other the larder, which opened into some dark subterranean place where the tripe was stored. Partly blocking the door of the larder there was a shapeless sofa upon which Mrs. Brooker, our landlady, lay permanently ill, festooned in grimy blankets. She had a big, pale yellow, anxious face. No one knew for certain what was the matter with her; I suspect that her only real trouble was over-eating. In front of the fire there was almost always a line of damp washing, and in the middle of the room was the big kitchen table at which the family and all the lodgers ate. I never saw this table completely uncovered, but I saw its various wrappings at different times. At the bottom there was a layer of old newspapers stained by Worcester Sauce; above that a sheet of sticky white oilcloth; above that a green serge cloth; above that a coarse linen cloth, never changed and seldom taken off. Generally the crumbs from breakfast were still on the table at supper. I used to get to know individual crumbs by sight and watch their progress up and down the table from day to day.

The shop was a narrow, cold sort of room. On the outside of the window a few white letters, relics of ancient chocolate advertisements, were scattered like stars. Inside there was a slab upon which lay the great white folds of tripe, and the grey flocculent stuff known as "black tripe," and the ghostly translucent feet of pigs, ready boiled. It was the ordinary "tripe and pea shop," and not much else was stocked except bread, cigarettes and tinned stuff. "Teas" were advertised in the window, but if a customer demanded a cup of tea he was usually put off with excuses. Mr. Brooker, though out of work for two years, was a miner by trade, but he and his wife had been keeping shops of various kinds as a side-line all their lives. At one time they had had a pub, but they had lost their licence for allowing gambling on the premises. I doubt whether any of their businesses had ever paid; they were the kind of people who run a business chiefly in order to have something to grumble about. Mr. Brooker was a dark, small-boned, sour, Irish-looking man, and astonishingly dirty. I don't think I ever once saw his hands clean. As Mrs. Brooker was now an invalid he prepared most of the food, and like all people with permanently dirty hands he had a peculiarly intimate, lingering manner of handling things. If he gave you a slice of bread-and-butter there was always a black thumb-print on it. Even in the early morning when he descended into the mysterious den behind Mrs. Brooker's sofa and fished out the tripe, his hands were already black. I heard dreadful stories from the other lodgers about the place where the tripe was kept. Blackbeetles were said to swarm there. I do not know how often fresh consignments of tripe were ordered, but it was at long intervals, for Mrs. Brooker used to date events by it. "Let me see now, I've had in three lots of froze (frozen tripe) since that happened," etc., etc. We lodgers were never given tripe to eat. At the time I imagined that this was because tripe was too expensive; I have since thought that it was merely because we knew too much about it. The Brookers never ate tripe themselves, I noticed.

The only permanent lodgers were the Scotch miner, Mr. Reilly, two old-age pensioners and an unemployed man on the P.A.C. named Joe— he was the kind of person who has no surname. The Scotch miner was a bore when you got to know him. Like so many unemployed men he spent too much time reading newspapers, and if you did not head him off he would discourse for hours about such things as the Yellow Peril, trunk murders, astrology, and the conflict between religion and science. The old-age pensioners had, as usual, been driven from their homes by the Means Test. They handed their weekly ten shillings over to the Brookers and in return got the kind of accommodation you would expect for ten shillings; that is, a bed in the attic and meals chiefly of bread-and-butter. One of them was of "superior" type and was dying of some malignant disease—

cancer, I believe. He only got out of bed on the days when he went to draw his pension. The other, called by everyone Old Jack, was an ex-miner aged seventy-eight who had worked well over fifty years in the pits. He was alert and intelligent, but curiously enough he seemed only to remember his boyhood experiences and to have forgotten all about the modern mining machinery and improvements. He used to tell me tales of fights with savage horses in the narrow galleries underground. When he heard that I was arranging to go down several coal mines he was contemptuous and declared that a man of my size (six feet two and a half) would never manage the "travelling"; it was no use telling him that the "travelling" was better than it used to be. But he was friendly to everyone and used to give us all a fine shout of "Good night, boys!" as he crawled up the stairs to his bed somewhere under the rafters. What I most admired about Old Jack was that he never cadged; he was generally out of tobacco towards the week, but he always refused to smoke anyone else's. The Brookers had insured the lives of both old-age pensioners with one of the tanner-a-week companies. It was said that they were overheard anxiously asking the insurance-tout "how long people lived when they'd got cancer."

Joe, like the Scotchman, was a great reader of newspapers and spent almost his entire day in the public library. He was the typical unmarried unemployed man, a derelict-looking, frankly ragged creature with a round, almost childish face on which there was a naïvely naughty expression. He looked more like a neglected little boy than a grown-up man. I suppose it is the complete lack of responsibility that makes so many of these men look younger than their ages. From Joe's appearance I took him to be about twenty-eight, and was amazed to learn that he was forty-three. He had a love of resounding phrases and was very proud of the astuteness with which he had avoided getting married. He often said to me, "Matrimonial chains is a big item," evidently feeling this to be a very subtle and portentous remark. His total income was fifteen shillings a week, and he paid out six or seven to the Brookers for his bed. I sometimes used to see him making himself a cup of tea over the kitchen fire, but for the rest he got his meals somewhere out of doors; it was mostly slices of bread-and-marg and packets of fish and chips, I suppose.

. . . .

When you go down a coal-mine it is important to try and get to the coal face when the "fillers" are at work. This is not easy, because when the mine is working visitors are a nuisance and are not encouraged, but if you go at any other time, it is possible to come away with a totally wrong impression. On a Sunday, for instance, a mine seems almost peaceful. The time to go there is when the machines are roaring and the air is black with coal dust, and when you can actually see what the miners have to do. At those times the place is like hell, or at any rate like my own mental picture of hell. Most of the things one imagines in hell are there—heat, noise, confusion, darkness, foul air, and, above all, unbearably cramped space. Everything except the fire, for there is no fire down there except the feeble beams of Davy lamps and electric torches which scarcely penetrate the clouds of coal dust.

When you have finally got there—and getting there is a job in itself: I will explain that in a moment—you crawl through the last line of pit props and see opposite you a shiny black wall three or four feet high. This is the coal face. Overhead is the smooth ceiling made by the rock from which the coal has been cut; underneath is the rock again, so that the gallery you are in is only as high as the ledge of coal itself, probably not much more than a yard. The first impression of all, overmastering everything else for a while, is the frightful, deafening din from the conveyor belt which carries the coal away. You cannot see very far, because the fog of coal dust throws back the beam of your lamp, but you can see on either side of you the line of half-naked kneeling men, one to every four or five yards, driving their shovels under the fallen coal and flinging it swiftly over their left shoulders. They are feeding it on to the conveyor belt, a moving rubber belt a couple of feet wide which runs a yard or two behind them. Down this belt a glittering river of coal races constantly. In a big mine it is carrying away several tons of coal every minute. It bears it off to some place in the main roads where it is shot into tubs holding half a ton, and thence dragged to the cages and hoisted to the outer air.

It is impossible to watch the "fillers" at work without feeling a pang of envy for their toughness. It is a dreadful job that they do, an almost super-human job by the standards of an ordinary person. For they are not only shifting monstrous quantities of coal, they are also doing it in a position that doubles or trebles the work. They have got to remain kneeling all the while—they could hardly rise from their knees without hitting the ceiling—and you can easily see by trying it what a tremendous effort this means. Shovelling is comparatively easy when you are standing up, because you can use your knee and thigh to drive the shovel along; kneeling down, the whole of the strain is thrown upon your arm and belly muscles. And the other conditions do not exactly make things easier. There is the heat—it varies, but in some mines it is suffocating—and the coal dust that stuffs up your throat and nostrils and collects along your eyelids, and the unending rattle of the conveyor belt which in that confined space is rather like the rattle of a machine gun. But the fillers look and work as though they were made of iron. They really do look like iron—hammered iron statues—under the smooth coat of coal dust which clings to them from head to foot. It is only when you see miners down the mine and naked that you realise what splendid men they are. Most of them are small (big men are at a disadvantage in that job) but nearly all of them have the most noble bodies: wide shoulders tapering to slender supple waists, and small pronounced buttocks and sinewy thighs, with not an ounce of waste flesh anywhere. In the hotter mines they wear only a pair of thin drawers, clogs and knee-pads; in the hottest mines of all, only the clogs and knee-pads. You can hardly tell by the look of them whether they are young or old. They may be any age up to sixty or even sixty-five, but when they are black and naked they all look alike. No one could do their work who had not a young man's body, and a figure fit for a guardsman at that; just a few pounds of extra flesh on the waist-line, and the constant bending would be impossible. You can never forget that spectacle once you have seen it—the line of bowed, kneeling figures, sooty black all over, driving their huge shovels under coal with stupendous force and speed. They are on the job for seven and a half hours, theoretically without a break, for there is no time "off." Actually they snatch a quarter of an hour or so at some time during the shift to eat the food they have brought with them, usually a hunk of bread and dripping and a bottle of cold tea. The first time I was watching the "fillers" at work I put my hand upon some dreadful slimy thing among the coal dust. It was a chewed quid of tobacco. Nearly all the miners chew tobacco, which is said to be good against thirst.

Probably you have to go down several coal-mines before you can get much grasp of the processes that are going on round you. This is chiefly because the mere effort of getting from place to place makes it difficult to notice anything else. In some ways it is even disappointing, or at least is unlike what you have expected. You get into the cage, which is a steel box about as wide as a telephone box and two or three times as long. It holds ten men, but they pack it like pilchards in a tin, and a tall man cannot stand upright in it. The steel door shuts upon you, and somebody working the winding gear above drops you into the void. You have the usual momentary qualm in your belly and a bursting sensation in the ears, but not much sensation of movement till you get near the bottom, when the cage slows down so abruptly that you could swear it is going upwards again. In the middle of the run the cage probably touches sixty miles an hour; in some of the deeper mines it touches even more. When you crawl out at the bottom you are perhaps four hundred yards under ground. That is to say you have a tolerable-sized mountain on top of you; hundreds of yards of solid rock, bones of extinct beasts, subsoil, flints, roots of growing things, green grass and cows grazing on it—all this suspended over your head and held back only by wooden props as thick as the calf of your leg. But because of the speed at which the cage has brought you down, and the complete blackness through which you have travelled, you hardly feel yourself deeper down than you would at the bottom of the Piccadilly tube.

What is surprising, on the other hand, is the immense horizontal distances that have to be travelled under ground. Before I had been down a mine I had vaguely imagined the miner stepping out of the cage and getting to work on a ledge of coal a few yards away. I had not realised that before he even gets to his work he may have to creep through passages as long as from London Bridge to Oxford Circus. In the beginning, of course, a mine shaft is sunk somewhere near a seam of coal. But as that seam is worked out and fresh seams are followed up, the workings get further and further from the pit bottom. If it is a mile from the pit bottom to the coal face, that is probably an average distance; three miles is a fairly normal one; there are even said to be a few mines where it is as much as five miles. But these distances bear no relation to distances above ground. For in all that mile or three miles as it may be, there is hardly anywhere outside the main road, and not many places even there, where a man can stand upright.

❧ ❧ ❧

When George Orwell died of tuberculosis in London in 1950, at the age of forty-six, he received high praise from many commentators and critics. "Today, without fear of contradiction," James Stern wrote, "we can say that England never produced a novelist more honest, more courageous, more concerned with the common man—and with common sense."[8] V. S. Pritchett said Orwell "was entirely without self-righteousness and lacked the conventional optimism; his socialism was independent, pungent, aggressive, but sweet to the taste like the British workman's favorite tobaccos."[9] A year after Orwell's death, Edmund Wilson called him "a Marxist who was disgusted by the fashionable socialism of the thirties; a product of the best schools [Eton] who tried to identify himself with the lower middle class."[10]

Stern and Wilson mentioned *Wigan Pier* in the *New York Times* and the *New Republic,* although the book would not be published in the United States until 1958. When it was, Robert Hatch said it could have been "another of those exhumations that publishers sponsor in the hope of getting one more play out of a famous name,"[11] but he was not really objecting; he pronounced the book "wonderfully alive." An anonymous *Time* magazine reviewer said Orwell wrote "in a style beside which today's Angry Young Men sound like a party of petulant pixies."[12] Earl W. Foell said *Wigan Pier* was what readers expected of Orwell—"fact slightly intensified by indignation."[13] Harrison Smith compared Orwell favorably to Charles Dickens,[14] a novelist whose works included sympathetic novels about the poor of England. (Orwell listed Dickens as one of his twelve favorite writers[15] and said he "was certainly a subversive writer, a radical, one might truthfully say a rebel.")[16] William Hogan said *Wigan Pier* was "an example of a brilliant socialist-minded writer and journalist's observations on a national disaster."[17] Alfred C. Ames said Orwell "had the power to make any subject vivid, to make any topic exciting. He was consistently perceptive, original and passionate about basic issues."[18]

Part II of *Wigan Pier* was praised because it shows Orwell's discovery of his feelings and attitudes,[19] feelings he did not realize he possessed. Part II, his criticism of socialism, was not a coming-of-age essay but an essay of atonement. "He wanted to wash himself—in dirt," Donald Barr wrote.[20] Orwell also wrote critically of the left, Richard Hoggart said, because he found it "intellectually and imaginatively self-indulgent."[21] But J. R. Hammond said Part II was "highly idiosyncratic," "contentious," "polemical," and "obtrusive."[22] "What is of enduring value in these chapters," Hammond wrote, "is the essential decency and morality of his conception of socialism and the patent honesty of his attempts to understand its opponents."[23]

The best part of the book is the beginning, for it is there that Orwell's ability as a researcher, observer, and writer really comes through. Bernard Crick noted that Orwell visited several homes in Wigan, made systematic notes, spent days in the local public library, checked other public records, and went into a mine—he "did his homework as a social investigator."[24] As Neville Braybrooke said after Orwell died: "On the road back from Wigan

Pier, Orwell travelled with first-hand knowledge."[25] Orwell got some of that firsthand knowledge doing something both dangerous and physically challenging—he went down in a mine. Like others, such as James Agee, Hunter Thompson, and Joan Didion, Orwell shows the reader the process he went through to report and write the book,[26] as when he says: "I think I can best give an idea of what conditions are like by transcribing a few extracts from my notebook, taken more or less at random."[27]

Orwell's style also received high praise. T. R. Fyvel said that in *Wigan Pier* Orwell "discovered the spare, puritan descriptive style he was to employ so effectively."[28] Look at the way Orwell describes Mrs. Brooker: "She had a big, pale yellow, anxious face."[29] Q. D. Leavis, writing in 1940, suggested Orwell was a dreary novelist but that "his equivalent works in non-fiction are stimulating."[30] "It took all of Orwell's literary craftsmanship," Richard Filloy wrote, "to bury his Eton education and his intellectualism and to render his perceptions and thoughts ordinary."[31]

Orwell's writing is deceptive. He can write at great length about something, and the prose is vivid and never tiring. But obversely some sentences within the long descriptive passages are examples of economic description. Recall the line about the Brookers as "the kind of people who run a business chiefly in order to have something grumble about." In other words, Orwell also has the sense of the one-liner or the soundbite.

Orwell typed and saved his notes, which were published after his death. You can see where the opening sentence of *Wigan Pier* came from:

18 FEBRUARY
In the early morning the mill girls clumping down the cobbled street, all in clogs, make a curiously formidable sound, like an army hurrying into battle. I suppose this is the typical sound of Lancashire. And the typical imprint in the mud the outline of a clog-iron, like one half of a cow's hoof. Clogs are very cheap. They cost about 5/- a pair and need not wear out for years because all they need is new irons costing a few pence.[32]

Fyvel noted that Orwell took poetic license late in Chapter 1, where he refers to having seen a woman from a train and then describes her, "builds up an entire character, an entire life."[33] Here is part of that:

> At the back of one of the houses a young woman was kneeling on the stones, poking a stick up the leaden waste-pipe which ran from the sink inside and which I supposed was blocked. I had time to see everything about her—her sacking apron, her clumsy clogs, her arms reddened by the cold. She looked up as the train passed, and I was almost near enough to catch her eye. She had a round pale face, the usual exhausted face of the slum girl who is twenty-five and looks forty, thanks to miscarriages and drudgery; and it wore, for the second in which I saw it, the most desolate, hopeless expression I have ever seen.[34]

In the diary, Orwell describes seeing the woman while he was walking:

> Passing up a horrible squalid side-alley, saw a woman, youngish but very pale and with the usual draggled exhausted look, kneeling by the gutter outside a house and poking a stick up the leaden wastepipe, which was blocked. I thought how dreadful a destiny it was to be kneeling in the gutter in a back-alley in Wigan, in the bitter cold, prodding a stick up a blocked drain. At that moment she looked up and caught my eye, and her expression was as desolate as I have ever seen; it struck me that she was thinking just the same thing as I was.[35]

So be it. Orwell's poetic license does not detract from the overall work, as Fyvel was quick to point out.

Hammond said *Wigan Pier* "has taken its place as one of the most significant social documents of the 1930s and as one of those works of reportage which is destined to outlive the immediate economic conditions which are its theme."[36] In proclaiming the book's longevity and universality, Hammond cited Orwell's distinctive voice, his mastery of the language, and his development as a politically conscious writer.[37] Along the same lines, Hoggart said the book is unforgettable and honest, with "a quality of perception and a style which isolates it.[38] Orwell's general concern for the working class and *Wigan Pier*'s evocative and descriptive prose invite comparison with James

Agee and his *Let Us Now Praise Famous Men*. Overall, *Wigan Pier* makes a major contribution to reportage and serves as a model for future writers.

ENDNOTES

1. George Orwell, *The Collected Essays, Journalism and Letters of George Orwell: An Age Like This 1920–1940*, ed. Sonia Orwell and Ian Angus (New York: Harcourt, Brace and World, 1968), 7.
2. See, for example, Joseph Epstein, "How Revolting," *New Yorker*, 14 July 1997, 81; Ted Gup, "The Curse of Coal," *Time*, 4 November 1991, 54; Glenn Frankel, "Coal Town Tries to Build on Grim Legacy," *Los Angeles Times*, 6 October 1991, p. 8; Stewart Dalby, "Hope Stirs in the Valleys," *Financial Times*, 17 September 1990, p. v; Paul Greenberg, "Only the names have changed," *Chicago Tribune*, 16 February 1990, p. 19; Melvin Maddocks, "Whatever became of the middle class?" *Christian Science Monitor*, 19 September 1986, p. 21; Nick Garner, "A double-sided picture," *Financial Times*, 8 October 1985, p. v. Retrieved from Nexis. (Also see n. 5.)
3. V. S. Pritchett, "George Orwell: An Appreciation," *New York Times Book Review*, 5 February 1950, 22.
4. Robert C. de Camara, "Homage to Orwell," *National Review*, 13 May 1983, 566.
5. Robert Hatch, "Books in Brief," *Nation*, 30 August 1958, 97.
6. Paul C. Wermuth, "Book Reviews," *Library Journal*, 15 September 1958, p. 2432.
7. Bernard Crick, *George Orwell: A Life* (Boston: Little, Brown and Company, 1980), 204.
8. James Stern, "Homage to George Orwell," *New Republic*, February 1950, 18.
9. Pritchett, *George Orwell: An Appreciation*, 22.
10. Edmund Wilson, "Grade-A Essays: Orwell, Sartre, and Highet," *New Yorker*, 13 January 1951, 76.
11. Hatch, "Books in Brief," 97.
12. "Notes from a Black Country," *Time*, 18 August 1958, 84.
13. Earl W. Foell, "Fact and Indignation," *Christian Science Monitor*, 21 August 1958, p. 4.
14. Harrison Smith, "England's Thirties: A Terrible Record of Evil," *Saturday Review*, 9 August 1958, 14.
15. George Orwell, *The Collected Essays, Journalism and Letters of George Orwell: An Age Like This 1940–1943*, ed. Sonia Orwell and Ian Angus (New York: Harcourt, Brace and World, 1968), 24. Orwell also listed William Shakespeare, Jonathan Swift, Henry Fielding, Charles Reade,

Samuel Butler, Emile Zola, Gustave Flaubert, James Joyce, T. S. Eliot, D. H. Lawrence, and Somerset Maugham. Of Maugham, Orwell wrote, "I admire [him] immensely for his power of telling a story straightforwardly and without frills."

16. Orwell, "Charles Dickens," in *Collected Essays, 1920–1940*, 414. This is an approximately 10,000-word essay Orwell wrote in 1939. It opens with: "Dickens is one of those writers who are well worth stealing." The essay is well worth reading.

17. William Hogan, "An Orwellian Report From the 1930s Reaches America," *San Francisco Chronicle*, 3 August 1959, p. 20.

18. Alfred C. Ames, "Mr. Orwell's Testament to Abiding Moral Values," *Chicago Sunday-Tribune*, 3 August 1958, Part 5, p. 6.

19. Richard Filloy, "Orwell's Political Persuasion," in *Literary Nonfiction: Theory, Criticism, Pedagogy*, ed. Chris Anderson (Carbondale: Southern Illinois University Press, 1989), 54.

20. Donald Barr, "The Answer to George Orwell," *Saturday Review*, 30 March 1957, 31.

21. Richard Hoggart, "George Orwell and *The Road to Wigan Pier*," in *Critical Essays on George Orwell*, ed. Bernard Oldsey and Joseph Browne (Boston: G. K. Hall, 1986), 182.

22. J. R. Hammond, *A George Orwell Companion* (London: Macmillan, 1982), 124, 127.

23. Ibid., 124.

24. Crick, *George Orwell: A Life*, 184.

25. Neville Braybrooke, "George Orwell," *Fortnightly*, June 1951, 407.

26. I am indebted to Laura A. Geueke, who raised this point in my spring 1998 literature of journalism class.

27. Orwell, *Wigan Pier*, 53, but also see 67.

28. T. R. Fyvel, "George Orwell and Eric Blair, *Encounter*, July 1959, 64.

29. George Orwell, *The Road to Wigan Pier* (New York: Harvest/HBJ, 1958), 7. This is the date of the first American edition. The original was published in England in 1937.

30. Q. D. Leavis, "Mr. George Orwell," *Scrutiny*, September 1940, 175.

31. Filloy, "Orwell's Political Persuasion," 66.

32. Orwell, "The Road to Wigan Pier Diary," *Collected Essays, 1920–1940*, 180.

33. Fyvel, "George Orwell and Eric Blair," 187.

34. Orwell, *Wigan Pier*, 18.

35. Orwell, *Collected Essays, 1920–1940*, 177–78.

36. Hammond, *George Orwell Companion*, 127.

37. Ibid., 127–28.

38. Hoggart, "George Orwell and *The Road to Wigan Pier*," 184.

Chapter 2

❖

Let Us Now Praise Famous Men

When he was sent to Alabama to write a story for *Fortune* magazine, James Agee knew he was going to write something different from the standard *Fortune* magazine article and that the magazine would not publish it.[1] That Agee, something of a communist, was even working for *Fortune*, a magazine that glorified capitalism, was in itself an interesting sidebar in the history of a journalist and novelist. But the co-founder of Time, Inc., Henry R. Luce, was less interested in a writer's politics than in the writer's ability, especially for business articles, where dull writing was the norm. "If he could put poets to work writing business stories," Laurence Bergreen wrote, "he gambled he could produce a lively product brimming with the romance of capitalism."[2]

So in 1936, Agee was teamed with Walker Evans, a photographer, and sent to Alabama to write about sharecroppers. During the eight weeks they were gone, though, Luce changed editors at *Fortune*, moving out Ralph Ingersoll, who had made the original assignment and "who had been instrumental in endowing the magazine with a social conscience,"[3] and replaced him with someone more pliable. The change worked to Agee's benefit, because the new managing editor, Eric Hodgins, rejected Agee's article out of hand and told him to write something more conventional. But Agee refused on the grounds that it was not his fault *Fortune*'s editorial direction had changed while he was on assignment; he had done what he had been told to do. Agee set about writing—but not for *Fortune*—what would become *Let Us Now Praise Famous Men*. (He had used that title once before on a never-published short story.)[4] The line comes from Ecclesiasticus, a book found in some Christian Bibles.

The following excerpt comes from the chapter titled "Clothing." Gudger, Ricketts, and Woods are the fictitious surnames Agee gave the families. Agee did not capitalize some proper nouns and his punctuation is not standard.

❧ ❧ ❧

Sunday, George Gudger:

Freshly laundered cotton gauze underwear.

Mercerized blue green socks, held up over his fist-like calves by scraps of pink and green gingham rag.

Long bulb-toed black shoes: still shining with the glaze of their first newness, streaked with clay.

Trousers of a hard and cheap cotton-wool, dark blue with narrow gray stripes; a twenty-five-cent belt stays in them always.

A freshly laundered and brilliantly starched white shirt with narrow black stripes.

A brown, green, and gold tie in broad stripes, of stiff and hard imitation watered silk.

A very cheap felt hat of a color between that of a pearl and that of the faintest gold, with a black band.

The hat is still only timidly dented into shape. Its lining is still brilliant and pearly, with only a faint shadow of oil. The sweatband, and the bright insole of the shoes, will seem untouched for a long time still, and the scarred soles of the shoes are still yellow.

The crease is still sharp in the trousers.

If he were an older man, and faithful in the rural tradition of dressing well rather than in that of the young men in towns, he would wear, not a belt, but suspenders, striped, or perhaps decorated with rosebuds.

These are the only socks he owns.

He does not wear or own a coat and would not want one. What he would like to wear is a pull-over sweater.

He has two suits of the underwear. He will sleep in this suit tonight and during the rest of the week. The other suit will go into the wash and he will put it on next Sunday.

His neck seems violently red against the tight white collar. He is freshly shaven, and his face looks shy and naked.

He wears the hat straight awhile, then draws it down a little, but conservatively, over one eye, then pushes it far back on his head so that it is a halo, then sets it on straight again. He is delicate with his hands in touching it.

He walks a little carefully: the shoes hurt his feet.

Saturday, Mrs. Gudger:

Face, hands, feet and legs are washed.

The hair is done up more tightly even than usual.

Black or white cotton stockings.

Black lowheeled slippers with strapped insteps and single buttons.

A freshly laundered cotton print dress held together high at the throat with a ten-cent brooch.

A short necklace of black glass beads.

A hat.

She has two pairs of stockings. She sometimes goes barelegged to Cookstown, on saturdays, but always wears stockings on sundays.

The dress is one of two she would not be ashamed to wear away from home: they are not yet worn-down or ineradicably spotted. In other respects it is like all her other dresses: made at home, of carefully selected printed cotton cloth, along narrow variants of her own designing, which differs from some we saw and is probably a modified inheritance from her mother: short sleeves, a rather narrow skirt several inches longer than is ordinary. No kind of flaring collar, but in some of them, an effort to trim with tape. They are all cut deep at the breast for nursing, as all her dresses must have been for ten years now. The lines are all long, straight, and simple.

The hat is small and shallow, crowned with a waved brim. She must have taken care in its choice. It is a distant imitation of 'gay' or 'frivolous' 'trifles.' It is made of frail glazed magenta straw in a wide mesh through which her black hair shows. It has lost its shape a little in rain. She wears it exactly level, on the exact top of her small and beautifully graven head.

No southern country woman in good standing uses rouge or lipstick, and her face is colorless. There are traces of powder at the wings of her nose and in the seamed skin just in front of her left ear.

She is keenly conscious of being carefully dressed, and carries herself stiffly. Her eyes are at once searching, shy, excited, and hopelessly sad.

Saturday is the day of leaving the farm and going to Cookstown, and from the earliest morning on I can see that she is thinking of it. It is after she has done the housework in a little hurry and got the children ready that she bathes and prepares herself, and as she comes from the bedroom, with her hat on, ready to go, her eyes, in ambush even to herself, look for what I am thinking in such a way that I want to tell her how beautiful she is; and I would not be lying.

She will carry herself in this stiff, gravely watchful, and hopeful way all during the day in town, taking care to straighten her hat, and retiring as deeply as possible behind the wagons to nurse her baby. On the way home in the slow, rattling wagon, she will be tired and drooped, her hat crooked, her eyes silent, and once she will take the smallest child intensely against her, very suddenly.

Sunday: it is not very different from Saturday, for she has no really 'Sunday' dress, no other dress shoes, no other hat, and no other jewelry. If she is feeling happy, though, she will set into her hair the pink celluloid comb I have spoken of, with the glass diamonds.

George, on Saturday, dresses not in his dress clothes but in the newest and cleanest of his work clothes; if there is time, if he is not working until noon, away from home, he shaves that morning and washes his feet. When there is no work to do, in winter and midsummer, he shaves twice a week.

Ricketts, on Sunday:

No socks.

Old, black Sunday shoes, washed off with water, and slashed with a razor at the broadest part of the feet.

Very old dark trousers with the compound creases of two ironings in them; nearly new white suspenders with narrow blue stripes down the sides and brown dots down the centers, the strap at the right attached to the trousers by a rusty nail.

A nearly new blue work shirt, worn perhaps twice before since laundering; the sleeves rolled down, the cuffs buttoned, the collar buttoned; no tie.

An open vest, too wide and short for him, of heavy, worn-out, gray-and-black wool; his watch and chain joining it across the waist.

A very old and carefully kept dark felt hat with a narrow band and a delicate bow.

A pair of horn-rimmed spectacles.

The spectacles are worn only on Sunday and are perhaps mainly symbolic of the day and of his dignity as a reader in church; yet, too, they have strong small lenses. He bought them at a five-and-ten-cent store in Cherokee City.

Woods, on Sunday:

Of the head covering I have no certain memory, yet two images. A hat of coarse-grained, strongly yellow straw, shaped by machine as felt hats are by the owner's hands, with a striped band. And: a nearly new, sober plaid, flat cap, of the sort which juts wide above the ears, and of a kind of crackling cheapness which one rain destroys.

Shoes: the oxfords which at one time were his dress shoes, and in which his wife has worked during the week.

Trousers such as seventeen-year-old boys of small towns select for best who can spend no money and want what flash they can get: a coarse-meshed and scratchy cotton-wool, stiffened with glue, of a bright and youthful yellow-gray crossed in wide squares by horizontals of blue-green and verticals of green-blue, and thinly pebbled with small nodules of red, orange, and purple wool. They are a little large for him. The original crease is entirely gone at the knee and is very sharp from knee to cuff. The suspenders are printed with spaced knots of small blue flowers; are worn out, and have been laundered.

A white shirt, starched; thin brown stripes. The sleeves have been cut off just above the elbows and coarsely hemmed. There are rust marks all over it, and the image of a flatiron is scorched just beneath the heart. An originally white piqué detachable collar, blue-gray from laundering, the fray scissored clean. A white cotton tie with two narrow black lines along each edge; about an inch wide throughout; both 'ends' out; the end next the body much longer than the outside end, and showing three or four inches of knitting-wear.

One day's beard; the mustache trimmed neat and short; the temples and the slender, corded, behind-head, trimmed nearly naked and showing the criss-crossed, quilting work of the scissors, and the meekness of the pallid scalp; scraped toast.

The children, washed and combed, barefooted, with clean feet and legs; clean clothes on: I will tell more of them later; so, too, of Mrs. Woods, and Mrs. Ricketts, and of the Ricketts girls: at present, more of the daily clothing.

On Monday Gudger puts on cleanly washed workclothes; the other two men, whose laundering is done less often, change their clothing in a more casual cycle, two to several weeks long: I want now to try to describe these work clothes: shoes, overalls, shirts, head coverings: variants, general remarks: and to speak here perhaps, not of these three men only, but a little more generally as well.

On all the clothing here to be spoken of there are, within the narrow range of availabilities, so many variants that one cannot properly name anything as 'typical,' but roughly align several 'types.' I could say, for instance:

Of shoes: ordinary work shoes, to be described later, may be called 'typical'; but only if you remember that old Sunday shoes, tennis sneakers, high tennis shoes, sandals, moccasins, bare feet, and even boots, are not at all rarely used: it should be known, too, that there are many kinds of further, personal treatment of shoes. Mainly, this: Many men, by no means all, like to cut holes through the uppers for foot-spread and for ventilation: and in this they differ a good deal between utility and art. You seldom see purely utilitarian slashes: even the bluntest of these are liable to be patterned a little more than mere use requires: on the other hand, some shoes have been worked on with a wonderful amount of patience and studiousness toward a kind of beauty, taking the memory of an ordinary sandal for a model, and greatly elaborating and improving it. I have seen shoes so beautifully worked in this way that their durability was greatly reduced. Generally speaking, those who do this really careful work are negroes; but again, by no means all of the negroes are 'artists' in this way.

Of overalls, you could say that they are the standard working garment in the country south, and that blue is the standard color. But you should add that old Sunday pants in varying degrees of decay are also perhaps half as much used: that striped and khaki overalls sometimes appear and mechanics' coveralls, and dungarees, and khaki work pants:

And again, speaking now of shirts, that though the blue workshirt is standard, there are also gray and brown workshirts; and besides these, old Sunday shirts (white or striped), and now and then a homemade shirt, and undershirts, polo shirts, and jerseys:

And again of these categories of body covering, that, though all the variants appear among whites, they are a good deal more frequent among negroes; and again, too, that among the negroes the original predilections for colors, textures, symbolisms, and contrasts, and the subsequent modifications and embellishments, are much more free and notable.

And of hats, you could say that the standard is the ordinary farmers' straw sold at crossroads stores: but here you would be wrong for several reasons. Perhaps half the tenants wear these straws, but even in that category there are many differences in choice of kind at the same price, ranging from hats as conservative in size and shape as the city felts they imitate, through the whole register of what is supposed to be 'typical' to the american farmer, to hats which are only slight modifications of the ten-gallon and of the sombrero. And besides these straws: again there are all kinds of variants: old Sunday hats being one whole class; another, caps emulous of small-town and city and factory men: baseball caps, the little caps which are the gifts of flour and paint companies, factory caps; imitation pith helmets imitative of foremen imitative of landowners imitative of the colonists in pith-helmet melodramas; occasionally, too, a homemade hat or cap: and here again, both in choice and in modification, the negroes are much the richer.

There will be no time, though, to go into these variants beyond their mention, nor any time at all to talk of negro work and Sunday clothing, which in every respect seems to me, as few other things in this country do, an expression of a genius distributed among almost the whole of a race, so powerful and of such purity that even in its imitations of and plagiarisms on the white race, it is all but incapable of sterility.*

But now having suggested varieties, I want to lay out and tell of 'types,' speaking of the white race.

In general, then: the shoes are either work shoes of one age or another or worn-out Sunday oxfords. The body garments are blue overalls and blue work shirts; again, with a wide range of age. The head coverings are straw hats or old Sunday hats, or occasionally some more urban form of cap. These things have been bought ready-made, so consistently that any homemade substitute calls for a note to itself. Now a few further notes, on overalls and work shirts.

So far as I know, overalls are a garment native to this country. Subject to the substitutions I have spoken of; they are, nevertheless, the standard or classical garment at very least (to stay within our frame) of the southern rural American working man: they are his uniform, the badge and proclamation of his peasantry. There seems to be such a deep classicism in 'peasant' clothing in all places and in differing times that, for instance, a Russian and a southern woman of this country, of a deep enough class, would be undistinguishable by their clothing: moreover, it moves backward and forward in time: so that Mrs. Ricketts, for instance, is probably

---

*There is a large class of sober, respectable, pious, mainly middle-aged negroes who in every way react intensely against the others of their race, and as intensely toward imitation of the most respectable whites. Their clothing, for instance, has no color in it anywhere, but is entirely black-and-white; and the patterns are equally severe. But even here, the whites are so blazing and starchedly white, and the blacks so waxed-ironed dead, and the clothes are borne in so profound, delicate, and lovely a sobriety, that I doubt the white race has ever approached it.

In all this on negroes, by the way, I am speaking strictly of small towns and of deep country. City negroes, even in the south, are modified; and those of the north are another thing again.

undistinguishable from a woman of her class five hundred years ago. But overalls are a relatively new and local garment.

Perhaps little can be said of them, after all: yet something. The basis: what they are: can best be seen when they are still new; before they have lost (or gained) shape and color and texture; and before the white seams of their structure have lost their brilliance.

⚜ ⚜ ⚜

In order to gather information for *Famous Men,* Agee and Evans spent some of their time living with and interviewing three families. The original book contained eighteen of Evans's photographs; the number was increased to sixty-two when the book was reissued in 1960. In the preface, Agee said "the photographs are not illustrative. They, and the text, are coequal, mutually independent, and fully collaborative." In the book proper, he wrote: "If I could do it, I'd do no writing at all here. It would be photographs."[5]

The reissued version has not only the value of Evans's additional photographs but also an Evans essay on Agee. "Agee worked in what looked like a rush and a rage," Evans wrote. "He was driven to see all he could of the families' day, starting, of course, at dawn. In one way, conditions there were ideal. He could live inside the subject, with no distractions."[6]

Agee himself wrote that he wanted "to recognize the stature of a portion of unimagined existence and to contrive techniques proper to its recording, communication, analysis, and defense."[7] He told the reader that the book should be read aloud and continuously, "as music is listened to or a film watched, with brief pauses only where they are self-evident."[8] Agee was trying to create something active and did not even want to describe the result as a book. "More seriously," he wrote, "it is an effort in human actuality, in which the reader is no less centrally involved than the authors and those of whom they tell."[9] In the language of a half-century later, the book was meant to be interactive.

Agee felt he had fallen short of his goal,[10] and many reviewers agreed. Peter H. Ohlin said later that the book was "an uncomfortably original work, and it is easier to say what it is not than what it is. It is not a novel, or a documentary, or a journal, or a philosophical treatise, or a sociological study."[11] George Barker[12] and Ronald Weber, writing four decades apart, said the book did succeed as documentation or, as Weber put it, "a monumental piece of detailed reporting."[13]

In the book, Agee had been immediate and blunt in his attack on journalism, even sniping indirectly at himself that he had the presumption to take on the assignment. He wrote very early in the book (the footnote is his, as well):

> It seems to me curious, not to say obscene and thoroughly terrifying, that it could occur to an association of human beings drawn together through need and chance and for profit into a company, an organ of journalism, to pry intimately into the lives of an undefended and appallingly damaged group of human beings, an ignorant and helpless rural family, for the purpose of parading the nakedness, disadvantage and humiliation of these lives before another group of human beings, in the name of science, of "honest journalism" (whatever that paradox may mean), of humanity, of social fearlessness, for money, and for a reputation for crusading and for unbias which, when skillfully enough qualified, is exchangeable at any bank for money (and in politics, for votes, job patronage, abelincolnism, etc.*); and that these people could be capable of mediating this prospect without the slightest doubt of their qualification to do an "honest" piece of work, and with a conscience better than clear, and in the virtual certitude of almost unanimous public approval.[14]

Later in the book he criticized journalism again (and included two footnotes):

> Who, what, where, when and why (or how) is the primal cliché and complacency of journalism: but I do not wish to appear to speak favorably of journalism. I have never yet seen a piece of journalism which conveyed more than the slightest fraction of what any even moderately reflective and sensitive person would mean and intend by those inachievable words, and that fraction itself I have never seen clean of one or another degree of patent, to say nothing of essential, falsehood. Journalism is true in the sense that everything is true to the state of being and to what

*Money.

conditioned and produced it* (which is also, but less so perhaps,
a limitation of art and science): but that is about as far as its
value goes. This is not to accuse or despise journalism for
anything beyond its own complacent delusion, and its enormous
power to poison the public with the same delusion, that it is
telling the truth even of what it tells of. Journalism can within its
own limits be 'good' or 'bad,' 'or 'false,' but it is not in the nature
of journalism, even to approach any less relative degree of truth.
Again, journalism is not to be blamed† for this; no more than a
cow is to be blamed for not being a horse. The difference is, and
the reason one can respect or anyhow approve of the cow, that
few cows can have the delusion or even the desire to be horses,
and that none of them could get away with it even with a small
part of the public. The very blood and semen of journalism, on
the contrary, is a broad and successful form of lying. Remove
that form of lying and you no longer have journalism.[15]

Like Orwell, Agee was biting the hand that fed him, but unlike
Orwell, he was also offering press criticism and at the same time
defending his innovative approach to the story. Conventional
journalism was not the vehicle to tell the story as Agee saw it.

But on publication, *Famous Men* received an unfavorable
review—from Ralph Thompson of the *New York Times*.
Thompson praised Evans's photographs but in the same sentence
obliquely condemned Agee's writing. "There never was a better
argument for photography," Thompson wrote, claiming that
Evans had said as much in his "several dozen photographs" as
Agee had in 150,000 words. Thompson also noted Agee's criticism
of the vulgarities and clichés of modern journalism but said that,
given Agee's "self-inspired, self-conscious and self-indulgent
prose," "a little more vulgar modern journalism would have done
no harm."[16]

Five days after Thompson's review, Ruth Lechlitner produced
the second newspaper review. Hers was much longer than
Thompson's, never snarly, more analytical. She too praised the
photographs, but then took time and space to examine Agee's

---

*Looked at this way a page of newspaper can have all the wealth of a sheet of
fossils, or a painting.
†Why not.

intention and result. She declared that he was "not only a poet but a corking good journalist when he needs to be." She felt that *Famous Men* was really two books and that the subjective portions should have been published separately.[17] Lechlitner was correct; it is, in fact, a book about the sharecroppers and also a book in which Agee ruminates about truth and life as he is writing about the sharecroppers. As she said in her conclusion, the book revealed as much about Agee as it did about the tenant farmers, and, of course, it is in the subjective portions that the revelations about Agee show up.

According to Bergreen, Agee's friends conspired to submit reviews to various journals as a way of combating the *Times* review.[18] Harvey Breit, whose wife had helped type Agee's manuscript,[19] called *Famous Men* "a rich, many-eyed book" that should be read.[20] Breit did acknowledge problems with the book, as did another Agee friend, Selden Rodman, who had published an excerpt of the book in *Common Sense,* his magazine.[21] In his review, Rodman said the book's greatness was "its structural failure, its over-all failure as the 'work of art' it does not aim or presume to be and which from moment to moment it is."[22]

The New Yorker's brief review acknowledged Agee's reporting and said: "Overdone in spots, and doesn't add up to a single effect, but superior, highly original, accurately poetic writing."[23] In other words, Agee was on to something but hadn't quite gotten there. Paul Goodman also wrote a mixed review. He praised Agee for describing some items "with extraordinary beauty and power and a kind of isolated truth." In the description of things, but not people, he said Agee was "sensitive often to the point of genius," but added that "the sense of their proportions, tradition, and social tone is more feeble."[24] But the excerpt displays not only good description of things, but also of people—"There are traces of powder at the wings of her nose and in the seamed skin just in front of her left ear"[25]—so there are exceptions to Goodman's negative observation. John C. Cort panned the book as "too repetitious, too obscure, too obsessed with irrelevant detail, and particularly too obsessed with the author's complex reactions to his subject and to everything else."[26] A perfect example of Cort's observation plays out in Agee's discussion of Emma Woods:

Each of us is attractive to Emma, both in sexual immediacy and as symbols or embodiments of a life she wants and knows she will never have; and each of us is fond of her, and attracted toward her. We are not only strangers to her, but we are strange, unexplainable, beyond what I can begin yet fully to realize. We have acted toward her with the greatest possible care and shyness and quiet, yet we have been open or 'clear' as well, so that she knows we understand her and like her and care for her almost intimately. She is puzzled by this and yet not at all troubled, but excited; but there is nothing to do about it on either side. There is tenderness and sweetness and mutual pleasure in such a 'flirtation' which would one would not for the world retrain or cancel, yet there is also an essential cruelty, about which nothing can be done, and strong possibility of cruelty through misunderstanding, and inhibition, and impossibility, which can be restrained, and which one would rather die than cause any of: but it is a cruel and ridiculous and restricted situation, and everyone to some extent realizes it.[27]

A reviewer at *Time*, one of *Fortune*'s sister publications, called *Famous Men* "the most distinguished failure of the season" and complained of "Agee's bad manners, exhibitionism and verbosity." But the reviewer was able to parse the book for its strong points and said: "Even his most myopic descriptions are a poet's."[28]

The review that Bergreen said established Agee in literary circles came from Lionel Trilling, then an English professor at Columbia University.[29] Trilling said that "nine out of every ten pages are superb," and that "the book is full of marvelous writing which gives a kind of hot pleasure that words can do so much."[30] Trilling did not specify any particular passage, but one phrase that evokes that hot pleasure comes early in the book, when Agee, Evans and another man had gone to the home of a foreman, who was entertaining relatives: "The foreman's male guests hovered quietly and respectfully in silence on the outskirts of the talk until they were sure what they might properly do . . . ."

Consider the way Agee structured the book—or the way critics analyzed the structure. In 1968, from a distance of nearly thirty years, Kenneth Seib said the book was "appallingly overwritten, yet it is seldom boring"[31]—and one wonders whether

Agee ever considered a tighter revision. Genevieve Moreau said the book was "composed like a symphony consisting of themes and variations" and called it "a mobile creation, an ongoing inquiry"[32]—and one is tempted to liken it to performance art. Victor Kramer saw an "aural or musical quality" in the text.[33] The book's organization also suggests a play. Agee provides a cast of characters and sites, which he titles "Persons and Places," and then provides the organization in a section titled "Design of Book Two." That section shows, among other things, a preamble, three parts, scenes demarcated by time or place, even an intermission in which Agee provides his answers to a questionnaire from *Partisan Review*—answers that would be of interest to Agee scholars but that have nothing to do with the main story.

Peter H. Ohlin made an unstated comparison with George Orwell's *Road to Wigan Pier* when he observed that Agee had a tendency to criticize both sides of the farmers' problem, the New Dealers and the Southern landowners. Orwell disagreed with his sponsors, the Left Book Club, and was not afraid to suggest that there was enough blame to go around. Disinterested observation is what good journalists strive to bring to their writing.

Agee never saw the three tenant families again. But forty-five years after Agee and Evans visited Alabama, Howell Raines of *The New York Times* visited the families and found that some were angry at Evans because he profited from the photographs, others at Agee because they believed he had "marketed their only possessions, their privacy and their suffering, and deprived them of a fair share of the profits, which they imagine to be enormous."[34] But the book sold only six hundred copies originally. It was not until it was reissued in 1960 that it sold well and stayed in print. By that time Agee was dead (he had died in 1955).* In the words of Bergreen, Agee "won greater acclaim in death than he had in life."[35]

Did James Agee produce a classic? One could argue that at the simple level—the level of vulgar journalism—the answer is no. The book demands the reader's attention and patience. But at another level, when one stands back and examines what Agee

---

*Evans died in 1975, five years before Raines wrote his article.

attempted, albeit unevenly, the book deserves attention. One can also see in Agee's lyrical and self-referential writing the presaging of other writers, such as Michael Herr and Tom Wolfe, who twenty-five years later would produce evocative journalism.

ENDNOTES

1. Laurence Bergreen, *James Agee: A Life* (New York: Dutton, 1984), 162.
2. Ibid., 107.
3. Ibid., 178.
4. Ibid., 126.
5. James Agee and Walker Evans, *Let us Now Praise Famous Men* (Boston: Houghton Mifflin, 1941), 13. I am relying on the reissued edition of 1960, which includes an essay by Evans on Agee.
6. Ibid., xi.
7. Ibid., xiv.
8. Ibid., xv.
9. Ibid., xvi.
10. James Agee, *Letters of James Agee to Father Flye* (New York: Braziller, 1962), 131.
11. Peter H. Ohlin, *Agee* (New York: Obolensky, 1966), 55.
12. George Barker, "Three Tenant Families," *Nation*, 27 September 1941, 282.
13. Ronald Weber, *The Literature of Fact: Literary Nonfiction in American Writing* (Athens: Ohio University Press, 1980), 59.
14. Agee and Evans, *Let us Now Praise Famous Men*, 7.
15. Ibid., 234–35.
16. Ralph Thompson, "Books of the Times," *New York Times*, 19 August 1941, 19.
17. Ruth Lechlitner, "Alabama Tenant Families," *New York Herald Tribune Books*, 10.
18. Bergreen, *James Agee: A Life*, 258.
19. Ibid.
20. Harvey Breit, "Cotton Tenantry," *The New Republic*, 15 September 1941, 348, 350.
21. Bergreen, *James Agee: A Life*, 258.
22. Selden Rodman, "The Poetry of Poverty," *Saturday Review*, 23 August 1941. (Rodman was the author of *The Poetry of Flight*, hence the headline on his review.)
23. "Briefly Noted," *New Yorker*, 13 September 1941, 75–76.
24. Paul Goodman, *Partisan Review*, January–February 1942, 86–87.
25. Agee and Evans, *Let us Now Praise Famous Men*, 259.
26. John C. Cort, *The Commonweal*, 12 September 1941, 499.

27. Agee and Evans, *Let us Now Praise Famous Men*, 61–62.
28. "Experiment in Communication," *Time*, 13 October 1941, 104.
29. Bergreen, *James Agee: A Life*, 259.
30. Lionel Trilling, "Greatness with One Fault in It," *Kenyon Review*, Winter 1942, 99–102.
31. Kenneth Seib, *James Agee: Promise and Fulfillment* (Pittsburgh: University of Pittsburgh Press, 1968), 41.
32. Genevieve Moreau, *The Restless Journey of James Agee* (New York: Morrow, 1977), 186, 199.
33. Victor Kramer, *James Agee* (Boston: Twayne, 1975), 78.
34. Howell Raines, "Let Us Now Revisit Famous Folk," *New York Times Magazine*, 25 May 1980, 31, 36. Yet another revisit came from Dale Maharidge and Michael Williams, who produced text and photos in a book titled *And Their Children After Them* (New York: Pantheon, 1989).
35. Bergreen, *James Agee: A Life*, 408.

Chapter 3

❖

JOHN HERSEY

Hiroshima

O
n August 6, 1945, the United States exploded an atomic bomb over the city of Hiroshima, Japan. The bombing was the first of two (the second was over Nagasaki three days later) that would end the fighting in the Pacific Theater of World War II and end the war. Most of what Americans learned about the death and destruction—78,150 people killed, 13,983 missing, and 37,425 injured—came from journalists who got their information from U.S. military and government sources. About two months later, John Hersey, on assignment for *Life* and *The New Yorker*, made a trip to China and Japan.[1] Out of that trip came a 31,347-word article[2] in *The New Yorker*, which was subsequently published as a book. What made the article and the book different from conventional war coverage was that they told the story from the victims' point of view[3]—and the victims were the enemy.

When the original book-length article on the bombing appeared by itself in a single issue of *The New Yorker*, it was the only article in the magazine, an unprecedented occurrence that William Shawn, then the managing editor, had suggested to the editor, Harold Ross.[4]

Forty years after the original book was published, Hersey published an updated version that contained an epilogue on the six people whose stories he had told in the original. The updated version contains five parts: "A Noiseless Flash (the impact)," "The Fire" (the first twelve hours), "Details Are Being Investigated" (the next few days), "Panic Grass and Feverfew" (the next few months and some of the year), and "The Aftermath" (the revised edition's epilogue). A modern reader might read the original in one sitting and then go back the next day and read the epilogue. "A Noiseless Flash" introduces the main characters and tells where each one was when the bomb exploded.

The following excerpt opens the book.

⚜ ⚜ ⚜

At exactly fifteen minutes past eight in the morning, on August 6, 1945, Japanese time, at the moment when the atomic bomb flashed above Hiroshima, Miss Toshiko Sasaki, a clerk in the personnel department of the East Asia Tin Works, had just sat down at her place in the plant office and was turning her head to speak to the girl at the next desk. At the same moment, Dr. Masakazu Fujii was settling down cross-legged to read the Osaka *Asabi* on the porch of his private hospital, overhanging one of the seven deltaic rivers which divide Hiroshima; Mrs. Hatsuyo Nakamura, a tailor's widow, stood by the window of her kitchen, watching a neighbor tearing down his house because it lay in the path of an air-raid-defense fire lane; Father Wilhelm Kleinsorge, a German priest of the Society of Jesus, reclined in his underwear on a cot on the top floor of his order's three-story mission house, reading a Jesuit magazine, *Stimmen der Zeit*; Dr. Terufumi Sasaki, a young member of the surgical staff of the city's large, modern Red Cross Hospital, walked along one of the hospital corridors with a blood specimen for a Wassermann test in his hand; and the Reverend Mr. Kiyoshi Tanimoto, pastor of the Hiroshima Methodist Church, paused at the door of a rich man's house in Koi, the city's western suburb, and prepared to unload a handcart full of things he had evacuated from town in fear of the massive B-29 raid which everyone expected Hiroshima to suffer. A hundred thousand people were killed by the atomic bomb, and these six were among the survivors. They still wonder why they lived when so many others died. Each of them counts many small items of chance or volition—a step taken in time, a decision to go indoors, catching one streetcar instead of the next—that spared him. And now each knows that in the act of survival he lived a dozen lives and saw more death than he ever thought he would see. At the time, none of them knew anything.

The Reverend Mr. Tanimoto got up at five o'clock that morning. He was alone in the parsonage, because for some time his wife had been commuting with their year-old baby to spend nights with a friend in Ushida, a suburb to the north. Of all the important cities of Japan, only two, Kyoto and Hiroshima, had not been visited in strength by *B-san*, or Mr. B, as the Japanese, with a mixture of respect and unhappy familiarity, called the B-29; and Mr. Tanimoto, like all his neighbors and friends, was almost sick with anxiety. He had heard uncomfortably detailed accounts of mass raids on Kure, Iwakuni, Tokuyama, and other nearby towns; he was sure Hiroshima's turn would come soon. He had slept badly the night before, because there had been several air-raid warnings. Hiroshima had been getting such warnings almost every night for weeks, for at that time the B-29s were using Lake Biwa, northeast of Hiroshima, as a rendezvous point, and no matter what city the Americans planned to hit, the Superfortresses streamed in over the coast near Hiroshima. The frequency of the warnings and the continued abstinence of Mr. B with respect to Hiroshima had made its citizens jittery; a rumor was going around that the Americans were saving something special for the city.

Mr. Tanimoto was a small man, quick to talk, laugh, and cry. He wore his black hair parted in the middle and rather long; the prominence of the frontal bones just above his eyebrows and the smallness of his mustache, mouth, and chin gave him a strange, old-young look, boyish and yet wise, weak and yet fiery. He moved nervously and fast, but with a restraint which suggested that he was a cautious, thoughtful man. He showed, indeed, just those qualities in the uneasy days before the bomb fell. Besides having his wife spend the nights in Ushida, Mr. Tanimoto had been carrying all the portable things from his church, in the close-packed residential district called Nagaragawa, to a house that belonged to a rayon manufacturer in Koi, two miles from the center of town. The rayon man, a Mr. Matsui, had opened his then unoccupied estate to a large number of his friends and acquaintances, so that they might evacuate whatever they wished to a safe distance from the probable target area. Mr. Tanimoto had had no difficulty in moving chairs, hymnals, Bibles, altar gear, and church records by pushcart himself, but the organ console and an upright piano required some aid. A friend of his named Matsuo had, the day before, helped him get the piano out to Koi; in return, he had promised this day to assist Mr. Matsuo in hauling out a daughter's belongings. That is why he had risen so early.

Mr. Tanimoto cooked his own breakfast. He felt awfully tired. The effort of moving the piano the day before, a sleepless night, weeks of worry and unbalanced diet, the cares of his parish—all combined to make him feel hardly adequate to the new day's work. There was another thing, too:

Mr. Tanimoto had studied theology at Emory College, in Atlanta, Georgia; he had graduated in 1940; he spoke excellent English; he dressed in American clothes; he had corresponded with many American friends right up to the time the war began; and among a people obsessed with a fear of being spied upon—perhaps almost obsessed himself—he found himself growing increasingly uneasy. The police had questioned him several times, and just a few days before, he had heard that an influential acquaintance, a Mr. Tanaka, a retired officer of the Toyo Kisen Kaisha steamship line, an anti-Christian, a man famous in Hiroshima for his showy philanthropies and notorious for his personal tyrannies, had been telling people that Tanimoto should not be trusted. In compensation, to show himself publicly a good Japanese, Mr. Tanimoto had taken on the chairmanship of his local *tonarigumi,* or Neighborhood Association, and to his other duties and concerns this position had added the business of organizing air-raid defense for about twenty families.

Before six o'clock that morning, Mr. Tanimoto started for Mr. Matsuo's house. There he found that their burden was to be a *tansu,* a large Japanese cabinet, full of clothing and household goods. The two men set out. The morning was perfectly clear and so warm that the day promised to be uncomfortable. A few minutes after they started, the air-raid siren went off—a minute-long blast that warned of approaching planes but indicated to the people of Hiroshima only a slight degree of danger, since it sounded every morning at this time, when an American weather plane came over. The two men pulled and pushed the handcart through the city streets. Hiroshima was a fan-shaped city, lying mostly on the six islands formed by the seven estuarial rivers that branch out from the Ota River; its main commercial and residential districts, covering about four square miles in the center of the city, contained three-quarters of its population, which had been reduced by several evacuation programs from a wartime peak of 380,000 to about 245,000. Factories and other residential districts, or suburbs, lay compactly around the edges of the city. To the south were the docks, an airport, and the island-studded Inland Sea. A rim of mountains runs around the other three sides of the delta. Mr. Tanimoto and Mr. Matsuo took their way through the shopping center, already full of people, and across two of the rivers to the sloping streets of Koi, and up them to the outskirts and foothills. As they started up a valley away from the tight-ranked houses, the all-clear sounded. (The Japanese radar operators, detecting only three planes, supposed that they comprised a reconnaissance.) Pushing the handcart up to the rayon man's house was tiring, and the men, after they had maneuvered their load into the driveway and to the front steps, paused to rest awhile. They stood with a wing of the house between them and the city. Like most homes in this part of Japan, the house consisted of a wooden frame and wooden walls supporting a heavy tile roof. Its front hall, packed with rolls of bedding and clothing, looked like a cool cave full of fat cushions. Opposite the house, to the right of the front door, there was a large, finicky rock garden. There was no sound of planes. The morning was still; the place was cool and pleasant.

Then a tremendous flash of light cut across the sky. Mr. Tanimoto has a distinct recollection that it travelled from east to west, from the city toward the hills. It seemed a sheet of sun. Both he and Mr. Matsuo reacted in terror—and both had time to react (for they were 3,500 yards, or two miles, from the center of the explosion). Mr. Matsuo dashed up the front steps into the house and dived among the bedrolls and buried himself there. Mr. Tanimoto took four or five steps and threw himself between two big rocks in the garden. He bellied up very hard against one of them. As his face was against the stone, he did not see what happened. He felt a sudden pressure, and then splinters and pieces of board and fragments of tile fell on him. He heard no roar. (Almost no one in Hiroshima recalls hearing any noise of the bomb. But a fisherman in his sampan on the Inland Sea near Tsuzu, the man with whom Mr. Tanimoto's mother-in-law and sister-in-law were living, saw the flash and heard a tremendous explosion; he was nearly twenty miles from Hiroshima, but the thunder was greater than when the B-29s hit Iwakuni, only five miles away.)

When he dared, Mr. Tanimoto raised his head and saw that the rayon man's house had collapsed. He thought a bomb had fallen directly on it. Such clouds of dust had risen that there was a sort of twilight around. In panic, not thinking for the moment of Mr. Matsuo under the ruins, he dashed out into the street. He noticed as he ran that the concrete wall of the estate had fallen over—toward the house rather than away from it. In the street, the first thing he saw was a squad of soldiers who had been burrowing into the hillside opposite, making one of the thousands of dugouts in which the Japanese apparently intended to resist invasion, hill by hill, life for life; the soldiers were coming out of the hole, where they should have been safe, and blood was running from their heads, chests, and backs. They were silent and dazed.

Under what seemed to be a local dust cloud, the day grew darker and darker.

❧ ❧ ❧

John Hersey's choice to tell his story by focusing on survivors was influenced by Thornton Wilder's *Bridge of San Luis Rey,* a novel about people joined by fate in a natural disaster.[5] He said forty years later that he went to Hiroshima "looking for the kinds of people who would fit into the pattern."[6] The first people he approached were German priests, whom he knew about because one of them had written a report on the bombing for the Holy See. Hersey interviewed approximately forty people before selecting the six individuals who appear in the book and spent about three weeks interviewing them for their stories of survival.[7] He chose the six he did because "he could bridge the language barrier more easily with them than he could with many other survivors whom he interviewed": two spoke English and Hersey had a translator for the other four.[8] These six survivors led him to other survivors.

The New Yorker's obituary on Hersey acknowledged that he "had a distinguished career as a novelist and another as a teacher, but he was above all a reporter" and that his article on the bombing "may be the most famous magazine article ever published."[9] Whether Hersey would have agreed with that comment will never be known, but he did leave a record of the distinction he made between fiction and journalism. "Journalism," Hersey once wrote, "allows its readers to witness history; fiction gives it readers an opportunity to live it."[10] But many would argue that in *Hiroshima,* Hersey—who once bemoaned the failure of the giant communications companies to communicate human truth[11]—accomplished both, and in doing so communicated human truth.

Many of Hersey's reviewers spoke of Hersey's plain style, a style more typical of a journalist than a novelist. "He just tells the story," said Bruce Bliven, who likened *Hiroshima* to Wilder's classic without giving any indication that he knew Wilder's writing had informed Hersey's.[12] Bliven did point out the absence of editorializing, which Ruth Benedict also praised.[13] The *New Yorker* obituary writer said: "Though [Hersey's writing] is imbued with a profound moral sense, it does not preach. It does not hector. It simply tells."[14] Another reviewer said *Hiroshima* was "unpleasant reading—told without emotion or flourish, and yet [it is] the most instructive and thought provoking publication that has come out of World War II."[15] One scholar referred to the original as "unsensational yet moving."[16] "The prose," Edward Weeks said, "is stark and stirring in its revelation of fortitude."[17] A decade and a half after it was published Truman Capote praised Hersey (and Thornton Wilder, among others) as a "styleless stylist . . . which is very difficult, very admirable, and *always* popular."[18]

Later Hersey was to say that he tried "to be deliberately quiet" because he thought that presenting the horror directly "would allow the reader to identify with the characters in a direct way."[19] Hersey also said he employed the devices of fiction to get away from the conspicuousness of a journalist, who, Hersey said, is always mediating between the material and the reader. He believed that the reader is conscious of the mediation and wanted to make his mediator's role disappear.[20]

The original publication of *Hiroshima* in *The New Yorker* provoked a largely positive reaction. Albert Einstein ordered a thousand copies, the Belgian Chamber of Commerce wanted five hundred, the United States Army sought reprints for educational purposes, and newspapers from around the world sought reprint rights. The entire article was read over the air on the American Broadcasting Company (radio) over four successive evenings. The BBC, Canadian networks, and Australian networks followed suit. The Book-of-the-Month Club distributed copies free to its members.[21] Hersey stipulated that reproduction of the book would be permitted as long as the entire book was reproduced; he charged fifteen dollars per ten thousand copies circulated as a permissions fee, and all proceeds were to go the Red Cross.[22]

The critical response was generally positive. Poore called it a "subtly contrapuntal text,"[23] referring to Hersey's interweaving of his characters' stories into a point-counterpoint, from which comes the tension that propels the narrative. Forty years later Chalmers M. Roberts said the book's "powerful effect came from the simplicity of the writing, a vivid, straightforward, non-polemical reportorial account of half a dozen survivors of the first atomic bomb."[24] Martin J. Sherwin said of the 1985 update that it "remains the classic, chilling account of the nightmare experience of nuclear war."[25]

An anonymous reviewer in the *Times Literary Supplement* (published, coincidentally, on the fifth anniversary of the Japanese bombing of Pearl Harbor) praised Hersey for his plain style and for letting the facts speak for themselves, but also complained that "they have not spoken loudly enough."[26] Other reviewers made similar comments. It is unfair to compare books and suggest that one writer should have imitated another; still, the way Orwell divided *Wigan Pier* between description and commentary does spring to mind. The difference, of course, is that Hersey wrote for a magazine and commentary wasn't part of the contract.

Hersey was also condemned for being artless and detached. Dwight Macdonald said Hersey was "feeble as an artist, with no style, no ideas, no feelings of intensity," so detached from his subjects "that they become objects of clinical description."[27] A month later Mary McCarthy responded that Hersey had minimized the bombing and made it appear no more out of place than fires, floods and earthquakes.[28] It seems that both Macdonald and McCarthy's commentaries are really aimed at *The New Yorker*, which both referred to with disdain.

Both the original article and the updated book, as the previous paragraph suggests, provoked more political discussion than critical discussion. (A similar reaction, though on a lesser scale, followed Michael Herr's Vietnam book, *Dispatches*.) More than half of Poore's review of *Hiroshima* was devoted to the issue Hersey's article raised—should the United States have dropped the atomic bomb at all? Some who had once favored the bombing had second thoughts after reading *Hiroshima*; those who had opposed the bombing were even more outraged because of Hersey's story.[29] Some were not happy with what they considered a compassionate portrayal of the enemy,[30] while others felt as John Toland did: "Riveted by the ghastly details, those of us who had hated the Japanese for almost five years finally realized that Mr. Hersey's six protagonists were fellow human beings."[31] (Toland, by the way, was the author of *The Rising Sun: The Decline and Fall of the Japanese Empire 1936–1945*, which is told largely from the Japanese point of view.)

Yet, *Hiroshima* was also praised for its non-preaching approach. Or, as Dan R. Jones said, "its journalistic credibility is not flawed by the injection of moralistic sentiment."[32] For roughly the same reason, Richard Rhodes did not like the update, saying that Hersey completed the story from the same point of view but failed to rethink the larger moral issues.[33] Others thought the original was perfectly clear. Louis Ridenour said, "It seems to me impossible for anyone to read 'Hiroshima' without drawing morals for himself."[34]

There is little doubt that Hersey was personally opposed to war. In 1965, during the early stages of the obviously escalating Vietnam War, Hersey and many other writers attended a White House celebration in honor of the arts. Various writers were asked to speak, and Hersey read from *Hiroshima*. Before he began the reading he made a statement about how people and nations can slip imperceptibly from one degree of violence to another and then not go back. "The end point of these little steps is horror and oblivion," he said. He cautioned against arrogance and against relying on military power rather than moral strength. "Wars have a way of getting out of hand," he said.[35]

The epilogue should be seen in the larger context of Hersey's public expressions on war. It recounts the fate of each of the six people from the original, although it focuses Kyoshi Tanimoto as the central character. Perhaps sensitive to the early criticism that the book did not take a stand, Hersey may have tried to compensate by focusing on Tanimoto, who had organized an antinuclear movement. He also interspersed among the stories brief details of subsequent nuclear explosions by the United States and other countries. He concluded with Tanimoto and these sentences: "He was slowing down a bit. His memory, like the world's, was getting spotty."*

It is difficult to believe anyone could read the updated book and not understand Hersey's position on nuclear weapons. The original stands as a straightforward, understated account of six survivors of an atomic bomb, and even then, as Ridenour said, it is not difficult to draw a moral from it. But the epilogue of the updated version shifts in tone and to a degree in style, clearly turning the book into an antinuclear statement. David Sanders called the epilogue "a sobering, often bitter assessment of the impact the bombings have had on the world's conscience over forty years."[36] *Hiroshima* stands as a classic piece of reportage on

---

*Tanimoto died of pneumonia at the age of 77 on September 28, 1986.

the results of war. And, as Sanders put it, if it turns out that because of this book no one ever uses a nuclear weapon again, "Hersey will have done all that a writer could have done to make it so."[37] Few writers can be so viewed.

ENDNOTES

1. Michael J. Yavenditti, "John Hersey and the American Conscience: The Reception of 'Hiroshima,'" *Pacific Historical Review*, February 1974, 34.
2. Eric Pace, "William Shawn, 85, Is Dead; New Yorker's Gentle Despot," *New York Times*, 9 December 1992, p. B13.
3. Yavenditti, "John Hersey," 33.
4. "Talk of the Town," *Newsweek*, 9 September 1946, 70.
5. Jonathan Dee, "The Art of Fiction XCII, John Hersey," *Paris Review*, Summer 1986, 226–27.
7. Ibid., 227.
7. Yavenditti, "John Hersey," 35–36. (Yavenditti's source is an interview he conducted with Hersey on 19 September 1967.)
8. David Sanders, *John Hersey Revisited* (Boston: Twayne, 1991), 15.
9. "John Hersey," *New Yorker*, 5 April 1993, 111.
10. John Hersey, "The Novel of Contemporary History," *Atlantic Monthly*, November 1949, 82. Also see "The Legend on the License," *The Yale Review*, Autumn 1980, 1–25.
11. Ibid., 80.
12. Bruce Bliven, "Hiroshima," *New Republic*, 9 September 1946, 300–01.
13. Ruth Benedict, "The Past and the Future," *Nation*, 7 December 1946, 656.
14. "John Hersey," *New Yorker*.
15. Rudolph Hirsch, "Book Review," *Library Journal*, 1 November 1946, 1539.
16. James Gray, "The Journalist as Literary Man," in *American Non-fiction, 1900–1950* (Westport, Conn.: Greenwood, 1952, 1970), 138.
17. Edward Weeks, "The Peripatetic Reviewer," *Atlantic Monthly*, January 1947, 106.
18. Pati Hill, "The Art of Fiction XVII, Truman Capote," *Paris Review*, Spring/Summer 1957, 47.
19. Dee, "The Art of Fiction XCII," 228.
20. Ibid.
21. Charles Poore, "The Most Spectacular Explosion in the Time of Man," *New York Times Book Review*, 10 November 1946, 7.
22. "Talk of the Town," 7.

23. Poore, "The Most Spectacular Explosion," 56.
24. Chalmers M. Roberts, "John Hersey Returns to Hiroshima," *Washington Post Book World,* 11 August 1985, 3.
25. Martin J. Sherwin, "Old issues in new editions," *Bulletin of Atomic Scientists,* December 1985, 40.
26. "The Second Fall of Man," *Times Literary Supplement,* 7 December 1946, 605.
27. Dwight Macdonald, "Hersey's 'Hiroshima,'" *Politics,* October 1946, 308.
28. Mary McCarthy, "The Hiroshima 'New Yorker,'" *Politics,* November 1946, 367.
29. Yavenditti, "John Hersey," 42.
30. Richard Rhodes, "Hersey still dodging the issue in epilogue to 'Hiroshima,'" *Chicago Tribune,* 4 August 1985, p. 31.
31. John Toland, "Beyond the Brink of Destruction," *New York Times Book Review,* 4 August 1985, 3.
32. Dan R. Jones, "John Hersey," *A Sourcebook of American Literary Journalism: Representative Writers in an Emerging Genre,* ed. Thomas B. Connery (New York: Greenwood, 1992), 216.
33. Rhodes, "Hersey still dodging," 34.
34. Louis Ridenour, "What Is the Crime of War?" *Saturday Review of Literature,* 2 November 1946, 16.
35. Quoted in Howard Taubman, "White House Salutes Culture in America," *New York Times,* 15 June 1964, 48.
36. David Sanders, *John Hersey* (New York: Twayne Publishers, Inc., 1967), p. 51.
37. Sanders, *John Hersey,* 22.

Chapter 4

❖

LILLIAN ROSS

Reporting

Before Tom Wolfe and his emphasis on status life and saturation reporting, before Truman Capote and his book-length reporting, there was Lillian Ross, who perhaps more than any other writer could stand as a model for good reporting in the second half of the twentieth century. Capote cited her *New Yorker* article "Picture" as an example of a nonfiction novella.[1] D. T. Max praised her for her fly-on-the-wall reporting. As Max pointed out, fly-on-the-wall reporting later became the standard, but when Ross did "Picture" it was new.[2]

She began her *New Yorker* career in 1948 and wrote for the "Talk of the Town" section, but she also wrote film criticism and fiction. She became known quite early for her nonfiction, especially "Picture" and "Portrait of Hemingway," both of which were also published as books and then republished in her collection, a book called *Reporting.* Both received praise and sharp criticism. The piece on Ernest Hemingway continued to rankle with critics fifteen years after it first appeared.

When *Portrait of Hemingway* was published as a book, Ross explained in the preface how she had first met Hemingway, how the profile had come about, and the outrage that had followed. She also said she considered the profile to be "a sympathetic piece, covering two days Hemingway spent in New York, in which I tried to describe as precisely as possible how Hemingway, who had the nerve to be like nobody else on earth, looked and sounded when he was in action, talking, between work periods—to give a picture of the man as he was, in his uniqueness and with his vitality and his enormous spirit of fun intact." In fact, the profile begins: "Ernest Hemingway, who may well be the greatest living American novelist and short-story writer, rarely comes to New York." As any journalist knows, the lead establishes the story.

The chronology gets a bit confusing. The Hemingway piece first appeared in 1950, "Picture" in 1952. But "Picture" was published as a book before "Portrait of Hemingway" was, and book reviews of *Picture* frequently criticized the Hemingway article.

The following excerpts come from "Picture" and "Portrait of Hemingway," as they appear in *Reporting*.

⚜ ⚜ ⚜

One day in the middle of December, Huston and James Agee, the novelist and former *Time* writer, who had been hired to collaborate with Huston on the script for "The African Queen," were working in the Horizon cottage, trying to finish the script in time for Huston's and Spiegel's departure for Africa, where the picture was to be filmed. In the front room of the cottage was a false fireplace containing a gas log. Huston's Academy Award statuettes stood on the mantel. Agee was saying, as Huston paced in small circles, that the trip the river captain, Humphrey Bogart, and the missionary's sister, Katharine Hepburn, would make together down the river on the captain's boat in "The African Queen" could symbolize the act of love.

"Oh, Christ, Jim," Huston said. "Tell me something I can understand. This isn't like a novel. This is a screenplay. You've got to demonstrate everything, Jim. People on the screen are gods and goddesses. We know all about them. Their habits. Their caprices. But we can't touch them. They're not real. They stand for something, rather than being something. They're symbols. You can't have symbolism within symbolism, Jim." He paced the floor and said he was going crazy. "I really hate the city," he said. "I've got to get out to the country and get on a horse. I get all mixed up in the city. You know where I'd like to be this very minute, Jim?" He spread his long arms along the mantel of the fireplace. "I'd like to be in Mexico. God!" He gave a stifled laugh, and said he guessed one of the best periods of his entire life had been spent, in his eighteenth year, in the Mexican cavalry. "What a time that was!" he said. "Always going places in Packards. You'd go the rounds of the cafes. Then you'd go to somebody's *finca*.

Then you'd play the next thing to Russian roulette. You'd cock a pistol and throw it up and hit the ceiling with it. It was great. Just great. I was their top jumping rider. God, those were wonderful days!"

Spiegel put his head in at the door. Huston stared at him for a moment without saying anything. Then he pretended to be shocked. "Christ, Sam'l, for a minute there you looked just like an act Dad used to do in vaudeville," he said in a menacing tone. Spiegel came into the room and looked from Huston to Agee with a hesitant smile. "I was six when I first saw Dad do this act!" Huston went on, in his special tone of amazement at his own words. "Dad played a house painter, come to paint this lady's house. There was a picture of her husband inside the front door. The husband's face would begin to make faces, and then this big head would shove through the door with electric lights for eyes. And I'd roar. And Dad would sing, 'I Haven't Got the Do-Re-Mi.' It was just wonderful. Ho! Ho! Ho!"

"So," said Spiegel. "How are things on the script?"

Huston said things were fine. "Only trouble is, Sam, we just demolished two weeks' work. Threw out every bit of it," he added lightly.

Spiegel swallowed hard. "When?" he asked.

"Just now," Huston said, with a forced grin.

"My ulcers are being formed," Spiegel said, and gave Agee an appealing look.

Agee seemed bewildered.

"We leave in four weeks," Spiegel said to Huston. "We must have the script before we leave."

"Don't worry, Sam'l," Huston said, in the reassuring tone he had used in talking with Reinhardt about the script for "The Red Badge of Courage."

Spiegel said, "Beneath this facade of worry is worry. Did you get anything done today?"

"Don't worry," said Huston. "There's nothing to worry about."

"I like to know what I'm worrying about," said Spiegel. "Now it's that I worry and I don't know why."

"John," Agee said, "when are you going to do the retakes for David Selznick?"

Spiegel wet his lips. "You expect to do retakes for Selznick?"

Huston nodded. "David is in a jam," he said.

"You can't. You have no time," Spiegel said. "Why? Is he offering you a fortune?"

"I'm doing it for nothing," Huston said.

Spiegel shook his head. "You can't do it," he said.
"When a pal of mine is in a jam, I do what I can to help," Huston said.
"You can't do it," said Spiegel.
"Like hell I can't," Huston said.
"No," Spiegel said.
Huston gave a choked laugh. "Your ulcers, Sam'l," he said softly.

⚜ ⚜ ⚜

The following excerpt, from "Portrait of Hemingway," begins
outside Hemingway's hotel. Ross and Hemingway have embarked
on a shopping trip. Hemingway was known to his friends as "Papa."

⚜ ⚜ ⚜

Hemingway balked for a moment in front of the hotel. It was a cool,
cloudy day. This was not good weather for him to be out in, he said sulkily,
adding that his throat felt kind of sore. I asked him if he wanted to see a
doctor. He said no. "I never trust a doctor I have to pay," he said, and
started across Fifth Avenue. A flock of pigeons flew by. He stopped,
looked up, and aimed an imaginary rifle at them. He pulled the trigger, and
then looked disappointed. "Very difficult shot," he said. He turned quickly
and pretended to shoot again. "Easy shot," he said. "Look!" He pointed
to a spot on the pavement. He seemed to be feeling better, but not
much better.

I asked him if he wanted to stop first at his optician's. He said no.
I mentioned the coat. He shrugged. Mrs. Hemingway had suggested that
he look for a coat at Abercrombie & Fitch, so I mentioned Abercrombie
& Fitch. He shrugged again and lumbered slowly over to a taxi, and we
started down Fifth Avenue in the afternoon traffic. At the corner of Fifty-
fourth, we stopped on a signal from the traffic cop. Hemingway growled.
"I love to see an Irish cop being cold," he said. "Give you eight to one he
was an M.P. in the war. Very skillful cop. Feints and fakes good. Cops
are not like they are in the Hellinger movies. Only once in a while." We
started up again, and he showed me where he once walked across Fifth
Avenue with Scott Fitzgerald. "Scott wasn't at Princeton any more, but he
was still talking football," he said, without animation. "The ambition of
Scott's life was to be on the football team. I said, 'Scott, why don't you cut

out this football?' I said, 'Come on, boy.' He said, 'You're crazy.' That's the end of that story. If you can't get through traffic, how the hell are you gonna get through the line. But I am not Thomas Mann," he added. "Get another opinion."

By the time we reached Abercrombie's, Hemingway was moody again. He got out of the taxi reluctantly and reluctantly entered the store. I asked him whether he wanted to look at a coat first or something else.

"Coat," he said unhappily.

In the elevator, Hemingway looked even bigger and bulkier than he had before, and his face had the expression of a man who is being forcibly subjected to the worst kind of misery. A middle-aged woman standing next to him stared at his scraggly white beard with obvious alarm and disapproval. "Good Christ!" Hemingway said suddenly, in the silence of the elevator, and the middle-aged woman looked down at her feet.

The doors opened at our floor, and we got out and headed for a rack of topcoats. A tall, dapper clerk approached us, and Hemingway shoved his hands into his pants pockets and crouched forward. "I think I still have credit in this joint," he said to the clerk.

The clerk cleared his throat. "Yes, sir," he said. "Want to see coat," Hemingway said menacingly.

"Yes, sir," said the clerk. "What kind of coat did you wish to see, sir?"

"That one." He pointed to a straight-hanging, beltless tan gabardine coat on the rack. The clerk helped him into it and gently drew him over to a full-length mirror. "Hangs like a shroud," Hemingway said, tearing the coat off. "I'm tall on top. Got any other coat?" he asked, as though he expected the answer to be no. He edged impatiently toward the elevators.

"How about this one, sir, with a removable lining, sir?" the clerk said. This one had a belt. Hemingway tried it on, studied himself in the mirror, and then raised his arms as though he were aiming a rifle. "You going to use it for *shooting*, sir?" the clerk asked. Hemingway grunted, and said he would take the coat. He gave the clerk his name, and the clerk snapped his fingers. "Of course!" he said. "There was *something . . .* " Hemingway looked embarrassed and said to send the coat to him at the Sherry-Netherland, and then said he'd like to look at a belt.

"What kind of belt, Mr. Hemingway?" the clerk asked.

"Guess a brown one," Hemingway said.

We moved over to the belt counter, and another clerk appeared.

"Will you show Mr. Hemingway a belt?" the first clerk said, and stepped back and thoughtfully watched Hemingway.

The second clerk took a tape measure from his pocket, saying he thought Hemingway was a size 44 or 46.

"Wanta bet?" Hemingway asked. He took the clerk's hand and punched himself in the stomach with it.

"Gee, he's got a hard tummy," the belt clerk said. He measured Hemingway's waistline. "Thirty-eight!" he reported. "Small waist for your size. What do you do—a lot of exercise?"

Hemingway hunched his shoulders, feinted, laughed, and looked happy for the first time since we'd left the hotel. He punched himself in the stomach with his own fist.

"Where you going—to Spain again?" the belt clerk asked.

"To Italy," Hemingway said, and punched himself in the stomach again. After Hemingway had decided on a brown calf belt, the clerk asked him whether he wanted a money belt. He said no—he kept his money in a checkbook.

Our next stop was the shoe department, and there Hemingway asked a clerk for some folding bedroom slippers.

"Pullman slippers," the clerk said. "What size?"

"'Levens," Hemingway said bashfully. The slippers were produced, and he told the clerk he would take them. "I'll put them in my pocket," he said. "Just mark them, so they won't think I'm a shoplifter."

"You'd be surprised what's taken from the store," said the clerk, who was very small and very old. "Why, the other morning, someone on the first floor went off with a big roulette wheel. Just picked it up and—"

Hemingway was not listening. "Wolfie!" he shouted at a man who seemed almost seven feet tall and whose back was to us.

The man turned around. He had a big, square red face, and at the sight of Hemingway it registered extreme joy. "Papa!" he shouted.

The big man and Hemingway embraced and pounded each other on the back for quite some time. It was Winston Guest. Mr. Guest told us he was going upstairs to pick up a gun, and proposed that we come along. Hemingway asked what kind of gun, and Guest said a ten-gauge magnum.

"Beautiful gun," Hemingway said, taking his bedroom slippers from the clerk and stuffing them into his pocket.

In the elevator, Hemingway and Guest checked with each other on how much weight they had lost. Guest said he was now down to two hundred and thirty-five, after a good deal of galloping around on polo ponies. Hemingway said he was down to two hundred and eight, after shooting ducks in Cuba and working on his book.

"How's the book now, Papa?" Guest asked as we got out of the elevator.

Hemingway gave his fist-to-the-face laugh and said he was going to defend his title once more. "Wolfie, all of a sudden I found I could write wonderful again, instead of just biting on the nail," he said slowly. "I think it took a while for my head to get rebuilt inside. You should not, ideally, break a writer's head open or give him seven concussions in two years or break six ribs on him when he is forty-seven or push a rear-view-mirror support through the front of his skull opposite the pituitary gland or, really, shoot at him too much. On the other hand, Wolfie, leave the sons of bitches alone and they are liable to start crawling back into the womb or somewhere if you drop a porkpie hat." He exploded into laughter.

Guest's huge frame shook with almost uncontrollable laughter. "God, Papa!" he said. "I still have your shooting clothes out at the island. When are you coming out to shoot, Papa?"

Hemingway laughed again and pounded him on the back. "Wolfie, you're so damn big!" he said.

Guest arranged to have his gun delivered, and then we all got into the elevator, the two of them talking about a man who caught a black marlin last year that weighed a thousand and six pounds.

"How do you like it now, gentlemen?" Hemingway asked.

"God, Papa!" said Guest.

On the ground floor, Guest pointed to a mounted elephant head on the wall. "Pygmy elephant, Papa," he said.

"Miserable elephant," said Hemingway.

Their arms around each other, they went out to the street. I said that I had to leave, and Hemingway told me to be sure to come over to the hotel early the next morning so that I could go with him and Patrick to the Metropolitan Museum. As I walked off, I heard Guest say, "God, Papa, I'm not ashamed of anything I've ever done."

"Nor, oddly enough, am I," said Hemingway.

I looked around. They were punching each other in the stomach and laughing raucously.

⚜ ⚜ ⚜

When *Portrait of Hemingway* was published as a book in 1961, Ross said in the preface that she, her editors, and Hemingway never expected the outrage that had followed the initial appearance of the profile as an article. Although Hemingway said he had found it "funny and good," Ross said some readers "reacted violently." She wrote that some felt she had ridiculed or attacked Hemingway because she had, among other things, quoted him using what she called "a kind of joke Indian language."

Some criticism of the Hemingway profile came in reviews of other Ross work. When Budd Schulberg analyzed *Picture,* for example, he also referred to the Hemingway profile, pointing out that it violated privacy and caught some people with their clichés down or their pretensions showing. He claimed that Ross, contrary to her publisher's claim, was neither tactful nor impartial. "Miss Ross' impartiality and tact," he wrote, "already are well known to *The New Yorker*'s readers of her gentle profile of Ernest Hemingway in 1950."[3]

When Ross published the Hemingway piece as a book, the famous novelist had just killed himself (on July 2, 1961, in Ketchum, Idaho). After Hemingway died and the book was published, Irving Howe wrote in an essay in *The New Republic* that Ross's interview was the cruelest act ever done to an American writer—that it was "a smear of vanity and petulence [*sic*] that only a journalistic Delilah would have put into print."[4] In a review of the book, Colin Campbell noted Ross's attempt to be as objective as a camera, but said that the profile had a "satiric thrust" and that Ross's juxtaposition of scenes caused "Hemingway to caricature himself."[5] Robert Manning said the profile, with its "peephole fascination," caught Hemingway "in an artificial and inattentive moment" and fell short of capturing the real person.[6] Granville Hicks, in reviewing a later Ross book, began by mentioning the Hemingway profile, which he said was "painfully revealing if not deliberately malicious." Hicks even imputed self-aggrandizing motives to Ross's writing, saying she "has a way of getting herself talked about."[7]

In her reply to Howe's essay, Ross spelled "petulance" correctly and said Howe's remarks were "irresponsible, rather sordid, and absolutely wrong."[8] She also quoted Hemingway as having written to her: "They can't understand you [meaning himself] being a serious writer and not be solemn." In her preface, she paraphrased that this way: "They couldn't under-stand his being a serious writer without being pompous." Part of her response forms the preface to the book and is quoted at the beginning of this chapter.[9]

In a letter to the editor, another letter writer also objected to Howe's characterization, saying Howe had missed the point of the profile, which was "not only a truly brilliant piece of reporting . . . but [also] a work of art."[10] A reviewer who defended Ross's work, Milton Hindus, said Ross had not been malicious and that she had "caught convincingly the note of fatuous self-satisfaction struck by the idol."[11] John Killinger said the profile was "probably the cleanest, most authentic, and most viable" of all the biographical material published and added: "It has caught the quintessence of Hemingway."[12]

Not everyone was negative. Herbert Mitgang said that in Ross's profile Hemingway "emerges as a far greater craftsman and intellectual than his current interpreters allow"[13]—in other words, that Ross did not get in the way of accurately portraying Hemingway's qualities. James Fixx said "there emerges a portrait clear enough to capture a man's complexity" and that Ross's style was "a manner of reporting that all but eliminates the reporter." Fixx also praised Ross for relying largely on facts rather than interpretation and for the steady and even tone of her writing.[14] Sandra Schmidt said Ross "is never cruel, merely detached." Likening her to a camera, Schmidt said: "One gets the impression that she is standing wide-eyed and slightly agape to one side of the door, carefully inconspicuous, taking it all uncritically in."[15]

When *Reporting* appeared, other critics commented on the Hemingway profile. Robert Manning, who had reviewed the profile as a book and hadn't changed his mind, wrote that her "pen struck with the thud of a tomahawk." He did not limit that description to the Hemingway profile. In addition to the Hemingway profile and "Picture," *Reporting* contains five other articles—"The Yellow Bus," "Symbol of All We Possess," "The Big Stone," "Terrific," and "El Único Matador." Manning said that in "Terrific," which is about the New York City Junior League's 1955 Mardis Gras Ball, and in "Symbol," which is about the Miss America competition of 1949, Ross "betrays the sound of meow and the sign of claws, but not to the detriment of eye and ear." In other words, Manning suggested that Ross was just a catty woman writing about other women, and would not give her her due as a good reporter. He called her "a disarmingly aggressive writer," which most journalists would consider a compliment but which Manning meant as a putdown. The headline on the review, "A deceptive style of needlework," suggests "woman's work."[16] John C. Pine said her "skillful reportorial technique can, of course, be devastating."[17] Even an admirer, Tom Wolfe, citing the Hemingway piece as an ancestor of the new journalism of the 1970s, referred to it as "Ross's famous evisceration of Ernest Hemingway."[18]

References to Hemingway surfaced again when "Picture" was published. Even before "Picture" became an article in *The New Yorker*, Hollywood was in a state of panic. Ross was attacked in *Partisan Review* by Hans Meyerhoff, who opened his essay by condemning her profile of Hemingway and ended defensively by saying that no matter what Ross wrote, it would not fairly portray Hollywood. Meyerhoff, whom *Newsweek* eventually identified as an assistant professor of philosophy at U.C.L.A. with only social connections to Hollywood,[19] made the peculiar argument that Hollywood could not be written about the same way Hemingway had been because they were two different subjects.[20] And all this was before the article even appeared in print.

When "Picture" was first published, it received criticism similar to that Ross had received for the Hemingway profile. Arthur Knight said Ross's articles had inspired heated comment. "For under her cold light," he wrote, "it is always the blemishes, the failings, the pettiness of her subjects that stand out."[21] Look back at the scene in which James Agee appears to discuss work on the screenplay for John Huston's next film, *The African Queen:* Ross has captured everyone in an unguarded moment, as some of the commentary on the article suggests. For example, James Hilton said that Ross had used all the selectivity of a novelist. He called it "the technique of the candid typewriter, which is no more truly candid than the candid camera, since neither clicks unless and until the operator chooses." Nevertheless, he suggested Hollywood had gotten what it deserved for giving Ross free access.[22]

Meyerhoff noted that Ross was a careful observer and took copious notes, "But she never seemed to say anything herself— except to ask questions."[23] The approach troubled Meyerhoff deeply because he felt that Ross's questions were simplistic and deceptive: she wanted to know what B-girls were, what a *Quattro-cento* was, what "The American Tragedy" (an upcoming movie) was. Meyerhoff suggested Ross already knew the answers to the questions, but apparently did not recognize Ross was taking care not to assume anything. She knew what a B-girl was, but she wanted to make sure the person with whom she was speaking had the same definition. The *Newsweek* article that identified Meyerhoff praised Ross for her documentary technique and her ear for dialogue, and said, "the girl from *The New Yorker* has caught Hollywood in a series of takes as keenly focused as those of any camera."[24]

As some of the preceding comments suggest, Ross was (quite rightly) a calculating reporter. In a letter to her managing editor, William Shawn, Ross explained how she saw the story taking shape as she was reporting it. She said she saw it becoming "a kind of novel-like book because of the way the characters may develop and the variety of relationships that exist among them."[25] After the story was published, Ross wrote: "Every time I was around my principal characters in the unfolding drama, I would hear their interchanges in terms of how they would sound in my evolving scenes. I felt as though I was being handed a bonanza. I thought I was the luckiest reporter in the history of journalism."[26]

Lucky or not, today *Picture* is the benchmark against which any other book on the making of a movie is measured. In 1992, Joseph Nocera, reviewing more recent books on Hollywood, called *Picture* a "shrewd, engaging, blow-by-blow chronicle," and faulted Ross only for her refusal to report anything she did not see, which almost caused her to miss a subplot in the story about the making of the movie.[27]

Reviews of Ross's subsequent books also describe Ross as a good reporter and writer. Reviewing *Talk Stories*, a collection of Ross's shorter *New Yorker* pieces, Irving Wallace talked about her "unique writing style—spare, direct, objective, fast—a style that disarms, seeming only full of wonder, but one that can suddenly, almost sneakily, nail a personality naked to a page."[28] Marya Mannes said Ross knew "how to record the revealing phrase, the defining gesture."[29] Alice S. Morris talked about Ross's "talent for high-fidelity observation."[30] And, yes, two of these three reviewers mentioned the Hemingway profile—but it was because they liked it.

The fact that people liked it should not come as a surprise. It is not the evisceration of Hemingway its early critics said it was. Instead, it is a fine piece of reporting that has held up quite well, and the book *Reporting*, as James Fixx stated, "deserves to be recommended to any reporter interested in a postgraduate course in his [or her] craft."[31]

ENDNOTES

1. Quoted in George Plimpton, "The Story Behind a Nonfiction Novel," *New York Times Book Review*, 16 January 1966, 2

2. D. T. Max, "'Picture' author Ross remembers it well," *Variety*, 24 May 1993, 63.

3. Budd Schulberg, "What Makes Hollywood Run?" *New York Times Book Review*, 23 November 1952, 4. Schulberg was the author of the novel *What Makes Sammy Run*, hence the headline on his review.

4. Irvin Howe, "Hemingway: The Conquest of Panic," *New Republic*, 24 July 1961, 19.

5. Colin Campbell, "Trio of Hemingway Portraits," *Christian Science Monitor*, 16 August 1962, p. 7.

6. Robert Manning, "A Profile, but Is It a Likeness?" *Herald Tribune Book Review*, 17 November 1961, 7.

7. Granville Hicks, "The Hi-Fi Hollow of Dr. Fifield," *Saturday Review*, 25 May 1963, 25.

8. Lillian Ross, "Correspondence: The Hemingway Profile," *New Republic*, 7 August 1961, 30–31.

9. According to the book, the preface was broadcast in abridged form by the BBC as part of a program, "Tribute to Ernest Hemingway," in July 1961. Lillian Ross, *Portrait of Hemingway* (New York: Simon and Schuster, 1961).

10. Julian I. Mazor, "Correspondence: The Hemingway Profile," *New Republic*, 7 August 1961, 31.

11. Milton Hindus, "The 'Papa' They Knew," *New York Times Book Review*, 4 March 1962, 16.

12. John Killinger, "When Paper Was Still in the Ring," *Saturday Review*, 13 January 1962, 59.

13. Herbert Mitgang, "The Art of Needle-Point Reportage," *New York Times*, 8 April 1964, 41.

14. James Fixx, "Books in Communications," *Saturday Review*, 14 March 1964, 133.

15. Sandra Schmidt, "The Girl With the Camera Eyes," *Christian Science Monitor*, 30 April 1964, p. 4.

16. Robert Manning, "A deceptive style of needlework," *Washington Post Book World,* 15 March 1964, 5.
17. John C. Pine, "Book Review," *Library Journal,* March 1964, 1090.
18. Tom Wolfe, *The New Journalism,* with an anthology edited by Tom Wolfe and E. W. Johnson (New York: Harper & Row, 1973), 46.
19. "Hollywood Profiled," *Newsweek,* 9 June 1952, 54.
20. Hans Meyerhoff, "'The New Yorker' in Hollywood," *Partisan Review,* September–October 1951, 574.
21. Arthur Knight, "Battle-orders In Beverly Hills," *Saturday Review,* 29 November 1952, 34.
22. James Hilton, "Hollywood: Ross'-Eye-View," *Herald Tribune Book Review,* 23 November 1952, 14.
23. Meyerhoff, "'New Yorker' in Hollywood," 571.
24. "Hollywood Profiled," 56.
25. Lillian Ross, *Here but Not Here,* (New York: Random House: 1998), 90.
26. Ibid., 91.
27. Joseph Nocera, "The Book in Hollywood," *GQ,* February 1992, 69, 70.
28. Irving Wallace, "Innocent Bystander," *New York Times Book Review,* 15 May 1966, 10.
29. Marya Mannes, "The Soft Facts," *Washington Post Book Week,* 1 May 1966, 4.
30. Alice S. Morris, "All the Tricks of the Trade," *New York Times Books Review,* 2 June 1963, 5.
31. Fixx, "Book in Communications," 133.

Chapter 5

❧

The Story of a Shipwrecked Sailor

T he Colombian destroyer *Caldas*[1] set sail from Mobile, Alabama, on February 24, 1955. Its voyage should have been a routine return trip through the Gulf of Mexico and the Caribbean Sea to Cartagena, Colombia. Instead, as the small ship moved into the Caribbean two days later, a large wave arose and swept overboard eight sailors who were on the deck. Only Luis Alejandro Velasco survived. He spent ten days drifting on a raft before coming ashore at Umbá, Colombia.[2]

The *Caldas*, meanwhile, had arrived in Cartagena within two hours of losing the eight men. The Colombian government announced that a storm had caused the loss of life. When Alejandro Velasco surfaced, the government kept him sequestered in a naval hospital and made him available only to journalists favorable to the regime of General Gustavo Rojas Pinilla, the dictator of Colombia. Alejandro Velasco was treated as a hero and cashed in on his fame, serving as a paid spokesman for, among other things, watches (his kept on ticking for the ten days he was lost a sea) and shoes (his sustained him as food).

But fame was fleeting. When most Colombians grew tired of Alejandro Velasco he turned to the Bogotá newspaper *El Espectador*, an opposition newspaper whose staff had no one older than thirty. The editor asked one of his reporters, Gabriel García Márquez (nicknamed "Gabo"), to interview Alejandro Velasco and write the story.

When it comes to interviewing, García Márquez has a view on tape recorders that is similar to Truman Capote's. Once an interview is being taped, he told an interviewer, the person being interviewed changes his attitude. He also said that a tape recorder betrays the person being interviewed because "it even records and remembers when you make an ass of yourself." "As a journalist," García Márquez said, "I feel that we still haven't learned how to use a tape recorder to do an interview." He advocated participating in a long conversation without taking notes, then afterward reminiscing about the conversation and writing it down as an impression of what the interviewer felt, not necessarily in the exact words of the interview itself.[3]

García Márquez interviewed Alejandro Velasco at length, boiled down his notes and wrote a fourteen-part series in the first person of Alejandro Velasco. This is the third part.

⚜ ⚜ ⚜

My first impression was that I was utterly alone in the middle of the ocean. Trying to stay afloat, I watched another wave crash against the destroyer. The ship, now about two hundred meters from me, plunged into an abyss and disappeared from sight. I thought it had gone under. And a moment later, as if to confirm what I had thought, all the crates of merchandise that had been loaded onto the destroyer in Mobile began to surface and floated toward me, one by one. I kept afloat by grabbing on to the crates of clothing, radios, refrigerators, and other household goods that bounced around, willy-nilly, battered by the waves. I had no idea what was happening; a bit stunned, I took hold of one of the bobbing crates and stupidly began to contemplate the sea. It was a perfectly clear day. Except for the choppy waves produced by the wind and the cargo scattered across the surface, there was no evidence of a shipwreck.

Soon I began to hear shouts nearby. Through the sharp whistling of the wind, I recognized the voice of Julio Amador Caraballo, the tall, well-built first warrant officer, who was yelling at someone: "Grab hold there, under the life preserver."

It was as if in that instant I had awakened from a moment's deep sleep. It dawned on me that I wasn't alone in the sea. There, only a few meters away, my mates were shouting to one another and trying to stay afloat. Quickly, I began to think. I couldn't swim in just any direction. I knew we were about fifty miles from Cartagena, but I was not yet frightened. For a moment I thought I could hold on to the crate indefinitely, until help arrived. It was reassuring to know that all around me other sailors were in the same predicament. That was when I saw the raft.

There were two life rafts about seven meters apart. They appeared unexpectedly on the crest of a wave, near where my mates were calling out. It seemed odd that none of them could reach the life rafts. In an instant, one of the rafts disappeared from view. I couldn't decide whether to risk swimming toward the other one or stay safely anchored to my crate. But before I had time to decide, I found myself swimming toward the one I could see, which was moving farther away from me. I swam for about three minutes. I lost sight of the raft momentarily, but I was careful not to lose my bearings. Suddenly, a rough wave pushed the raft alongside me— it was huge, white, and empty. I struggled to grab the rigging and jump aboard. I made it on the third try. Once on the raft, panting, whipped by the wind, immobilized and freezing, I found it hard to sit up. Then I saw three of my mates near the raft, trying to reach it.

I recognized them immediately. Eduardo Castillo, the quartermaster, had a firm grip around Julio Amador Caraballo's neck. Caraballo, who had been on watch when the accident occurred, was wearing his life jacket. He yelled: "Hold on tight, Castillo." They floated amid the scattered cargo, about ten meters away.

On the other side was Luis Rengifo. Only a few minutes before, I had seen him on the destroyer, trying to stay above water with his headphones aloft in his right hand. With his habitual calm, with that good sailor's confidence that allowed him to boast that the sea would get seasick before he did, he had stripped off his shirt so that he could swim better, but he had lost his life jacket. Even if I hadn't seen him, I would have recognized his cry: "Fatso, paddle over here."

I quickly grabbed the oars and tried to get closer to the men. Julio Amador, with Eduardo Castillo clinging to his neck, neared the raft. Much farther away, looking small and desolate, was the fourth of my mates: Ramón Herrera, who was waving at me while he held on to a crate.

If I had had to decide, I wouldn't have known which of my mates to go after first. But when I saw Ramón Herrera, of the revel in Mobile, the happy young man from Arjona who had been with me on the stern only a few moments before, I began to paddle furiously. But the life raft was almost two meters long. It was very heavy in that lurching sea, and I had to row against the wind. I don't think I managed to advance more than a meter. Desperate, I looked around once more and saw that Ramón Herrera had disappeared. Only Luis Rengifo was swimming confidently toward the raft. I was sure he would make it. I had heard him snoring below my bunk, and I was convinced that his serenity was stronger than the sea.

In contrast, Julio Amador was struggling with Eduardo Castillo, so that Castillo wouldn't let go of his neck. They were less than three meters away. I figured that if they got just a little closer, I could hold out an oar for them to grab. But at that moment a gigantic wave lifted the raft, and from the top of the huge crest I could see the mast of the destroyer, heading away from me. When I came down again, Julio Amador had vanished, with Eduardo Castillo hanging on to his neck. Alone, two meters away, Luis Rengifo was still swimming calmly toward the raft.

I don't know why I did this absurd thing: knowing I couldn't move forward, I put the oar in the water as though trying to prevent the raft from moving, trying to anchor it in place. Luis Rengifo, exhausted, paused a moment, then raised his arm as he had when he held his headphones aloft, and shouted again: "Row over here, Fatso!"

The wind was blowing from his direction. I yelled that I couldn't row against the wind, that he should make another try, but I felt he hadn't heard me. The crates of cargo had disappeared and the life raft danced from side to side, battered by the waves. In an instant I was five meters away from Luis Rengifo and had lost sight of him. But he appeared in another spot, still not panicking, ducking underwater to prevent the waves from sweeping him away. I stood up, holding out the oar, hoping Luis Rengifo could get close enough to reach it. But then I could see he was tiring, losing heart. He called to me again, sinking: "Fatso! Fatso!"

I tried to row, but . . . it was as hopeless as the first time. I made a last try so that Luis Rengifo could reach the oar, but the raised hand, which a few minutes earlier had been trying to keep the headphones from sinking, sank forever, less than two meters from the oar.

I don't know how long I stayed like that, balancing in the life raft, holding out the oar. I kept searching the water, hoping that someone would surface soon. But the sea was clear and the wind, getting stronger, blew against my shirt like the howl of a dog. The cargo had disappeared. The mast, growing more distinct, proved that the destroyer hadn't sunk, as I had first thought. I felt calm. I thought that in a minute they would come looking for me. I thought that one of my mates had managed to reach the other life raft.

There was no reason they shouldn't have reached it. The rafts weren't provisioned—in fact, none of the destroyer's life rafts was outfitted. But there were six of them, apart from the rowboats and the whalers. It was reasonable to believe that some of my mates had reached the other life rafts, as I had reached mine, and perhaps the destroyer was searching for us.

Very soon I was aware of the sun. A midday sun, hot and metallic. Stupefied, not fully recovered, I looked at my watch. It was noon on the dot.

The last time Luis Rengifo had asked me the time, on the destroyer, it was 11:30. I had checked the time again, at 11:50, and the disaster had not yet occurred. When I looked at my watch on the life raft, it was exactly noon. It had taken only ten minutes for everything to happen—for me to reach the life raft, and try to rescue my shipmates, and stand motionless in the raft, searching the empty sea, listening to the sharp howl of the wind. I thought it would take them at least two or three hours to rescue me.

Two or three hours, I calculated. It seemed an extraordinarily long time to be alone at sea. But I tried to resign myself to it. I had no food or water, and by three in the afternoon I would surely have a searing thirst. The sun burned my head and my skin, which was dry and hardened by salt. Since I had lost my cap, I splashed water on my head, and I just sat on the side of the raft, waiting to be rescued.

It was only then that I felt the pain in my right knee. The thick, blue drill fabric of my trouser leg was wet, so I had a hard time rolling it up. But when I did, I was startled: I saw a deep, half-moon-shaped wound on the lower part of my knee. I didn't know if I had gashed it on the side of the ship, or if it had happened when I hit the water, for I didn't notice it until I was seated in the life raft. Though the wound burned a little, it had stopped bleeding and was completely dry, because of the salt water, I imagine.

Uncertain as to what to do, I decided to make an inventory of my belongings. I wanted to figure out what I could count on in my solitude at sea. First of all, I could rely on my watch, which kept perfect time, and which I couldn't stop glancing at every two or three minutes. In addition, I had my gold ring, which I'd bought in Cartagena the year before, and a chain with a medal of the Virgin of Carmen on it, also purchased in Cartagena, from another sailor for thirty-five pesos. In my pockets I had nothing but the keys to my locker on the destroyer and three business cards I had been given at a store in Mobile one day in January when I had gone out shopping with Mary Address. Since I had nothing to do, I read the cards over and over to distract myself until I was rescued. I don't know why the cards seemed like the messages in bottles that shipwrecked sailors pitch into the sea. I think if I had had a bottle at that moment I would have put one of the cards into it, playing shipwrecked sailor, just to do something amusing to tell my friends about in Cartagena.

⚜ ⚜ ⚜

García Márquez had hit pay dirt. He had come upon a story for which there was an official version, and then discovered, during the twenty days he spent interviewing Alejandro Velasco, that there was another version, a version that indicated malfeasance on the part of the ship's officers (one of whom died in the disaster) and a larger moral decay in the government. García Márquez discovered the truth on the fourth day when he asked Alejandro Velasco to describe the storm that had caused the disaster.

"There was no storm," García Márquez recorded Alejandro Velasco as responding.[4] What García Márquez learned from Alejandro Velasco was that the ship had been overloaded with contraband—refrigerators, television sets and washing machines—the members of the crew intended to resell in Colombia. Because military equipment is to be used for military purposes only, that cargo was in itself illegal. Because of the contraband, as well, the ship was overweight and could not be maneuvered to rescue the sailors. "As his cultural level was only fair," García Márquez reported later, "he didn't realize the extreme importance of many of the details he told me spontaneously, and was surprised at my being so struck by them."[5]

Since the opening of the series did not tip off the government that the navy was about to be exposed, the series, even though it was appearing in an opposition newspaper, was allowed to run with government approval. And once the truth was out, the government, in García Márquez's words, would have been "politically dishonest" to halt the publication. When the series ended, the government did deny the story, so the staff of *El Espectador* tracked down *Caldas* sailors who had photographs of the contraband on the overloaded ship. One week after the series appeared, the newspaper reprinted it in a special supplement— with photographs. This time the government reacted, taking steps that eventually led to shutting down the newspaper, and García Márquez began a lengthy exile from his native Colombia.

Over the years he developed an international reputation as a novelist. In 1982 he was awarded the Nobel Prize for Literature. Around 1970, a Spanish publisher engaged him to issue the Alejandro Velasco story as a book; then, as García Márquez's fame grew, the story was translated and published in English— after he won the Nobel prize. "I find it depressing," García Márquez wrote in the preface, "that the publishers are not so much interested in the merit of the story as in the name of the author, which, much to my sorrow, is also that of a fashionable writer." But he is also a very good writer, one who has never given up practicing journalism,[6] which he has called "the noblest profession in the world."[7]

The writing in *Sailor* is simple. Campbell Geeslin said the book is "straightforward, without literary pretension, and it provides exciting entertainment in less time than it takes to watch a television miniseries."[8] Robert Louis Sims also used a television analogy. He said that García Márquez had merged "the *seen* and the *lived* to create what is called in electronic journalism 'live coverage' in which the words of the reporter are broadcast without being scripted."[9] Richard Eder, who saw the publication of the book as more of a publishing event than a literary one, said the story was told unremarkably, although the ordeal was extraordinary.[10] But Bruce Allen called the book "this small gem of storytelling."[11] Barbara Hillman said it was "truly spellbinding" and that the language had "a precision and vividness of detail that make it very immediate."[12]

Even in his fiction, García Márquez has been praised for his vivid writing, which critics generally attribute to his journalistic background. When he won the Nobel Prize he was praised "for his novels and short stories, in which the fantastic and the realistic are combined in a richly composed world of imagination, reflecting a continent's life and conflicts."[13] In analyzing *A Chronicle of a Death Foretold*, Raymond L. Williams called that novel's opening sentence "arresting"—"On the day they were going to kill him, Santiago Nasar got up at five-thirty in the morning to wait for the boat the bishop was coming on"— and suggested it was typical of García Márquez's fiction and journalism.[14] Bill Buford said *Chronicle* was "written in the manner of investigative journalism and in a conspicuously flattened, unadorned prose."[15]

García Márquez's work has been referred to as "bigeneric writing" and "narrative journalism."[16] Unlike some successful novelists who would rather forget their journalistic origins, García Márquez happily connects them. "Journalism helps maintain contact with reality, which is essential to literature," he once said. "And vice versa: literature teaches you how to write."[17]

Sailor is also a reconstruction, or what is known in Spanish journalese as a "refrito" (literally "refried").[18] It should come as no surprise, then, that García Márquez considers John Hersey's *Hiroshima*, also a reconstruction, "an exceptional piece" of journalism.[19] Sims confirmed the relationship between the two books and invited inclusion of others in their category, including Qian Gang's *Great China Earthquake*, when he said of García Márquez: "Human beings produce events and journalism, among other mass media, transmits these events, but all too often the facts suppress the voices and shroud the human content. Freeing the voices is a subversive act in itself, especially when it involves governments and other official institutions which want to establish and impose a monolithic concept of reality."[20]

That is a perfect description of *Sailor*. Because *Sailor* was written for an opposition newspaper, García Márquez could not write the story directly, say as an inverted pyramid with a lead proclaiming that lives were lost because of incompetence and corruption. Because the story appeared in an opposition newspaper, government supporters might discount such muckraking. By using the narrative and telling the story in the words of the surviving sailor, however, *El Espectador* would function as the messenger, not the message. Of course, the newspaper lost its upper hand when it reprinted the story with photographs. That was a direct attack on the government, albeit a commendable one.

As a newspaper series, *Sailor* ended each day with what is called a cliffhanger. That device worked for Piers Paul Read,[21] but not for Michiko Kakutani,[22] who both wrote reviews in the *New York Times*. In a book, the cliffhanger ending for each chapter might seem contrived, because the book appears before the reader as one package. But in a newspaper, made up of (relatively) shorter stories, the cliffhanger seems to fit, to be part of the discontinuity so typical of the news. In the 1990s, in fact, newspaper serials, which had already been around for 150 years (albeit it as fiction in the early decades), appeared to be making a comeback.

Kakutani's review ended by saying that the book "remains a fairly ephemeral piece of journalism and only a very provisional blueprint for what Mr. García would accomplish in the years ahead." In 1986 García Márquez did write a similar book, titled *Clandestine in Chile: The Adventures of Miguel Littín,* which told the story of how Littín, an exiled film director, sneaked into Chile in disguise and shot 100,000 feet of film.* Again, García Márquez interviewed the subject extensively, then wrote in the first person of Littín. García Márquez converting 600 pages of transcript into 150 pages of text.[23] For *Sailor,* García Márquez interviewed Alejandro Velasco intensively and asked trick questions to see whether Alejandro Velasco would contradict himself. With Littín, García Márquez was at least as intense, although more trusting. "I underwent a relaxed but very precise interrogation," Littín said later, recalling that García Márquez asked him to remember how people dressed, the weather, the smells. "Then he'd give me homework. He'd say he wanted more details on my itinerary, what train I took, and so on."[24]

García Márquez probably used the same approach for *News of a Kidnapping,* which was published in Spanish in 1996 and in English in 1997. That book focuses on the story of ten people, most of them Colombian journalists, who were kidnapped in 1990 by the Medellín drug boss Pablo Escobar. Told from the omniscient point of view, the book is rich in detail that García Márquez pulled from the survivors and their relatives during extensive interviews. The novelist Muriel Spark praised the book for being "deeply researched and verified" and said that it had "realism that no mere journalist but only a true artist could achieve"[25]—an observation that might also be made about *The Story of a Shipwrecked Sailor,* written four decades earlier. Additional praise for García Márquez's realism came from Joan Didion. who quoted from *The Autumn of the Patriarch* in *Salvador*

---

*Chilean military authorities burned fourteen thousand copies, according to the Associated Press (25 January 1987).

and then said she had begun to see García Márquez "in a new light, as a social realist."[26]

The Story of a Shipwrecked Sailor demonstrates a technique not common in journalism—writing in the first person of the main subject of the story—but that does not diminish the book as a journalistic enterprise. The book also functions as a subtle piece of subversive journalism in attempting to present the truth from the point of view of the participant rather than from the perspective of the investigator or official sources. Good journalism does that.

ENDNOTES

1. Perhaps named after Franciso José Caldas (1770–1816), who was, among other things, a Colombian general, author, and journalist. He was executed under the orders of a Spanish general sent to put down a rebellion in Colombia.
2. Unless otherwise noted, the information in this introduction comes from Gabriel García Márquez, *The Story of a Shipwrecked Sailor* (New York: Vintage, 1986), v–ix.
3. Peter H. Stone, "The Art of Fiction," *Paris Review,* Winter 1981, p. 47.
4. García Márquez, *Shipwrecked Sailor,* vii.
5. Quoted in Rita Guibert, *Seven Voices* (New York: Knopf, 1973), 309.
6. Marlise Simons, "Storyteller with Bent for Revolution," *New York Times,* 22 October 1982, p. A10.
7. Robert Lewis Sims, *The First García Márquez* (Lanham, Md.: University Press of America, 1992), 3. Sims attributes this quotation, which he translated, to Victor Rodríguez Núñez, "La peregrinación de la jirafa. García Márquez: su periodismo costeño," *Casa de las Américas* 23:137 March–April 1983, 27–8.
8. Campbell Geeslin, "The story of a shipwrecked sailor," *People,* 2 June 1986, 23.
9. Sims, *The First García Márquez,* 171.
10. Richard Eder, "Book Review Desk," *Los Angeles Times,* 27 April 1986, p. 3.
11. Bruce Allen, "Early Work Foretells a Nobel Prize," *Chicago Tribune,* 27 April 1986, p. 44. No doubt the headline is a play on García Márquez's *Chronicle of a Death Foretold.*
12. Barbara Hillman, "Book Reviews," United Press International, 12 May 1986. Retrieved via Nexis.
13. John Vinocur, "Garcia Marquez of Colombia Wins Nobel Literature Prize," *New York Times,* 22 October 1982, p. 1.

14. Raymond L. Williams, *Gabriel García Márquez* (Boston: Twayne, 1984), 135.
15. Bill Buford, "Haughty falconry and collective guilt," *Times Literary Supplement,* 10 September 1982, 965.
16. Sims, *The First García Márquez,* 147, 154. Sims attributes the phrase "narrative journalism" to Pedro Sorela, *El otro García Márquez: Los años difíciles* (Madrid: Mondadori, 1988).
17. Quoted in Edith Grossman, "Truth Is Stranger Than Fact," *Latin American Literature and Arts Review,* September–December 1981, 72. Grossman translated the quotation from Francisco Fajardo, "El último opus de García Márquez," *Lu Mañana,* Montevideo, 10 May 1981.
18. Sims, *The First García Márquez,* 123. Sims is citing Sorela.
19. Stone, "The Art of Fiction," 49.
20. Sims, *The First García Márquez,* 155.
21. Piers Paul Read, "The Hero Who Lived to Regret It," *New York Times Book Review,* 27 April 1986, 11.
22. Michiko Kakutani, "Early García Márquez," *New York Times,* 26 April 1986, p. 10.
23. Alan Riding, "A Chilean Exile Returns in Disguise," *New York Times,* 22 October 1982, p. A10.
24. Quoted in Ibid.
25. Muriel Spark, "International Books of the Year," *Times Literary Supplement,* 8 December 1997, 8.
26. Joan Didion, *Salvador* (New York: Washington Square Press, 1983), 59.

Chapter 6

❖

A. J. LIEBLING

The Earl of Louisiana

S omeone wrote anonymously in *The New Yorker*, upon the death of A. J. Liebling, "He wrote with real joy."[1] That joy shows time and again in Liebling's essays on eating and the press, in his reportage on a variety of events and places, and in his profiles of characters such as Colonel John R. Stingo and Earl Long. Long was a member of a Louisiana political dynasty and the last major subject on which Abbott Joseph Liebling practiced his joy of writing.

Earl Long was the younger brother of Huey, who was assassinated in 1935. In 1959, during his second term as governor, Earl Long started behaving strangely and his wife had him committed to a sanitarium in Texas. Liebling's wife, the short-story writer Jean Stafford, who had lived in Louisiana with her first husband, Robert Lowell, in the early 1940s, told Liebling about Long in front of William Shawn, who at the time was the editor of *The New Yorker* and trying to talk Liebling out of taking a job at *Newsweek*. With the background Stafford provided on Long, Shawn became interested and asked Liebling to pursue the story. Liebling never left *The New Yorker*.[2]

Before Liebling arrived at *The New Yorker* in 1935, he had jobs at various newspapers—"intermittent employment as a newspaperman" was the way the anonymous *New York Times* obituary writer put it[3]—among them, the *New York Times*, the *Evening Bulletin* of Providence, Rhode Island, the *New York World*, and the *New York World-Telegram and Journal*.

At *The New Yorker*, Liebling had a reputation for being a good interviewer. Brendan Gill wrote that Liebling would sit silently facing the person he was supposed to interview until the subject, no longer able to bear the silence, would begin to talk.[4] He used other approaches, too, especially the one of doing enough research on the subject of an interview to know, in Liebling's words, "what questions are likely to stimulate a response."[5]

Liebling was particularly proud of the preparation he had done for an interview with the jockey Eddie Arcaro, who launched into a virtual non-stop reply to Liebling's opening question: "How many holes longer do you keep your left stirrup than your right?" Liebling knew most jockeys ride that way. The question eventually led Arcaro to say: "I can see you've been around riders a lot." Only for a week before the interview, Liebling admitted later.

Horses and the track also figured in Liebling's approach to Earl Long. He realized Long was not going to grant him, a northerner from a liberal magazine, an interview. So at a news conference, Liebling waited until others had asked questions, then wrangled an introduction to Long: "Governor," Liebling said, "I am not a newspaperman. I am with you all the way about publishers. Nor am I primarily interested in politics. I came all the way down here to find out your system for beating the horses."[6] Taken aback, Long replied: "I got no particular system." He then talked for a paragraph on how he saw betting—"a good thing to take your mind off your troubles and keep you out in the air." Liebling followed up with another betting question. Within a few minutes Long had invited him and Stafford (the "Northern lady" in the following excerpt) to stay for dinner.

The following excerpt is Chapter 8 in the book, which is titled "BLAM-BLAM-BLAM." Readers are cautioned that the excerpt reveals a patronizing attitude toward African-Americans that was common at the time and place, as well as a condescending view of "redneck" southerners.

⚜ ⚜ ⚜

There had been so many people in the room, and for so long, that they had taken the snap out of the air-conditioning. The men staying on for dinner—about fifteen of us—took off their coats and laid them down on chairs and sofas.

One of the women guests, a Northerner, inadvertently sat on a jacket a political gent had laid aside. It was a silvery Dacron-Acrilan-nylon-airpox miracle weave nubbled in Danish-blue asterisks. She made one whoop and rose vertically, like a helicopter. She had sat on his gun, an article of apparel that in Louisiana is considered as essential as a zipper. Eyebrows rose about as rapidly as she did, and by the time she came down she decided that comment would be considered an affectation.

A colored man brought a glass wrapped in a napkin to the Governor—"Something for my throat," the latter explained and the members of his inner council gathered at his flanks and knees for the powwow on catfish bait. One of the bills Earl had in mind would give individual members of the Legislature scholarship funds to allot personally to young people in their districts. Another would raise the salaries of assistant attorney generals, whose friends in the Legislature might be expected to respond. There were various local baits, funds for construction. The compounders kept their voices low and mysterious, as if saying "One-half pint of fish oil, one ounce of tincture of asafetida, one ounce of oil of rhodium—that will fetch them," or "Mix equal parts of soft Limburger cheese and wallpaper cleaner—never fails." Sometimes a conspirator would be unable to suppress a laugh.

A Mr. Siegelin, a political catfisherman arriving late, brought with him two children, a girl of about ten and a boy of five.

"Give them Cokes," the Governor said, and while a state cop hurried off to fill the order, he said to the little girl, "I hope you ain't going steady yet."

The little girl shook her head, and Uncle Earl said, "That's right. I went with more than a hundred before I made up my mind."

Made it up too soon at that, he probably thought, as he wondered about Miz Blanche and the mortgage money.

The children took their Cokes and settled down on facing identical love seats to drink them, while their father, a fair man in shirt sleeves, sat down to join in the bait suggestions, with his equivalent of "Cut smoked herring into bits. Soak in condensed milk several days." The group was still in the midst of bait-mixing when a plug-ugly, either a state trooper or a bodyguard from civilian life, came to the top of the steps leading to the dining room and shouted, "It's ready!" By his tone I judged him ravenously hungry.

The catfishermen remained engrossed in their concoctive deliberations, and the plug-ugly shouted at Mrs. Dixon, whom he judged less engaged, "C'mawn, *Maggie!*"

Mrs. Dixon rose, and the catfishermen, Southern gentlemen after all, perforce rose too and rushed toward the dining room in her wake, the Governor dragging the two children.

The ballroom smacked of Bachelors' Hall, lacking the touch of a woman's fastidious hand, but the dining end of the Mansion, I was happy to see, was well kept up. The long table under the great chandelier was covered with a mountain range of napkins folded into dunce caps, with streams of table silver in the valleys between them, and the iced tea, Sargassified with mint and topped with cherry, was pretty near *Ladies' Home Journal* color-ad perfection. Negro waiters and waitresses swarmed about, smiling to welcome Odysseus home. None of them, either, seemed to miss Penelope. The wanderer, his heart expanding in this happy atmosphere, propelled me to a seat at the head of the table.

He took his place at my left, with the Northern lady across the table from him. Around the longboard crouched plug-uglies in sports shirts, alternating with the guests: Tom, Mrs. Dixon, Senator Fredericks, Siegelin, the two Siegelin children clutching Coca-Cola bottles, and half a dozen politicians I hadn't met. The colossal figure of Mr. Joe Arthur Sims, the Governor's personal counsel, dominated the other end of the table. Mr. Sims had his right arm in a plaster cast that kept his hand above his head, as if perpetually voting Aye. He had sustained an odd sort of fracture on July 4, he explained.

It had followed hard on his stump speech for the Governor, a great oratorical effort, but he denied that he had thrown the arm out of joint. He said he was in an auto crash.

The Governor said, "We don't serve hard liquor here. Da church people wouldn't like it. But I'll get you some beer. Bob," he called to one of the somber seneschals, "get da man some beer." Quickly, the waiter fetched a can, two holes newly punched in the top, ready for drinking, and set it down on the table.

The beer bore an unfamiliar label, and the Governor said, "Dat looks like some of dat ten-cent beer from Schwegmann's." (He had probably bought it himself, on one of his raids for bargains.) "Dat looks like some of da stuff dat when da brewers got an overstock, dey sell it to da supermarkets. Get da man some good beer. And bring a glass—hear?"

He looked so healthy now that I ventured a compliment.

"You fooled those doctors, all right," I said. "You're like that Swede Johansson—you have your own way of training."

"You see dat fight?" the Governor asked, suspending his attack on the salad, which he was tossing between his dentures with the steady motion of a hay-forker. I said I had.

"I didn't see it, but I would have if I thought da fellow had a chance to lick Patterson," the Governor said. "Patterson's pretty good." (If he looked at the return fight, he was let down again.)

"I hear they've got a law here in Louisiana that a white boy can't even box on the same card with colored boys," I said.

"Yeah," said the Governor, "but dat kind of stuff is foolish. If dere's enough money in it, dey're bound to get together."

I recognized the theory of an economic resolution of the race conflict.

He sat there like a feudal lord, and his *maisnie*, the men of his household, leaned toward him like Indians around a fire. The trenchers went around, great platters of country ham and fried steak, in the hands of the black serving men, and sable damsels toted the grits and gravy. There was no court musician, possibly because he would have reminded the Earl of Jimmie Davis, but there was a court jester, and now the master called for a jape.

"Laura, Laura," he called out to one of the waitresses, "set your tray down—dere, hand it to Bob. Tell us what your husband does for a living."

"Prize fighter, sir," the girl said.

"Show us how he does when he goes in da ring," the Governor ordered.

The girl, long, thin and whippy, was instantly a-grin. This was evidently a standard turn, and she loved the spotlight. She got rid of the tray and showed how her husband climbed through the ropes, lifting her right knee high to get over the imaginary strand, and holding the hem of her short skirt against the knee as a boxer sometimes holds his robe to keep it from getting in his way. Once inside, she danced about the ring, waving her clasped hands at friends in the imaginary crowd. Then she retired to a corner and crouched on an imaginary stool until the Governor hit the rim of a glass with a gravy spoon.

The girl came out, sparring fast, dancing around the ring and mugging for friends at ringside, with an occasional wink. The opposition didn't amount to much, I could see. Laura's husband, impersonated by Laura, was jabbing him silly. Then her expression changed; the other man was beginning to hit her husband where he didn't like it. Her head waggled. She began to stagger. Even the bodyguards, who must have seen the act often, were howling.

"Show us how your husband does when he gets tagged," the Governor ordered, and Laura fell forward, her arms hanging over the invisible ropes, her head outside the ring, her eyes bulged and senseless.

The feudal faces were red with mirth. I applauded as hard as I could. Laura stood up and curtsied.

"You gonna let him keep on fightin'?" the Governor asked.

"I don't want him to," Laura said, "don't want him get hurt. But I don't know if he'll quit."

"Is he easier to live with when he loses?" a state senator asked.

"Yes, sir, he is," the jester said, and took her tray back from the colleague who had been holding it.

The meal went on.

"Dat's da way some a dese stump-wormers going to be when dis primary is over," Uncle Earl said. "Hanging on da ropes. If it's a pretty day for the primary, I'll win it all. I'll denude dem all, da *Times-Picayune* included."

Outside the air-conditioned keep the enemy might howl, but inside, the old vavasor held his court without worrying.

"Da voting machines won't hold me up," he said. "If I have da raight commissioners, I can make dem machines play 'Home Sweet Home.'" He laughed confidingly. "Da goody-goodies brought in dose machines to put a crimp in da Longs," he said. "Da first time dey was used, in 1956, I won on da first primary. Not even my brother Huey ever did dat.

"Da machines is less important dan who's allowed to vote," he said. "I appointed a man State Custodian of Voting Machines here dat run up a bill of a hundred and sixty-three thousand dollars for airplane hire in one year, just flying around da state, inspecting da machines. Good man, Southern gentleman—da *Times-Picayune* recommended him and I thought I'd satisfy dem for once. Den he got an appropriation from da Legislature to keep da machines in repair, but it said in da contract with da voting-machine company dat da company had to keep dem in repair for one year for free. So he split da money wit da company—dey sent him six thousand dollars, and den another six thousand, but I grabbed half of da second six thousand for my campaign fund. Should have took it all."

The cellarer he had sent for the name-brand beer returned with a report that none except the supermarket kind was cold.

"Dey keeping da good beer for demself," the Governor said indulgently. "You drink dis." It tasted fine.

The Northern woman, who had listened with awe to the career of the voting-machine man, asked, "What happened to him?"

"I denuded him," the Governor said. "It's an elective office now."

"And where is he now?" the woman asked, expecting, perhaps, to hear that he was confined in a *cachot* beneath the Mansion.

"He's hypnotizing people and telling fortunes and locating oil wells," the Governor said, "and he got himself a fine blonde and built her a big house and quit home."

Outside of the *Lives of the Troubadours*, which was compiled in the thirteenth century, I had never known a better-compressed biography. I felt that I knew the denuded hypnotist well. I remembered the comparable beauty of the Governor's account of the last day of a beloved uncle in Winnfield: "He got drunk and pulled a man out of bed and got into bed with the man's wife, and the man got mad and shot my poor uncle, and he died."

I asked him what he thought of Governor Faubus of north-neighboring Arkansas, who had won a third term by closing the schools, and he said Faubus was a fine man, but nobody had told him about the Civil War.

"Fellas like Faubus and Rainach and Leander Perez and da rest of da White Citizens and Southern Gentlemen in dis state want to go back behind Lincoln," he said. "And between us, gentlemen, as we sit here among ourselves," he said, arresting a chunk of fried steak in mid-air and leaning forward to give his statement more impetus, "we got to admit dat Lincoln was a fine man and dat he was right."

Then as he turned back to the steak, skewering it against a piece of ham before swallowing both, he caught my look of astonishment and cried, too late, "But don't quote me on dat!"

Since he has won his last primary, I disregard his instructions. It was a brave thing for a Governor of Louisiana to say and would have made a lethal headline in his enemies' hands: "Long Endorses Lincoln; Hints War Between States Ended."

We had up another can of beer, and the Governor and I shared it with a sense of double complicity.

"Laura, Laura," the Governor called to his jester, "get rid of dat tray."

"Yes, sir, Mister Governor," and the star turn passed the grits to a co-worker.

"Now, Laura," the Governor said, "can you make a speech like Mr. McLemore?" (McLemore had been the White Citizens' candidate in '56.)

This was plainly another well-used bit of repertory. The Prize Fighter and Mr. McLemore may be Laura's *Cavalleria* and *Pagliacci*, always done as a double bill. But I'd love to hear her sing Jimmie Davis.

She took a stance, feet wide apart and body stick-straight, looking as foolish as she could.

"Ladies and gentlemen," she said, "do not vote for Mr. Earl Long, because he has permitted da Supreme Court of da United States to make a decision by which, by which, Little White Johnny will have to attend da same school with Little Black Mary. If you wish to prevent dis, vote for, vote for—" and she hesitated, like a man fumbling in his mind for his own name. Then, running her hands over her body, she located, after some trouble, a white card in her breast pocket. The card, a planted prop, showed she had expected to perform. She took the card, peered at it, turned it around and finally read, "McLemore. Dat's it. Vote for McLemore."

The Earl howled, and so did all his guests and men-at-arms. I do not imagine that Penelope would have found it all that funny. She probably cramped his style.

The meal ended with a great volume of ice cream. The Governor, in high humor and perhaps still thinking of the frustrated voting machines, said to the lady across from him, "Would you mind if I told you a semi-bad story?"

She said she would not mind, and the Governor began: "There was an important man once who had a portable mechanical-brain thinking machine that he carried everywhere with him. Da machine was about as big as a small model of one of dose fruit machines dey have in a Elks club-house. When he wanted a answer: How many square feet in a room by so and so much? or, Has dat blonde a husband and is he home? he submitted his question and da machine answered it correctly. He would write out da question on a piece of paper and put it in a slot, da machine would read it, and pretty soon it would go blam, blam, blam—blam, blam, blam—dat was da brain working, and it would give him a printed slip with da correct answer. Well, finally da man got jealous of dis machine, it was such a Jim-cracker, and he thought he take it down a little for its own good.

"So he wrote out a message: 'Where is my dear father at this minute, and what is he doing?' He put it in da slot, and da machine says, 'Blam, blam, blam,' very calm, like he had asked it something easy, and it write out da answer, 'Your dear father is in a pool hall in Philadelphia, *Penn*sylvania, at dis moment, shooting a game of one hundred points against a man named Phil Brown. Your dear father is setting down watching, and Phil Brown has da cue stick and is about to break.'"

"Philadelphia, *Penn*sylvania," had the romantic sound in the Governor's mouth of Coromandel in Sinbad's.

The Governor's manner changed, and his voice became indignant. "'Why,' da man says, 'dat's da most unmitigated libelous slander I ever heard of. My dear father is sleeping in da Baptist cemetery on da side of da hill in *Pitts*burgh, Pennsylvania, and has been for da last five years. I am sure of dates because my dear Mother who is still living reminded me of da anniversary of his death and I telegraphed ten dollars worth of flowers to place on his grave. I demand a *re*-investigation and an *apology*.'

"And he writes it out and puts it in da slot. 'Dis time I got you,' he says. 'You ain't nothing but a machine anyway.'

"Da machine reads da message and gets all excited. It says 'Blam, *Blam*' and 'Blam, *blam*,' like it was scratching its head, and den 'Blam, blam, blam, blam . . . blam, blam, blam, blam,' like it was running its thoughts through again, and den 'BLAM!' like it was mad, and out comes da message."

All eyes were on the Governor now, as if the ladies and men-at-arms half expected him to materialize the ticker tape.

"Da message said, 'REPEAT,'" the Governor said. "It said 'REPEAT' and den, 'RE-REPEAT. Your dear father is in a pool hall at Philadelphia, *Penn*sylvania, playing a game with a man named Phil Brown. YOUR MOTHER'S LEGALLY WEDDED HUSBAND is in the Baptist cemetery on the side of the hill in *Pitts*burgh, *Penn*sylvania, and has been there these last five years, you BASTARD. The only change in the situation is that Phil Brown has run fourteen and missed, and your old man now has the cue stick. I predict he will win by a few points.'"

It broke everybody up, and soon the Governor said to the outsiders politely, "Y'all go home. We got a lot to do tonight." But he said he might be able to see me at nine next morning.

I arose at that hour and got over there, but there were already so many cars on the driveway that if it hadn't been morning I would have guessed there was a cockfight in the basement. Inside the Mansion, the nearly bookless library on the right of the door that serves as a waiting room was full of politicians, all wearing nubbly suits and buckskin shoes, and each sporting the regulation enlargement of the left breast beneath the handkerchief pocket. (This group included no left-handed pistol shot.) The length of the queue demonstrated that the public reaction to the speeches had been favorable, and that the sheiks who had raided the herds in Earl's absence were there to restore the stolen camels.

A Negro in a white jacket came in and asked the ritual "Y'all have coffee?" Since I had no deal to offer, I just had coffee and went.

Odysseus ruled in Ithaca again.

❧ ❧ ❧

The Earl of Louisiana did not get many reviews. Sokolov said it would have been a better book if Long had still been alive when it was published. But Long had died and the end of the book, Sokolov pointed out, is more epilogue than a symmetrical conclusion. Nor did the book sell well. "The old codger," Sokolov wrote, "had pulled Liebling down with him." But two decades later, Sokolov said, the book had "acquired the status of a minor classic of journalism about the South."[7] In 1990 when Victor Gold reviewed another biography of Long he paid homage to Liebling's "rollicking book," called it a "tour de farce," and said the authors of the book he was reviewing had not matched Liebling's artistry.[8] Malcolm Jones, echoing a criticism made of Joan Didion, wrote of Liebling: "He has been accused of missing greatness because he dodged writing about great issues, but that is like criticizing chicken because it doesn't taste like fish."[9]

Some contemporary reviews were very positive. Noting that Democratic politics in Louisiana had attracted writers of varying talent for decades, Victor Wilson praised Liebling's book for being unique. "He also has the ability to make the atmosphere of a place, smelly or otherwise, pop out at you from the printed page. Good qualities, these, for reporting Louisiana politics."[10]

As the excerpt shows, the book captures the mood quickly and holds the reader. The excerpt also shows some of Liebling's artful writing. Look at the way he describes the jacket that Stafford sits on—"silvery, Dacron-Acrilan-nylon-airpox miracle weave nubbled in Danish-blue asterisk." And consider his introductory clause about who is sitting at the table: "Around the long board crouched plug-uglies in sports shirts, alternating with the guests." And take note of the way he describes Long and his entourage: "He sat there like a feudal lord, and his *maisnie*, the men of his household, leaned toward him like Indians around a fire."

Another positive review came from Wert Williams, who pronounced *Earl* "the best nonfictional account of contemporary Louisiana" since 1941, "clearly one of 1961's most exciting, entertaining, witty and intelligent books." He called the book "a warm and friendly defense of Earl Long."[11] Samuel L. Simon said

Liebling had provided a "lively and sympathetic portrait which has caught the circus personality and native shrewdness of Earl Long."[12] *Kirkus Reviews* called it a "breezy portrait" and "a forceful and vital book and politically more real than *All the King's Men*"[13] (a biography of Earl Long's brother, by Robert Penn Warren). *Booklist* said Liebling had furnished "a vivid picture of Long, political contemporaries in Louisiana, and state politics at that time."[14]

Although not quite as high on Long as Liebling was, William L. Rivers said "this curiously valuable book provides a better perspective than the headlines." Rivers pointed out that, because Liebling tended to meander into other topics, the book was somewhat self-indulgent, suggesting—and one can readily see this—that Liebling and Long were "a biographer and a subject who were made for each other."[15] The *New York Times* obituary made a similar point about Liebling's writing in general, saying that "as his style matured it became convoluted, subtle and abounding in unlikely allusions."[16] A later critic opined, however, "You can read Liebling just for the digressions."[17] Harnett T. Kane complained because parts of the book were undeveloped and needed more background. Though he called *Earl* "an honest book," he ended his review by saying that Liebling, because he was such a good writer, should have written a better book.[18] In other words, it is lousy chicken because it does not taste like fish.

The Earl of Louisiana was one of Liebling's last books. He died on December 28, 1963, at the age of fifty-nine. Just nine months before that, he had written an introduction to a collection of his essays, *The Best of A. J. Liebling*. "Painters often have retrospective shows," he wrote, "and there is no reason to suspect writers of being less vain."[19] Liebling deserved all the collections he could publish, but as Fred Warner complained thirty years after Liebling's death: "It is high time that his works become known at last, to readers in and out of colleges who know a truly good writer when they see one."[20] In his eulogy, one of Liebling's friends, Joseph Mitchell, said: "Every time anyone anywhere in all the years to come takes down one of his books and reads or rereads one of his wonderful stories, he will live again."[21] Mitchell was more of a prophet than he could have known. In the 1990s, proof of Liebling's endurance surfaced in the reissuing of five of his books, prompting this headline over one review: "The Timeless A. J. Liebling."²² Liebling had deservedly come back from the dead. He and Earl Long no doubt were having a last laugh and another can of beer.

ENDNOTES

1. "A. J. Liebling," *New Yorker,* 11 January 1964, 107.
2. Raymond Sokolov, *Wayward Reporter: The Life of A. J. Liebling* (New York: Harper & Row, 1980), 300. The term "Wayward" appears in various references to Liebling because *The New Yorker*'s press criticism column, written primarily by Liebling between 1945 and 1963, was published under the heading "The Wayward Press."
3. "A. J. Liebling, Journalist and Critic, Dies at 59," *New York Times,* 29 December 1963, p. 42.
4. Brendan Gill, *Here at The New Yorker* (London: Michael Joseph, 1974), 320.
5. A. J. Liebling, *The Best of A. J. Liebling,* ed. William Cole (London: Methuen, 1965), 196–97.
6. A. J. Liebling, *The Earl of Louisiana,* (Baton Rouge: Louisiana State University Press, 1970), 129.
7. Sokolov, *Wayward Reporter,* 303.
8. Victor Gold, "The Saga of Crazy Earl," *American Spectator,* December 1990, 38–39.
9. Malcolm Jones, Jr., "The Timeless A. J. Liebling," *Newsweek,* 26 November 1990, 76.
10. Victory Wilson, "Liebling Report on a Wayward Governor," *Herald Tribune,* 7 May 1961, "Lively Arts," p. 32.
11. Wert Williams, "Off—and On—His Crumpet," *New York Times Book Review,* 30 July 1961, 7.
12. Samuel L. Simon, "Book Review," *Library Journal,* July 1961, 2463.
13. "The Earl of Louisiana," *Kirkus Reviews,* 1 April 1961, 354.
14. "Biography," *Booklist,* 1 June 1961, 605.
15. William L. Rivers, "Spectacular Eccentric," *Saturday Review,* 15 July 1961, 35.
16. "A. J. Liebling, Journalist and Critic, Dies at 59."
17. Jones, "Timeless," 76
18. Harnett T. Kane, "'Ole Earl' Long," *Chicago Tribune,* 7 May 1961, Sec. 4, p. 3.
19. A. J. Liebling, *The Best of A. J. Liebling,* ed. William Cole (London: Methuen, 1965), 15.

20. A. J. Liebling, *Liebling at the New Yorker,* ed. James Barbour and Fred Warner (Albuquerque: University of New Mexico Press, 1994), xiv.
21. Quoted in "A. J. Liebling," *New Yorker,* 11 January 1964, 108.
22. Jones, "Timeless," 76.

Chapter 7

ALEX HALEY

The Autobiography of Malcolm X

While it may seem a contradiction to write about an autobiography of one man and another man as the author, *The Autobiography of Malcolm X* presents such a situation. *The Autobiography of Malcolm X* is the late black leader's story, but it is Alex Haley's book. Or, as a British reviewer said it: "The modest hero of this book is really Alex Haley."[1]

Haley is probably better known for *Roots*, the story of Haley's search for his African roots, which was published in 1976, more than a decade after *Malcolm X*. Various essays on Haley begin by citing *Roots*[2] and barely mention *Malcolm X*, and many of his obituaries mention *Roots* and only later *Malcolm X*. Both books are excellent, however. Charles Johnson, a National Book Award winner, said when Haley died in 1992. "You have two classics and that's pretty hard to pull off—and that by a man who was primarily a journalist."[3]

Both books, while originally published as nonfiction, are sometimes labeled otherwise. One essayist correctly listed *Roots* as "long fiction" and *Malcolm X* incorrectly as "edited text."[4] Both labels underplay Haley's role in bringing the stories to life, for "serving as an admirably unobtrusive and astute organizer of the material."[5]

Malcolm X was born Malcolm Little on May 19, 1925, in Omaha, Nebraska. The family eventually moved to Lansing, Michigan, where Little was elected president of his seventh-grade class. Discouraged by a white teacher from even thinking about becoming a lawyer because of his race, with his family life unsettled because the state of Michigan had institutionalized his mother, Little joined a half-sister in Boston. Eventually he ended up in prison. There, he converted to the Muslim religion as preached by the Elijah Muhammad of the Nation of Islam, which held that whites were evil and that blacks should have a nation of their own. The conversion also brought about Malcolm X's change in name, as X "replaced the white slavemaster name of 'Little' which some blue-eyed devil named Little had imposed upon my paternal forebears."[6] Malcolm X rose quickly through the ranks of the Nation of Islam. He and Haley met when Haley wanted to write a story about the group. Eventually, Malcolm X and Elijah Muhammad had a falling out. Malcolm X was assassinated on February 21, 1965.

The following excerpt comes from Chapter 1, which is titled "Nightmare." Malcolm X tells of his father, the Reverend Earl Little, and his death; his mother, Louise Little; the Universal Negro Improvement Association; the Ku Klux Klan; his six siblings, among them, Wilfred and Philbert; and his family life during the economic straits of the Great Depression.

❦ ❦ ❦

Then, about in late 1934, I would guess, something began to happen. Some kind of psychological deterioration hit our family circle and began to eat away our pride. Perhaps it was the constant tangible evidence that we were destitute. We had known other families who had gone on relief. We had known without anyone in our home ever expressing it that we had felt prouder not to be at the depot where the free food was passed out. And, now, we were among them. At school, the "on relief" finger suddenly was pointed at us, too, and sometimes it was said aloud.

It seemed that everything to eat in our house was stamped Not To Be Sold. All Welfare food bore this stamp to keep the recipients from selling it. It's a wonder we didn't come to think of Not To Be Sold as a brand name.

Sometimes, instead of going home from school, I walked the two miles up the road into Lansing. I began drifting from store to store, hanging around outside where things like apples were displayed in boxes and barrels and baskets, and I would watch my chance and steal me a treat. You know what a treat was to me? Anything!

Or I began to drop in about dinnertime at the home of some family that we knew. I knew that they knew exactly why I was there, but they never embarrassed me by letting on. They would invite me to stay for supper, and I would stuff myself.

Especially, I liked to drop in and visit at the Gohannas' home. They were nice, older people, and great churchgoers. I had watched them lead the jumping and shouting when my father preached. They had, living with them—they were raising him—a nephew whom everyone called "Big Boy," and he and I got along fine. Also living with the Gohannases was old Mrs. Adcock, who went with them to church. She was always trying to help anybody she could, visiting anyone she heard was sick, carrying them something. She was the one who, years later, would tell me something that I remembered a long time: "Malcolm, there's one thing I like about you. You're no good, but you don't try to hide it. You are not a hypocrite."

The more I began to stay away from home and visit people and steal from the stores, the more aggressive I became in my inclinations. I never wanted to wait for anything.

I was growing up fast, physically more so than mentally. As I began to be recognized more around the town, I started to become aware of the peculiar attitude of white people toward me. I sensed that it had to do with my father. It was an adult version of what several white children had said at school, in hints, or sometimes in the open, which really expressed what their parents had said—that the Black Legion or the Klan had killed my father, and the insurance company had pulled a fast one in refusing to pay my mother the policy money.

When I began to get caught stealing now and then, the state Welfare people began to focus on me when they came to our house. I can't remember how I first became aware that they were talking of taking me away. What I first remember along that line was my mother raising a storm about being able to bring up her own children. She would whip me for stealing, and I would try to alarm the neighborhood with my yelling. One thing I have always been proud of is that I never raised my hand against my mother.

In the summertime, at night, in addition to all the other things we did, some of us boys would slip out down the road, or across the pastures, and go "cooning" watermelons. White people always associated watermelons with Negroes, and they sometimes called Negroes "coons" among all the other names, and so stealing watermelons became "cooning" them. If white boys were doing it, it implied that they were only acting like

Negroes. Whites have always hidden or justified all of the guilts they could by ridiculing or blaming Negroes.

One Halloween night, I remember that a bunch of us were out tipping over those old country outhouses, and one old farmer—I guess he had tipped over enough in his day—had set a trap for us. Always, you sneak up from behind the outhouse, then you gang together and push it, to tip it over. This farmer had taken his outhouse off the hole, and set it just in *front* of the hole. Well, we came sneaking up in single file, in the darkness, and the two white boys in the lead fell down into the outhouse hole neck deep. They smelled so bad it was all we could stand to get them out, and that finished us all for that Halloween. I had just missed falling in myself. The whites were so used to taking the lead, this time it had really gotten them in the hole.

Thus, in various ways, I learned various things. I picked strawberries, and though I can't recall what I got per crate for picking, I remember that after working hard all one day, I wound up with about a dollar, which was a whole lot of money in those times. I was so hungry, I didn't know what to do. I was walking away toward town with visions of buying something good to eat, and this older white boy I knew, Richard Dixon, came up and asked me if I wanted to match nickels. He had plenty of change for my dollar. In about a half hour, he had all the change back, including my dollar, and instead of going to town to buy something, I went home with nothing, and I was bitter. But that was nothing compared to what I felt when I found out later that he had cheated. There is a way that you can catch and hold the nickel and make it come up the way you want. This was my first lesson about gambling: if you see somebody winning all the time, he isn't gambling, he's cheating. Later on in life, if I were continuously losing in any gambling situation, I would watch very closely. It's like the Negro in America seeing the white man win all the time. He's a professional gambler; he has all the cards and the odds stacked on his side, and he has always dealt to our people from the bottom of the deck.

About this time, my mother began to be visited by some Seventh Day Adventists who had moved into a house not too far down the road from us. They would talk to her for hours at a time, and leave booklets and leaflets and magazines for her to read. She read them, and Wilfred, who had started back to school after we had begun to get the relief food supplies, also read a lot. His head was forever in some book.

Before long, my mother spent much time with the Adventists. It's my belief that what mostly influenced her was that they had even more diet restrictions than she always had taught and practiced with us. Like us, they were against eating rabbit and pork; they followed the Mosaic dietary laws. They ate nothing of the flesh without a split hoof, or that didn't chew a cud. We began to go with my mother to the Adventist meetings that were held further out in the country. For us children, I know that the major attraction was the good food they served. But we listened, too. There were a handful of Negroes, from small towns in the area, but I would say that it was ninety-nine percent white people. The Adventists felt that we were living at the end of time, that the world soon was coming to an end. But they were the friendliest white people I had ever seen. In some ways, though, we children noticed, and, when we were back at home, discussed, that they were different from us—such as the lack of enough seasoning in their food, and the different way that white people smelled.

Meanwhile, the state Welfare people kept after my mother. By now, she didn't make it any secret that she hated them, and didn't want them in her house. But they exerted their right to come, and I have many, many times reflected upon how, talking to us children, they began to plant the seeds of division in our minds. They would ask such things as who was smarter than the other. And they would ask me why I was "so different."

I think they felt that getting children into foster homes was a legitimate part of their function, and the result would be less troublesome, however they went about it.

And when my mother fought them, they went after her—first, through me. I was the first target. I stole: that implied that I wasn't being taken care of by my mother.

All of us were mischievous at some time or another, I more so than any of the rest. Philbert and I kept a battle going. And this was just one of a dozen things that kept building up the pressure on my mother.

I'm not sure just how or when the idea was first dropped by the Welfare workers that our mother was losing her mind. But I can distinctly remember hearing "crazy" applied to her by them when they learned that the Negro farmer who was in the next house down the road from us had offered to give us some butchered pork—a whole pig, maybe even two of them—and she had refused. We all heard them call my mother "crazy" to her face for refusing good meat. It meant nothing to them even when she explained that we had never eaten pork, that it was against her religion as a Seventh Day Adventist.

They were as vicious as vultures. They had no feelings, understanding, compassion, or respect for my mother. They told us, "She's crazy for refusing food." Right then was when our home, our unity, began to disintegrate. We were having a hard time, and I wasn't helping. But we could have made it, we could have stayed together. As bad as I was, as much trouble and worry as I caused my mother, I loved her.

❖ ❖ ❖

The Autobiography of Malcolm X has a collateral history.[7] Haley and Malcolm X had had a contract with Doubleday, announced in the September 2, 1963, *Publishers Weekly*,[8] and an excerpt of the book titled "I'm Talking to You, White Man" had appeared in *The Saturday Evening Post* on September 12, 1964. The book was in galleys and Doubleday announced in *Publishers Weekly* on March 8, 1965—two weeks after Malcolm X's death—that the book would be published in late August or early September.[9] At that time, though, Doubleday owned a chain of about forty bookstores. According to one source, Nelson Doubleday, Jr., the company's executive vice president and secretary, was fearful for the safety of clerks selling a book about a man murdered by political rivals in a controversial sect and decided not to publish the book.

Haley and Malcolm X were allowed to keep the advance they had received. They took the book to Grove Press, where Haley and Malcolm X's widow received a $15,000 non-returnable advance.[10] Grove advertised the book on its fall list in the August 30, 1965, *Publishers Weekly*.[11] By January, *Publishers Weekly* reported that *Autobiography* had reached a fourth printing, with twenty-five thousand copies in print, and that sales were "picking up momentum."[12]

The copyright page for the *Autobiography of Malcolm X* describes copyright as belonging first to Alex Haley and Malcolm X, then passing to Haley and Malcolm X's widow, Betty Shabazz. An anonymous entry in the *1977 Current Biography Yearbook* calls Haley "the under-appreciated amanuensis behind *The Autobiography of Malcolm X*."[13] One essayist unjudgmentally refers to the book as "dictated to the journalist Alex Haley."[14] But if it was dictated to Haley, why is *Malcolm X* Haley's book?

To answer that question, we need some modest background to establish how Haley came to know Malcolm X and how Haley approached interviewing someone who was less than willing to be interviewed. Haley had been a chief journalist in the United States Coast Guard, which he had entered as a messboy (later they were called "stewards"), When he retired from the Coast Guard in 1959,[15] chief was the highest level an enlisted person could reach. Afterwards, as a freelance writer, he conducted and wrote the first *Playboy* interview, which was with Miles Davis, a well known jazz trumpeter. In all, Haley would do eleven interviews for *Playboy*, including one with Malcolm X and one with George Lincoln Rockwell, an anti-black, anti-Semitic neo-Nazi who believed in white supremacy. When Haley talked over the telephone to Rockwell about doing an interview, he first had to assure him that he wasn't Jewish. Haley did not volunteer that he was an African-American.[16]

By they time they met, Rockwell had been told that Haley was an African-American. Rockwell did not smile or offer to shake hands. And when they sat down to begin the interview, "he took out a pearl-handled revolver, placed it pointedly on the arm of his chair, sat back and spoke for the first time: 'I'm ready if you are.'" Rockwell told Haley the revolver was merely a precaution, given, Rockwell said, the many threats against his life."[17] Rockwell further attempted to disrupt Haley's professional demeanor by calling him a "nigger." Haley replied: "I've been called 'nigger' many times, Commander, but this is the first time I'm being *paid* for it. So you go right ahead. What have you got against us 'niggers'?"

Three years before, Haley had interviewed Malcolm X (and also Cassius Clay and Martin Luther King, among others), but that interview was also not their first meeting. Haley had earlier written a story about the Nation of Islam for *Reader's Digest*[18] and co-authored another article on the subject for the *Saturday Evening Post*.[19] The *Playboy* interview led a publisher to suggest that Haley write Malcolm X's autobiography.

Malcolm X required that Haley sign a strict agreement. "Nothing can be in this book's manuscript that I didn't say," Malcolm X dictated in one agreement, "and nothing can be left out that I want in it."[20] Unfortunately, that meant Haley could not independently verify information and change errors caused by the memory lapses that occur with the passage of time. That does not mean Haley was not concerned about the veracity of the story. He once told Malcolm X that some people had wanted to know "if you're really telling the truth." Malcolm X replied: "What lies could be as disgraceful as what I'm telling you?"

Still, Haley wrote in an early draft of the afterword, he would test Malcolm X by asking him questions about "some trivial point about some incident he had recounted as much as a year before," and Malcolm X "always re-told the same even small details." Haley wrote: "Either the story was true, or it was painstakingly memorized. His memorizing a whole book's countless incidents seemed unlikely, so I wrote believing that he was telling the truth."[21]

Fortunately, Malcolm X also agreed to let Haley add a chapter of his own comments that would not be subject to Malcolm X's review.[22] In fact, Haley found himself making what he called "side notes" in a second notebook, which would become a record of Haley's "various personal observations."[23] Haley used the epilogue to tell not only how the book came about, but also about events that followed the last interview, including the assassination of Malcolm X on February 21, 1965. Although an epilogue can sometimes read like an afterthought or a quick summary, Haley's original came in at something like forty thousand words[24] and was reduced by at least 25 percent.[25] Robert Penn Warren pointed out that Haley's epilogue, by showing how Haley slowly gained Malcolm X's confidence and how Malcolm X discovered his need to tell his story, became an integral part of the book.[26]

Haley conducted lengthy interviews—"talking marathons," a *Times Literary Supplement* reviewer called them[27]—over a period of a year. The writing would take another year. "We got off to a very poor start," Haley wrote.[28] Eventually, the two overcame many obstacles, among them Malcolm X's belief that the FBI had bugged Haley's studio* and Malcolm X's attitude toward Haley, manifested when he would stiffly address Haley as "Sir!"[29] Haley did not get much out of his subject until he noticed that Malcolm X, while talking, was scribbling with his red-ink pen on any available paper. So Haley began leaving two white napkins for Malcolm X whenever Haley served coffee and

---

*Actually, someone from the Justice Department did talk to Haley about Malcolm X. [Peter Louis Goldman, *The Death and Life of Malcolm X* (New York: Harper & Row, 1973), 212] Citing a CIA file on Malcolm X, one biographer reports that the FBI asked Haley whether Malcolm X was being financed by a foreign government, "but Haley informed him that Malcolm X was strapped for cash." [Karl Evanzz, *The Judas Factor: The Plot to Kill Malcolm X* (New York: Thunder's Mouth Press, 1992), 294.]

collecting the napkins afterwards. From reading the scribblings he realized that Malcolm X might be talking about one thing but thinking of something else. Haley used the scribblings as tips to questions he might ask. Haley unknowingly found another way to get Malcolm X to talk in more depth when he asked this question: "I wonder if you'd tell me something about your mother?" Malcolm X began to talk and the story began to come out with fewer fits and starts.

In addition to getting Malcolm X to tell his story, Haley had to preserve the story. At one point, he had to talk Malcolm X out of rewriting the book to reflect his current state of thinking rather than leaving the manuscript the way Haley had originally written it, which would show the evolution of his thinking. After Malcolm X became a Muslim, he had what Haley described as a father-son relationship with Elijah Muhammad, the founder of the Nation of Islam. Ultimately, however, Malcolm X was expelled from the Nation of Islam and edited the manuscript in a way that turned it into a polemic against Elijah Muhammad. When Haley objected, Malcolm X said ("gruffly," Haley reported): "Whose book is this?" But Haley explained that the changes would wreck the book's narrative thread. Eventually Malcolm X apologized and agreed to Haley's original plan.[30]

Some reviewers examined the role of the "author" to see whether Haley was more than just a tape-recorder, whether there was a balance between subject and writer. More than one reviewer noted the book's "carefully symmetrical structure," to quote David P. Demarest, Jr.[31] Paul John Eakin recognized the major role Haley played and saluted him for being more than a scribe. Eakin pointed out, too, that Haley recognized what was happening in the Nation of Islam before it happened, "was one to read between the lines," and thus preserved the drama of Malcolm X's changing relationship with Elijah Muhammad.[32] Michael Cooke said "the willingness to let the past stand as it was" was the book's "distinctive feature."[33] These are, of course, some of the aspects of the book Malcolm X had wanted to change and which Haley talked him out of. Doris Lessing compared the evolving subject-author relationship to the one Truman Capote had with the two murderers—"bound to be suspicious, resistant, hostile, then over-confiding."[34] Lessing would have preferred Haley not to have served as a ghost, but as a "straight biographer," for she felt the "shrewd and compassionate Haley" would have knitted the story together better. By contrast, Demarest saw the best of both worlds. *"The Autobiography,"* he wrote, "may avoid the problems of both the autobiographer's lack of objectivity and the biographer's limited knowledge."[35] Anthony Adair saw more of Malcolm X than Haley in the book, saying that it lacked "sedate detachment" and reflected "more the urgency and nervous tension of a direct conversation with Malcolm X."[36] Likewise, Berthoff said: "It is a personal authority that comes through to us and makes the difference."[37] "It is," Colin MacInnes wrote, "Malcolm's thought and voice we are hearing all the time."[38] Given that so much of what the world knew about Malcolm X when his autobiography was published had been filtered through white reporters, it is to Haley's credit that many reviewers recognized Malcolm X's voice, not Haley's. One scholar, analyzing a book "whose authorship is clouded by collaboration,"[39] said: "Malcolm has created a work which is formally consistent, authentically autobiographical, and yet rhetorically effective."[40]

In general, the book received mixed reviews. Those who liked it, such as Truman Nelson, said: "You can hear and feel Malcolm in this book."[41] Demarest referred to the book's achievement as "showing the fullness of Malcolm as a man."[42] An *Economist* reviewer said the book "shows that he was vastly more complex, subtle, warm and thoughtful than white people realised him to be."[43] Carol Ohmann likened the book to Benjamin Franklin's *Autobiography.* She said it should not be limited to courses in African-American literature, but included in American literature courses.[44] Eliot Fremont-Smith, enthusiastically praising the book, said Haley's estimate of Malcolm X in the epilogue is "candid and perceptive."[45] Geoffrey Godsell called the book "a document to history by a man who helped make it."[46] Emile Capouya said the book "has considerable importance as a historical document."[47] Albert E. Stone praised the book fifteen years later "for recapturing both the vertical and horizontal axes of the unique yet deliberately representative life of a contemporary urban black man."[48]

Those who were critical generally said that the book did not bring out the inner life of its subject.[49] An anonymous *Newsweek* reviewer said the book was an "external record, a verbal kine-scope that sheds little light on Malcolm's tormented soul."[50] Bayard Rustin said that Malcolm X's "conflicting roles in the civil rights movement are described rather than analyzed,"[51] which in part reflects Haley's role as a scribe and speaks, in part, to the difference between autobiography and biography, with the latter providing an analytical view. I. F. Stone complained that Malcolm X's message was muted, "perhaps because Alex Haley, its writer, is politically conventional." Stone, a political icono-clast, contrasted it with another book, published by a group of Trotzkyists, that he said did not mute Malcolm X's message.[52] John Henrik Clarke said the *Autobiography* read "like the first draft of what could have been the most exciting autobiography of our time."[53]

The criticisms are valid, but should be taken in context. They speak to the filter that all writers are. Haley was a journalist and says at the end of the book: "I tried to be a dispassionate chronicler."[54] As noted earlier, he was contractually restricted regarding the content and did not verify anything with other sources, as a biographer would do. Furthermore, Haley was upper middle class in his origins; when he was born in 1921, both of his parents were in their first year of graduate school.[55] His experiences were not the same as Malcolm X's, whose father apparently was murdered by the Ku Klux Klan. So Haley was not only professionally but experientially detached.

Could Haley have done one more draft? Contractually, no. Malcolm X had signed off on the book and Haley was obligated to finish it, which he did about two weeks before Malcolm X was assassinated.[56] Having earned Malcolm X's trust, Haley was not about to go back on his word and suggest a different approach.

Malcolm X continues to play a role in the African-American community. When the book was first published, for example, it was adopted in college literature courses and shared the SR-Anisfield-Wolf Award, which is given to books that make a significant contribution toward improving relations among people.[57] As Tamara Hareven has put it, "Negro autobiography is survival literature":[58] such books provide models and hope for African-Americans. Valerie Boyd said *Malcolm X* was "one of those books that all budding African-American scholars must time the W. E. B. Du Bois Professor of the Humanities at Harvard University, recalled that another Muslim, Kareem Abdul-Jabbar, said in his own autobiography that *Malcolm X* had meant more to him than any other book and that all black Americans should read it.[60] Actually, because it is a story of how one can fall and redeem oneself, it is a story everyone should read.

The man who wrote *The Autobiography of Malcolm X* had a reputation as a storyteller in the tradition of the African narrator and oral historian, a person called a griot (gree-oh). Many people who heard Haley talk at length marveled at his ability, as Noel Holston put it, "to weave his magic."[61] Haley's widow, Myra, reflecting on his life, said she marveled at his ability "to take the most mundane subject and turn it into magic."[62] Howard Rosenberg said "Haley was an amazing storyteller not only in print but also in person."[63] And one student who heard Haley speak three months before his sudden death on February 10, 1992, said: "I loved it. He intended it to be inspirational and I thought it was. I was close to tears."[64]

Haley's inspirational speaking was in sharp contrast to his humility and self-deprecation. In a turnabout *Playboy* interview in which Haley was the subject, not the interviewer, he told a story about returning to his Henning, Tennessee, home after he had become famous. He recounted running into an elderly man who knew his parents. After Haley identified himself, the elderly man asked him what he did. Haley said he was a writer, and the old man asked him to write something. Haley said it wasn't that easy. After some thought, the old man said: "Well, if you was to tell me you was a lightnin' bug, I'd 'spect you to light up."

Haley said that whenever he began to feel important, he would remember that conversation. "Henning is what keeps me honest," he said.[65]

Alex Haley died owing $1.5 million.[66] A three-day auction was held to sell his effects. Haley's working manuscript of *Malcolm X*, containing editing by Haley (in green ink) and Malcolm X (red ink), was sold for $100,000. The manuscript for three chapters[67] that were not in the final book sold for $21,500. The forty-page *Playboy* interview, with each page signed in approval by Malcolm X, sold for $27,500. A napkin containing some of Malcolm X's scribblings from Haley's interviews for the book sold for $21,000.

No one should ignore the story of Malcolm X. But nor should anyone forget that it was Alex Haley, humble journalist, who through research, patience, and endurance, brought the story to the printed page.

ENDNOTES

1. Colin MacInnes, "Malcolm," *Spectator*, 27 May 1966, 668.
2. See, for example, Marilyn Kern-Foxworth, "Alex Haley," *Dictionary of Literary Biography, African-American Writers After 1955: Humanists and Prose Writers* (Detroit, Mich.: Gale Research, 1985) and Frances Carol Locher, ed., *Contemporary Authors* (Detroit, Mich.: Gale Research, 1979).
3. Quoted in Dee Norton and Donn Fry, "Alex Haley Dies," *Seattle Times*, 10 February 1992, p. 1. At the time, Johnson was a creative writing professor at the University of Washington.
4. James Baird, "Alex Haley," *Cyclopedia of World Authors II*, vol. 2 (Pasadena, Calif.: Salem Press, 1989), 658.
5. Nat Hentoff, "The odyssey of a black man," *Commonweal*, 28 January 1966, 511.
6. Alex Haley, *The Autobiography of Malcolm X* (New York: Grove Press, 1965), 229.
7. Unless otherwise noted, the source of the Doubleday information in these paragraphs comes from a telephone interview with Lisa Drew on June 16, 1997. Ms. Drew was the assistant to Kenneth Dale McCormick, the editor-in-chief at Doubleday. Ms. Drew, now vice president and publisher, Lisa Drew Books, Scribners', also read a version of what appears here and confirmed the information. McCormick died June 27, 1997.
8. "Tips," *Publishers Weekly*, 2 September 1963, 56, 58.
9. "Tips," *Publishers Weekly*, 8 March 1965, 47.
10. A copy of the Grove Press contract, dated April 6, 1965, can be found in the Grove Press Archive at Syracuse University.
11. "Tips," *Publishers Weekly*, 30 August 1965, 67.
12. "Tips," *Publishers Weekly*, 24 February 1966, 284. Doubleday did publish *Roots*, which was Haley's decision. Because Doubleday decided not to publish *Autobiography*, Haley could have chosen another publisher, but according to Lisa Drew, chose to stay with Doubleday.
13. Charles Moritz, ed., *Current Biography Yearbook 1977*, (New York: H. W. Wilson, 1977), 184.
14. Warner Berthoff, "Witness and Testament: Two Contemporary Classics," *New Literary History*, Winter 1971, 316.

15. Alex Haley, *Roots* (Garden City, N.Y.: Doubleday, 1976), 668.
16. Alex Haley, *The Playboy Interviews*, ed. Murray Fisher (New York: Ballantine, 1993), 173.
17. Haley, *Interviews*, 175.
18. "Mr. Muhammad Speaks," *Reader's Digest*, March 1960, 100–04. In the article, Haley refers to Malcolm X as "Muhammad's tall, whip-smart assistant" (101).
19. Haley, *Autobiography*, 441, 443.
20. Ibid., 445.
21. The copyedited manuscript is available in the Grove Press Archive at Syracuse University.
22. Haley, *Autobiography*, 446.
23. Ibid., 464.
24. Alex Haley letter to Harry Braverman, Grove Press Archives, 31 May 1965.
25. Harry Braverman letter to Alex Haley, Grove Press Archives, 8 June 1965.
26. Robert Penn Warren, "Malcolm X: Mission and Meaning," *Yale Review*, December 1966, 163–64.
27. "Remember Us in the Alley," *Times Literary Supplement*, 9 June 1966, 507.
28. Haley, *Autobiography*, 446.
29. Ibid., 446–47.
30. Ibid., 476.
31. David P. Demarest, Jr., "*The Autobiography of Malcolm X:* Beyond Didacticism," *CLA Journal* 16 (1972), 180.
32. Paul John Eakin, "Malcolm X and the Limits of Autobiography," *Criticism* 18 (1976), 239.
33. Michael G. Cooke, "Modern Black Autobiography in the Tradition," in *Romanticism: Vistas, Instances, Continuities*, ed. David Thorburn and Geoffrey Hartman (Ithaca, N.Y.: Cornell University Press, 1973), 274.
34. Doris Lessing, "Allah Be Praised," *New Statesman*, 27 May 1966, 775.
35. Demarest, "Beyond Didacticism," 184.
36. Anthony Adair, "Malcolm X," *Contemporary Review*, July 1966, 49.
37. Berthoff, "Witness and Testament," 320.
38. MacInnes, "Malcolm," 668.
39. Thomas W. Benson, "Rhetoric and Autobiography: The Case of Malcolm X," *Quarterly Journal of Speech* 60:1 (February 1974), 2.
40. Ibid., 13.
41. Truman Nelson, "Delinquent's Progress," *Nation*, 8 November 1965, 337.
42. Demarest, "Beyond Didacticism," 187.
43. "Epitaph for Malcolm," *Economist*, 18 June 1966.
44. Carol Ohmann, "*The Autobiography of Malcolm X:* A Revolutionary Use of the Franklin Tradition," *American Quarterly* 22:2 (Summer

1970), 132. Another possibility would be a course on comparative autobiography. H. Porter Abbot, for example, has contrasted *The Autobiography of Malcolm X* with St. Augustine's *Confessions.*

45. Eliot Fremont-Smith, "An Eloquent Testament," *New York Times,* 5 November 1965, p. 35.

46. Geoffrey Godsell, "The hard way," *Christian Science Monitor,* 11 November 1965, p. 11.

47. Emile Capouya, "A Brief Return from Mecca," *Saturday Review,* 20 November 1965, 42–44.

48. Albert E. Stone, "Collaboration in Contemporary American Autobiography," *Revue Français d'Études Américaines,* May 1982, 159.

49. Ohmann, "A Revolutionary Use," 134.

50. "Satan in the Ghetto," *Newsweek,* 15 November 1965, 130.

51. Bayard Rustin, "Making His Mark," *Washington Post Book Week,* 14 November 1965, 16.

52. I. F. Stone, "The Pilgrimage of Malcolm X," *New York Review of Books,* 11 November 1965, 5.

53. John Henrik Clarke, "The Man and His Mission," *Freedomways* 6 (1966), 52.

54. Haley, *Autobiography,* 523.

55. Kern-Foxworth, "Alex Haley," 115.

56. Haley, *Roots,* 669.

57. James F. Fixx, "Books that Change Men's Minds," *Saturday Review,* 11 June 1966. One of the other books sharing the award was *Manchild in the Promised Land,* by Claude Brown, which Readers' Subscription had chosen as its alternate selection to *Autobiography.*)

58. Tamara K. Hareven, "Step-Children of the Dream," *History of Education Quarterly* 9:4, (Winter 1969), 505.

59. Valerie Boyd, "Focus: Black Classics," *Atlanta Constitution,* 16 February 1992, p. N8.

60. Henry Louis Gates, Jr., "Malcolm, the Aardvark and Me," *New York Times Book Review,* 21 February 1993, 11.

61. Noel Holston, "TV was good to Haley, but you should have heard him speak," *Minneapolis Star Tribune,* 16 February 1992, p. 2F.

62. Quoted in "'Roots' author eulogized by friends, family," *Atlanta Constitution,* 16 February 1992, p. A12.

63. Howard Rosenberg, "Alex Haley, A Griot for Modern Times," *Los Angeles Times,* 12 February 1992, "Calendar," p. 9.

64. Orlana M. Darkins, "Haley's family history, stories inspire audience," *Daily Collegian,* 8 November 1991, pp. 1, 10. I was present at this talk and agree with Darkins's assessment that Haley was a marvelous storyteller. It was after this talk that Haley autographed my copy of *Roots:* "11/7/91 To Tom Brotherly Love! Alex Haley."

65. Haley, *Interviews,* 393.

66. The information is this paragraph is derived from two newspaper stories: "Pulitzer for 'Roots' Goes for $50,000 at Haley Sale" in *New York Times*, 4 October 1992, p. 33, and "Malcolm X's widow sues Haley's brother for proceeds," an Associated Press story in the *Centre Daily Times*, State College, Pa., 22 November 1992, p. 6A.
67. United Press International, March 18, 1993. The three chapters were titled: "The Negro," "The End of Christianity," and "20 Million." The last was supposed to have been the final chapter.

Chapter 8

❖

A Mother in History

Jean Stafford is remembered primarily as a novelist and short-story writer, and as the winner of a Pulitzer Prize in fiction. One bibliography, however, also lists fifteen articles, mostly profiles of women, that could be classified as journalism and one nonfiction book, *A Mother in History*. The book is an expansion of an article commissioned by *McCall's* after one of the magazine's editors learned that Stafford had attended a talk by Marguerite Oswald. Oswald's son, Lee Harvey Oswald, assassinated President Kennedy on November 22, 1963.

For the *McCall's* article, Stafford had decided she would borrow the interviewing technique she had seen A. J. Liebling use to break the ice with Louisiana Governor Earl Long.[1] What she admired in Liebling's technique was that he paved the way for interviewing the governor with a question about betting on horses, thus ingratiating himself to Long and winning an invitation to dinner. Stafford thought she would also begin her interview with Mrs. Oswald obliquely—"maybe asking her her recipe for Brownies." But, Stafford reported a year after the article was published, Mrs. Oswald never gave Stafford a chance to ask an opening question; instead she launched into what became three days of monologues that Stafford tape-recorded and then published with some commentary and description interspersed.

Stafford's quip about the recipe for brownies aside, she did actually attempt a Liebling-like approach to Mrs. Oswald. Knowing that Mrs. Oswald had lived in New Orleans, which is near Baton Rouge, where Stafford had once lived, Stafford asked Mrs. Oswald about New Orleans. "But if she had any nostalgia for that most raffish and romantic and sweet and sinful city, she had suppressed it," Stafford writes in the book, "and she brushed me aside as if there were no time for frivolous parentheses when the business at hand was history."[2] The book is so dominated by Mrs. Oswald that one reviewer called it a self-portrait.[3] Stafford says in the book that Mrs. Oswald so overwhelmed her "I felt like a flop on a junior high debating team who hadn't a prayer of reaching the semifinals."[4]

The following excerpt, which includes several of Mrs. Oswald's incomplete or convoluted sentences, comes from the first monologue.

⚜ ⚜ ⚜

The room was still cool, but the air was heavy, imbued with the second-hand mustiness of air-conditioning and the smoke from my cigarettes. I was tired and headachy, but Mrs. Oswald was as fresh and kinetic as she had been when she greeted me, and she persevered like a long-distance runner.

"You know, there was a violent campaign against me as well as my son in magazines, newspapers, and written literature. Most all the papers pictured me in a sort of a bad light, but really I'm not that way at all and never was. I should say I'm very outspoken, I'm aggressive, I'm no dope. Let's face it, if you step on my toes I'm gonna fight back, and I don't apologize for that. This was my training along with Lee's father, who, as we all know, is now deceased."

(Although I should have been used to it by now, I was surprised each time she used the royal or tutorial "we," and only the most tenuous hold on reality kept me from glancing from left to right to see who besides me was attending the lecture.)

"When my older boy first went to school, he came home one day crying that the children had taken his pennies away from him. Mr. Oswald took his little hand and started teaching him how to fight back, and I listened and I thought it was a wonderful thing. I remember him saying 'If you ever start a fight, you're gonna be whipped, but if they ever start a fight with you and you don't fight back, I'm gonna whip *you*.' Let me give you one little instance with Lee and the next-door neighbor boy. They were approximately the same age, and if not, they were the same height, and Lee had a dog. He loved his shepherd collie dog. It was named Sunshine.

He used to romp in the back yard with his dog and took him every place he went, and this little boy was throwing rocks over the fence at Lee's dog. Well, my kitchen window had a view to the back yard. And I watched my son Lee for approximately three days telling the little boy over the fence he better stop throwing rocks at his dog. Well, I was amused, and I was just waiting to find out what happened. Finally, one day when I came home from work the father called me on the phone. It seemed his son was very badly beaten up—in a child's way. My son Lee had finally taken upon himself, after much patience, I thought, to confront the little boy enough to fight him, and the father didn't approve. I told the father what happened, and since the boys were approximately the same age and height, let them fight their own battles.

"Now my boys were never tied to my apron strings. And Lee, Lee wanted to know all there was about life. Talking about going to Russia. He never did tell me why he went to Russia. I have my own opinion. He spoke Russian, he wrote Russian, and he read Russian. Why? Because my boy was being trained as an agent, that's why. Another thing I found out in some book where it said he was placed in another hut because he couldn't get along with someone. He was placed with a Cuban, and he was learning Spanish. I think he was spying on that Cuban. It's just so obvious. How many Marines are going around reading Russian and getting Russian newspapers? One and one make two to me. That boy was being trained."

I asked her what she thought Lee would have done with his life if he had not been killed, and she answered at once, as if she had answered the question many times before. "From what I know of my boy, and of course you have to understand that actually the last time I was very close to Lee was before he joined the service in 1956. After that, it was just through correspondence and on his leaves home from the Marines that I knew him. But every time he came home he talked and talked about the Marines and nothing else. I know when he came back from Japan he said, 'Oh, what a wonderful experience, what a wonderful trip!' He said, 'Do you know it cost my government over two thousand dollars to send me there? I could never afford it on my own.' I think he was doing with his life what he wanted to do. And I'm gonna say he was working for his country as an agent. I think that at age sixteen he became involved, that at age sixteen Lee Harvey Oswald was being trained as a government agent. And this brings up Russia and, of course, Marina."

I was glad she had broached the subject of her daughter-in-law. I had been shy of doing so myself because I knew that there was bad blood between the two women.

"Let's have some more coffee before I go into that," she said. "We'll *need* it." She went once again to the kitchen, where, with her back to me as she went about the business of the coffee, she honed her scalpels for the vivisection of Marina.

"Of course I don't know too much about Marina. She lived with me the one month when they came back from Russia. She was a very humble foreign girl, and she never smoked in front of me. Everything was 'Momma' and the baby, and we got along fine. Now this person never smoked in front of me for a reason, because she did smoke, and she smoked in Russia. The testimony of the Presidential report showed that she knew Americans before she knew Lee, and they taught her how to smoke. Now I smoked for twenty years, and Lee never did say a word to me about smoking—maybe he had respect because I was a mother. But he objected to his wife smoking. And she evidently thought I never smoked, because she never smoked in front of me. I didn't know Marina smoked, until the assassination."

(At the moment, like a white rat in some unprecedented experiment, I had a lighted cigarette in my hand, and another was burning in the ashtray.)

"And you see, I wouldn't be that type. I would be natural and do what I have to do, and there again we get into she's not a true person. If I smoke, I smoke in front of everybody. Of course, I would ask permission of an older person."

There was a moment's silence, and I tried to remember if I had minded my manners at the beginning and asked if I could smoke; I thought I had, but at this point I could be sure of nothing except that I was a white rat.

"To me, Marina is not a true person," she said with fair-minded deliberation. "And this is hard to explain. I have to ask myself who Marina Oswald really is. I'd like to see her marriage certificate some time, and I'd like to know more about her. Oh, when Marina went to Washington, Washington fell in love with Marina Oswald, and Chief Justice Warren was her grandfather, but when I went to Washington—'Don't listen to her. Momma hadn't seen Lee in a year, and she doesn't know anything, blah, blah, blah.' Everything was against me. Yet *I* was the mother. Now I don't say that Marina is necessarily guilty of anything, but both she and Mrs. Paine* have lied, lied continuously. Maybe they are not guilty, but why is it necessary to lie? When it first happened, Marina did not identify the rifle.

---

*A neighbor of Lee Harvey and Marina Oswald. R.T.B.

She said, 'Yes, Lee had rifle,' but when they showed it to her she said she couldn't say whether that was his. Now this is understandable. If your husband had a rifle, and particularly if he had it as they say he had it, wrapped up in a blanket and never using it, would the wife be able to identify it? Yet a few weeks later, when she had taken oath and been brainwashed by the Secret Service, she identified the rifle as Lee's. And at first she said, 'Lee good man, Lee no shoot anybody.' And then she changed her testimony. Marina seems French to me."

"French!"

"Yes, sweetheart, that's what I said, Marina Oswald seems French to me. Oh, definitely." She came back with our coffee, and as she put it down beside me, she said, "But that will have to be continued in our next. You'll have to drink up, honey, your driver's here."

I had not heard a car, and shrubbery obscured the window that looked onto the street, but when I peered through the interstices of the privet, I saw that she was indeed right and the car to take me back to Dallas, where I was staying, was at the curb. I began to respect the sixth sense she had several times laid claim to. ("I have a very unusual extrasensory perception," she had said once, "so doesn't it stand to reason that if my boy shot the President I would have *known* at the time it happened?") I respected, also, her dramatic sense of timing, and I wondered how I would hang to the cliff until I heard about Marina's French origins.

As I got up to go, I asked if she would object to my bringing a tape recorder the following day; she said that, on the contrary, she would be glad if I did, if, that is, I brought two machines, since she wanted one tape to preserve "for history." She had made many recordings, she told me, for "mass mediums" and for her own purposes; she knew that she spoke at the rate of a hundred and eighty words a minute, and I was to tell that to the man I rented the machines from. An operator would not be necessary, because she knew how "to work 'em all."

I started toward the bedroom to fetch my Neiman-Marcus rain cape, and my eye drifted willy-nilly toward the scroll over the desk. I did not look at it directly but instead at a tempera on wood of a baroque orange and chestnut newel post (a detail from backstairs at Blenheim Castle? from Marion Davies' house?), which she dismissed: "A little decorator thing. I thought it would go with the chair. But now this, this is important, this is what you should see," and she took the scroll down from its hook.

"I was gonna show you this," she said. "Here, the man can wait—I guess he's getting paid, isn't he? You get out your notebook and copy it down, and be sure you get the words right."

The legend, cut into copper, read,

MY SON—
LEE HARVEY OSWALD EVEN AFTER HIS
DEATH HAS DONE MORE FOR HIS COUNTRY
THAN ANY OTHER LIVING HUMAN BEING
MARGUERITE C. OSWALD

As I was writing down this abstruse manifesto (I could not get a purchase on the syntax), Mrs. Oswald brought my things and smiled disarmingly. "Of course, I'm not a writer like you," she said. "But I like how that sounds. That's what I said at the year period when I went to the grave. Newspaper reporters came by the galore and asked if I had anything to say, and I said this. And every word of it is true. I'm proud of my son, and why not? My son is an unsung hero."

I remembered that she had petitioned to have Lee Harvey buried in Arlington Cemetery.

I thanked her for giving me so much of her time, and I thanked her for the coffee. Her handclasp was firm and straightforward, and her eyes shone with zeal and satisfaction and optimism. "We're going to win in the end."

I was not sure whether the "we" was editorial or whether I had now been initiated into a coterie whose adversaries were "they."

On the drive back, I browsed through some matter Mrs. Oswald had lent me. One was a paperback book by Kerry Thornley, who had known Lee Harvey in the Marines and had dedicated his "iconoclastic critique on how America helped Oswald to become what he did" to "Clint Bolton, who first said to me: 'Go home and write—ya bum!'" I did not get much further than that. The other was a pamphlet proving that it was ballistically impossible for Oswald to have killed Kennedy; this was a compilation of diagrams and of copies of letters that had been sent, accompanying the diagrams, to leading magazines and to people of position—the letters, significantly, had gone unanswered or had been brushed aside; a ferocious admonition in the beginning of the text prevents me from quoting any part of it.

Soon after the assassination, my husband got a good many letters addressed to him in his role as critic of the press; most of them told him how to go about his reporting, and most of them went into the wastepaper basket. He was, as a matter of fact, at work on one of his "Wayward Press" analyses for *The New Yorker* just before he died, a little more than a month after the President was killed. He brought home for me to read one of the letters, whose author implored, "Mr. Liebling, go to Dallas and tell us the truth. You might of course get killed in Texas, but if you get killed, the world shall know that somebody from the right (be it Birchers or Southern Democrats) wants to hide the truth."

Exegetes of the Dallas murders sprang up like mushrooms in a pinewoods after a soaking rain; the mycelium at the round earth's four corners was rich and ready. Many of the toadstools that appeared were harmless but without flavor, some were tasty and even delicious, many more were as noxious as the amanita verna. In the cities, in whose purlieus these mycologists' wonderlands flourished, kangaroo courts met round the clock, and some of the judges and some of the jurors were responsible people, and the opinions they handed down were persuasive. They were shooting in the dark, but they managed to convince themselves and millions of others that their shots dispelled the darkness and everything was limpidly illuminated; theory, creative and flexible, made mincemeat of circumstantial evidence. The name of the prisoner in the dock was legion; he had every pigmentation and every shape of jaw known to anthropology; he was a member of every political organization, every religious fraternity, every business, scientific, criminal, occult conclave of every country on the face of the earth. In some of these courtroom spectaculars (the remarks from the peanut gallery were deafening; the confusion was such that one could not remember which were the good guys and which the bad ones among Mark Lane, Perry Mason, Melvin Belli, and The Defenders' man, let alone which belonged to the bar association and which to the American Federation of Radio and Television Artists), Lee Harvey Oswald was convicted of having pulled the trigger, but at the instigation of a highly organized and dangerous gang; in other reenactments of the drama, he was not even on the premises, but was under a haystack, fast asleep. In Europe, where there has never been an assassination of a political figure for an apolitical, individual reason, the idea that Oswald, obscure, untutored, could have acted on his own was insupportable, and the most important papers of the most important capitals carried stories categorically proving conspiracy.

As we entered Dallas and drove along the route of the President's caravan, I observed, as I had the other two times I had been over this same ground, that the distance between the sixth-floor window of the Texas Book Depository and the place where the car, slowing for a turn, had been, seemed to be much less than it had appeared in photographs. I was struck, moreover, by the fact that between the window and the target there was no obstruction of any kind to challenge aim or deflect the attention, no eave or overhang or tree. The drop shot, from a steadied rifle, was fired on a day of surpassing clarity; the marksmanship of the gunner did not have to be remarkable.

❧ ❧ ❧

As reviews and letters to the editor of *McCall's* reflected, *A Mother in History,* like the article that spawned it, was difficult to assess. Letter writers condemned *McCall's* for publishing the article, condemned Mrs. Oswald for being a bad mother and failing to get on with her life, suggested she was commercializing on her son's deed, and said Stafford could find subjects more worthy of her talent. Some letters praised Stafford, but as she reported in *Library Journal* a year after the article appeared and in *Esquire* a decade later,[5] she also received a great number of critical epistles that ran the gamut from criticizing her for destroying motherhood to being anti-Semitic, anti-Catholic, anti-Kennedy, and a dupe of the Warren Commission, which had investigated the assassination. It seemed like one of those situations in which the messenger was blamed for the message, as Stafford recognized. "Apparently," she subsequently wrote, "I can't win by telling the truth."

Among reviewers, reactions were less venomous but just as diverse. *Harper's* said the book would be compared with Truman Capote's *In Cold Blood* "no matter what the difference in size and intent"[6] while Annette K. Baxter praised Stafford for not writing a *Blood*-type book and said Stafford had returned "to a classic journalistic mode."[7] Even though *Harper's* pooh-poohed its own Capote comparison, one wonders why the question even arose; clearly, *Mother* is not a nonfiction novel. Capote did, however, take credit indirectly for Stafford getting the assignment. He also boasted that other novelists would get similar assignments and be offered huge commissions.[8] One Stafford biographer said the book sold ten thousand copies in three months and that "assignment offers flooded in." But instead of capitalizing on the opportunities, Stafford was unproductive for two years, although "financially, she was able to coast for awhile on her Oswald earnings."[9]

Those reviewers who praised *Mother* recognized that Stafford could have turned Mrs. Oswald into a comic figure, thus diminishing the larger issues,[10] or that Stafford's interspersions, which gave context to Mrs. Oswald's monologue, represented Stafford's "laconic good sense."[11] Marya Mannes saw the book working on two levels, the first being Mrs. Oswald's state and the second Stafford's ability "to convey the trauma of her own involvement with this woman without ever raising her voice."[12] Barbara La Rosa praised Stafford for her "asides and apt comments"[13]— the one about feeling like a white rat is just one example in the excerpt. Jean Holzhauer suggested that Stafford had done her objective best on a distasteful assignment.[14]

On the negative side, Karl Miller considered Stafford's asides to represent a self-preoccupation that was poetic license; but, then, he asked, what did one expect when a novelist was "adverted to matters of fact and required to show their paces?"[15] Paul Richard said that putting the *McCall's* article between covers resulted in "a petty and altogether disagreeable little book." He was bothered that the "neurotic verbiage that other reporters had listened to and then tastefully ignored" was now in print, but ended his review by saying that if Mrs. Oswald hanged herself in Stafford's book, it was because the author "has given her the rope and the opportunity to do so."[16] Grace Dole advised that the book could be read out of curiosity, "but it does not add much to our knowledge of this case." She was, of course, condemning Stafford for not writing a different book than the one she set out to write—something like condemning chicken for not tasting like fish, to borrow Malcolm Jones's defense of Liebling.[17] Eliot Fremont-Smith expressed a view somewhat similar to Dole's: "I suppose it has some value . . . but it is wounding all the same" and concluded his review by saying that anyone who reads the book is "completely assaulted."[18] In some ways, that comment is a credit to Stafford for having stayed out of the book enough to let Mrs. Oswald show through.

Retrospective commentary on Stafford's literary career mentioned that Stafford had ridiculed her own mother and so the "cruel portrait, executed pitilessly" was something of a Stafford motif.[19] An obituary writer said that a recurring theme in Stafford's work was of people imprisoned by their own personalities.[20] That comment certainly describes *A Mother in History*. Mary Ellen Williams Walsh proposed that Mrs. Oswald could have come from Stafford's fiction, theorizing that the portrait of Mrs. Oswald "suggests the conclusion that Stafford the novelist might have reached—the fatherless orphan sought his revenge by killing the most powerful representative figure of the father that he could approach."[21]

But actually Stafford was drawn to the story because of Liebling's original interest in the press coverage of Kennedy's assassination: the story found her. That *A Mother in History* fits a literary theme should not surprise us, because many pieces of writing—fiction and nonfiction alike—can be shown to fit ancient themes. Stafford's contribution to journalism, if small and brief, nevertheless owns a niche that it will occupy for a long time.

ENDNOTES

1. Jean Stafford, "Truth in Fiction," *Library Journal*, 1 October 1966, 4564.
2. Jean Stafford, *A Mother in History* (New York: Pharos Books, 1992), 12. (Originally published by Farrar, Straus and Giroux in 1966.)
3. Eliot Fremont-Smith, "How Oswald Happened," Eliot Fremont-Smith, *New York Times*, 23 February 1966, p. 37.
4. Stafford, *Mother in History*, 22.
5. Jean Stafford, "Somebody out There Hates Me," *Esquire*, August 1974, 108–09, 156. Passim.
6. "The New Books," *Harper's*, April 1966, 123.
7. Annette K. Baxter, "Mom Talks," *New York Times Book Review*, 13 March 1966, 16.
8. Quoted in Barbara Long, "In Cold Comfort," *Esquire*, June 1966, 179.
9. David Roberts, *Jean Stafford: A Biography* (Boston: Little, Brown, 1988), 357.
10. Granville Hicks, "Mother of the Accused," *Saturday Review*, 5 March 1966, 34.
11. Florence Casey, "Her 'why?' gets no answer," *Christian Science Monitor*, 3 March 1966, 5.
12. Marya Mannes, "Woman behind the gun," *Washington Post Book World*, 27 February 1966, 4.
13. Barbara La Rosa, "A Mother in History," *America*, 19 March 1966, 390.

14. Jean Holzhauer, "A Mother in History," *Commonweal,* 13 May 1966, 234.
15. Karl Miller, "Moving Around," *New Statesman,* 30 September 1966, 486.
16. Paul Richard, "Mother's Day in Fort Worth," *New Republic,* 26 March 1966, 22–23.
17. Malcolm Jones Jr., "The Timeless A. J. Liebling," *Newsweek,* 26 November 1990, 76.
18. Fremont-Smith, "How Oswald Happened," 37.
19. Ann Hulbert, *The Interior Castle: The Art and Life of Jean Stafford* (New York: Knopf, 1992), 341–42.
20. J. Y. Smith, "Jean Stafford, Author, Dies," *Washington Post,* 29 March 1979, p. B6.
21. Mary Ellen Williams Walsh, *Jean Stafford* (Boston: Twayne, 1985), 84.

Chapter 9

❖

In Cold Blood

Truman Capote, who was a literary star at age twenty-three, had an idea that he wanted to write a major piece of nonfiction. All he lacked was the subject matter. Then, while he was reading the *New York Times* one day in 1959, he saw a story[1] about the murder of a Kansas farmer, his wife, and two of their children—Herbert W. Clutter; his wife, Bonnie; a daughter, Nancy; and their only son, Kenyon. The murders had been committed, everyone would learn later, by Perry Smith and Richard Hickock. Capote had his subject matter. Within one month he arrived in Holcomb, Kansas, the site of the murders.[2]

In Cold Blood was serialized over four issues of *The New Yorker*, beginning with the September 15, 1965, issue. The editor at the time, William Shawn, reportedly said that he had second thoughts later and "almost wished he hadn't published it,"[3] although when he died the *New York Times* attributed him with editorial acumen for having done so.[4] Each part contained this editor's note: "All quotations in this article are taken either from official records or from conversations, transcribed verbatim, between the author and the principals."

Many readers saw the book, Capote said later, "as a reflection on American life—this collision between the desperate, ruthless, wandering, savage part of American life, and the other, which is insular and safe, more or less."[5]

The following excerpt comes from early in the book, shortly after Capote has introduced the main the killers and their victims. Perry and Dick are the killers. Kenyon and Nancy are the Clutter children who will soon be murdered.

❖   ❖   ❖

By midafternoon the black Chevrolet had reached Emporia, Kansas—
a large town, almost a city, and a safe place, so the occupants of the car
had decided, to do a bit of shopping. They parked on a side street, then
wandered about until a suitably crowded variety store presented itself.

The first purchase was a pair of rubber gloves; these were for Perry,
who, unlike Dick, had neglected to bring old gloves of his own.

They moved on to a counter displaying women's hosiery. After a spell
of indecisive quibbling, Perry said, "I'm for it."

Dick was not. "What about my eye? They're all too light-colored to
hide that."

"Miss," said Perry, attracting a salesgirl's attention. "You got any black
stockings?" When she told him no, he proposed that they try another
store. "Black's foolproof."

But Dick had made up his mind: stockings of any shade were unnec-
essary, an encumbrance, a useless expense ("I've already invested enough
money in this operation"), and, after all, anyone they encountered would
not live to bear witness. "*No* witnesses," he reminded Perry, for what
seemed to Perry the millionth time. It rankled in him, the way Dick
mouthed those two words, as though they solved every problem; it was
stupid not to admit that there might be a witness they hadn't seen. "The
ineffable happens, things do take a turn," he said. But Dick, smiling boast-
fully, boyishly, did not agree: "Get the bubbles out of your blood. Nothing
can go wrong." No. Because the plan was Dick's, and from first footfall to
final silence, flawlessly devised.

Next they were interested in rope. Perry studied the stock, tested it.
Having once served in the Merchant Marine, he understood rope and
was clever with knots. He chose a white nylon cord, as strong as wire
and not much thicker. They discussed how many yards of it they required.
The question irritated Dick, for it was part of a greater quandary, and he
could not, despite the alleged perfection of his over-all design, be certain
of the answer.

Eventually, he said, "Christ, how the hell should I know?"

"You damn well better."

Dick tried. "There's him. Her. The kid and the girl. And maybe the
other two. But it's Saturday. They might have guests. Let's count on eight,
or even twelve. The only *sure* thing is every one of them has got to go."

"Seems like a lot of it. To be so sure about."

"Ain't that what I promised you, honey—plenty of hair on them-those walls?"

Perry shrugged. "Then we'd better buy the whole roll."

It was a hundred yards long—quite enough for twelve.

Kenyon had built the chest himself: a mahogany hope chest, lined with cedar, which he intended to give Beverly* as a wedding present. Now, working on it in the so-called den in the basement, he applied a last coat of varnish. The furniture of the den, a cement-floored room that ran the length of the house, consisted almost entirely of examples of carpentry (shelves, tables, stools, a ping-pong table) and Nancy's needlework (chintz slip covers that rejuvenated a decrepit couch, curtains, pillows bearing legends: HAPPY? and YOU DON'T HAVE TO BE CRAZY TO LIVE HERE BUT IT HELPS). Together, Kenyon and Nancy had made a paint-splattered attempt to deprive the basement room of its unremovable dourness, and neither was aware of failure. In fact, they both thought their den a triumph and a blessing—Nancy because it was a place where she could entertain "the gang" without disturbing her mother, and Kenyon because here he could be alone, free to bang, saw, and mess with his "inventions," the newest of which was an electric deep-dish frying pan. Adjoining the den was a furnace room, which contained a tool-littered table piled with some of his other works-in-progress—an amplifying unit, an elderly wind-up Victrola that he was restoring to service.

Kenyon resembled neither of his parents physically; his crew-cut hair was hemp-colored, and he was six feet tall and lanky, though hefty enough to have once rescued a pair of full-grown sheep by carrying them two miles through a blizzard—sturdy, strong, but cursed with a lanky boy's lack of muscular coordination. This defect, aggravated by an inability to function without glasses, prevented him from taking more than a token part in those team sports (basketball, baseball) that were the main occupation of most of the boys who might have been his friends. He had only one close friend—Bob Jones, the son of Taylor Jones, whose ranch was a mile west of the Clutter home. Out in rural Kansas, boys start driving cars very young; Kenyon was eleven when his father allowed him to buy, with money he had earned raising sheep, an old truck with a Model A engine—the Coyote Wagon, he and Bob called it. Not far from River Valley Farm there is a mysterious stretch of countryside known as the Sand Hills; it is like a beach without an ocean, and at night coyotes slink among

---

*His older sister. R.T.B.

the dunes, assembling in hordes to howl. On moonlit evenings the boys would descend upon them, set them running, and try to outrace them in the wagon; they seldom did, for the scrawniest coyote can hit fifty miles an hour, whereas the wagon's top speed was thirty-five, but it was a wild and beautiful kind of fun, the wagon skidding across the sand, the fleeing coyotes framed against the moon—as Bob said, it sure made your heart hurry.

Equally intoxicating, and more profitable, were the rabbit roundups the two boys conducted: Kenyon was a good shot and his friend a better one, and between them they sometimes delivered half a hundred rabbits to the "rabbit factory"—a Garden City processing plant that paid ten cents a head for the animals, which were then quick-frozen and shipped to mink growers. But what meant most to Kenyon—and Bob, too—was their weekend, overnight hunting hikes along the shores of the river: wandering, wrapping up in blankets, listening at sunrise for the noise of wings, moving toward the sound on tiptoe, and then, sweetest of all, swaggering homeward with a dozen duck dinners swinging from their belts. But lately things had changed between Kenyon and his friend. They had not quarreled, there had been no overt falling-out, nothing had happened except that Bob, who was sixteen, had started "going with a girl," which meant that Kenyon, a year younger and still very much the adolescent bachelor, could no longer count on his companionship. Bob told him, "When you're my age, you'll feel different. I used to think the same as you: Women—so what? But then you get to talking to some woman, and it's mighty nice. You'll see." Kenyon doubted it; he could not conceive of ever wanting to waste an hour on any girl that might be spent with guns, horses, tools, machinery, even a book. If Bob was unavailable, then he would rather be alone, for in temperament he was not in the least Mr. Clutter's son but rather Bonnie's child, a sensitive and reticent boy. His contemporaries thought him "stand-offish," yet forgave him, saying "Oh, *Kenyon*. It's just that he lives in a world of his own."

Leaving the varnish to dry, he went on to another chore—one that took him out-of-doors. He wanted to tidy up his mother's flower garden, a treasured patch of disheveled foliage that grew beneath her bedroom window. When he got there, he found one of the hired men loosening earth with a spade—Paul Helm, the husband of the housekeeper.

"Seen that car?" Mr. Helm asked.

Yes, Kenyon had seen a car in the driveway—a gray Buick, standing outside the entrance to his father's office.

"Thought you might know who it was."

"Not unless it's Mr. Johnson. Dad said he was expecting him."

Mr. Helm (the late Mr. Helm; he died of a stroke the following March) was a somber man in his late fifties whose withdrawn manner veiled a nature keenly curious and watchful; he liked to know what was going on. "Which Johnson?"

"The insurance fellow."

Mr. Helm grunted. "Your dad must be laying in a stack of it. That car's been here I'd say three hours."

The chill of oncoming dusk shivered through the air, and though the sky was still deep blue, lengthening shadows emanated from the garden's tall chrysanthemum stalks; Nancy's cat frolicked among them, catching its paws in the twine with which Kenyon and the old man were now tying plants. Suddenly, Nancy herself came jogging across the fields aboard fat Babe—Babe, returning from her Saturday treat, a bathe in the river. Teddy, the dog, accompanied them, and all three were water-splashed and shining.

"You'll catch cold," Mr. Helm said.

Nancy laughed; she had never been ill—not once. Sliding off Babe, she sprawled on the grass at the edge of the garden and seized her cat, dangled him above her, and kissed his nose and whiskers.

Kenyon was disgusted. "*Kissing* animals on the mouth."

"You used to kiss Skeeter," she reminded him.

"Skeeter was a horse." A beautiful horse, a strawberry stallion he had raised from a foal. How that Skeeter could take a fence! "You use a horse too hard," his father had cautioned him. "One day you'll ride the life out of Skeeter." And he had; while Skeeter was streaking down a road with his master astride him, his heart failed, and he stumbled and was dead. Now, a year later, Kenyon still mourned him, even though his father, taking pity on him, had promised him the pick of next spring's foals.

"Kenyon?" Nancy said. "Do you think Tracy will be able to talk? By Thanksgiving?" Tracy, not yet a year old, was her nephew, the son of Eveanna, the sister to whom she felt particularly close. (Beverly was Kenyon's favorite.) "It would thrill me to pieces to hear him say 'Aunt Nancy.' Or 'Uncle Kenyon.' Wouldn't you like to hear him say that? I mean, don't you *love* being an uncle? Kenyon? Good grief, why can't you *ever* answer me?"

"Because you're silly," he said, tossing her the head of a flower, a wilted dahlia, which she jammed into her hair.

Mr. Helm picked up his spade. Crows cawed, sundown was near, but his home was not; the lane of Chinese elms had turned into a tunnel of darkening green, and he lived at the end of it, half a mile away. "Evening," he said, and started his journey. But once he looked back. "And that," he was to testify the next day, "was the last I seen them. Nancy leading old Babe off to the barn. Like I said, nothing out of the ordinary."

⚜ ⚜ ⚜

As a person, Capote was different. The antithesis of what a journalist should be—quiet, reserved, off to the side, unnoticed—Capote stood out in a crowd. At the time *Blood* was published, a news magazine said Capote had arrived in Kansas "in his Army-styled visored cap, sheepskin coat and moccasins, his high-pitched child's voice, and his trunk full of French wine and Life cigarettes."[6] Twenty-five years after the murder, one Holcomb resident recalled: "He was very short, of course, and had a fur coat on, fur hat, and he was sort of swallowed up in it."[7] Capote was not an ordinary person, and he did an extraordinary job in reporting and then writing *In Cold Blood.*

A *New Yorker* profile on Marlon Brando[8] followed by *The Muses Are Heard,* a nonfiction account of a musical troupe's tour of Russia,[9] had made Truman Capote realize he wanted to do something on a larger scale. That something eventually became *In Cold Blood,*[10] described by one critic as "a seminal work of new journalism that remains the highlight of Capote's career."[11] Generally known as a novelist and short story writer (although Tom Wolfe would say later that when Capote took on the Clutter murder, his "career had been in the doldrums"),[12] Capote in 1958 had signaled his intention "to prove that I could apply my style to the realities of journalism."[13] As part of his preparation, Capote grilled Lillian Ross about the way she had reported and written *Picture.* Four decades later Ross wrote that Capote had quizzed her about the mechanics of her reporting but that she had told him that the mechanics were irrelevant—that the key elements were the characters and their interactions, dramatic developments, and backgrounds.[14] Capote obviously took her advice to heart.

Within three days of reading about the quadruple murder, Capote was making plans to go to Kansas with his child-hood friend, Harper Lee, who had just completed *To Kill a Mockingbird*.[15] It would be six years before the results of Capote's prodigious reporting effort—six thousand pages of notes[16]—was published. *In Cold Blood* has since been turned into two movies and an opera.

Capote's journalistic methods deserve special mention. He never recorded an interview: not with a tape recorder (tape recorders were large and bulky at the time) or even with a notepad and pencil, because he felt they intruded on the inter-view.[17] Instead, he memorized interviews, then returned to his hotel room and typed them up. He would later claim that he had trained himself to do this by memorizing books read aloud to him until he was able to repeat 95 percent[18] of the contents—a figure that varied from 90 percent[19] to 97 percent[20] in interviews he gave after the publication of *Blood*.

Before he began the research for *Blood*, he had memorized a seven-hour monologue by Marlon Brando, which became the heart of a profile in *The New Yorker*. Capote eventually revealed that he began the interview by talking in very open terms about himself. Brando later said: "The little bastard spent half the night telling me all his problems. The least I could do was tell him a few of mine."[21] Of his technique, Capote once wrote: "The secret to the art of interviewing—and it is an art—is to let the other person think he's interviewing you. You tell him about yourself, and slowly you spin your web so that he tells you everything."[22]

Capote verified everything he could. In one instance, he wanted to interview the driver of a car who had picked up the murderers—Perry Smith and Richard Hickock—so he wrote the man a letter, using the address from the business card the man had given the murderers. No response. He wrote to the personnel manager of the company* and was told by return mail that while such a person existed, Capote must be mistaken about him picking up hitchhikers because it was against company policy to do that. Capote called the man, who claimed he did not know

---

*The telephone had not yet become the ubiquitous and inexpensive method of communication it is today.

what Capote was talking about. So Capote drove to Omaha, went to the man's office, and put photographs of the two murderers on his desk. Obviously, the man didn't want his company to know that he had violated policy,[23] but when Capote told him that the two murderers had in fact intended to murder him, he finally admitted to having picked them up. He was not murdered because he pulled over to pick up yet another hitchhiker as Smith was about to smash in his head.

Capote extended his verification to retracing the route Smith and Hickock took after they murdered the Clutters. Miami Beach. Mexico City. Las Vegas. Smith and Hickock, who were kept separate from each other, had told Capote where they had gone. In addition to cross-checking their accounts, Capote verified as much as he could himself. In checking out the murderers' story, he learned that Hickock had an extraordinary memory—for "names and addresses of any hotel or place along the route where they'd spent maybe just half a night."[24]

Capote covered the story as it was unfolding. He was in Holcomb within a month of the murders and witnessed much of their aftermath. In fact, it was not until the murderers were caught that townspeople felt comfortable talking to Capote.[25]

But what did Capote write?

He called *In Cold Blood* a "nonfiction novel" ("an appallingly harmful phrase," John Hersey said),[26] although he admitted the term was a *non sequitur*. "But what I wanted to do was bring to journalism the technique of fiction, which moves both horizontally and vertically at the same time"—"horizontally" with the external story and "vertically" in the sense of getting inside the minds of the characters.[27] In an interview, Capote said a reporter had to extend his imaginative range by writing about people he would normally have ignored. Capote felt it was only possible to do that in a journalistic situation."[28]

In Cold Blood arrived to much advance publicity—"twelve articles in national magazines, two half-hour television programs, and an unparalleled number of radio shows and newspaper stories."[29] When the book was serialized by *The New Yorker,* approximately four months before it was published as a book, "it broke the magazine's record for newsstand sales."[30] There was an eighteen-page spread in *Life,* which included photographs by

Richard Avedon. An anonymous caption writer for the photo essay wrote that no American book since *Look Homeward Angel* had "excited as much advance notice and excitement as Truman Capote's *In Cold Blood*."[31] Some publicity reported that Capote would make an unprecedented $2 million,[32] including $1 million from paperback and film rights alone.[33] Within two years, in fact, Capote had earned $3 million from the book and an additional $500,000 from the movie rights.[34] Added to the publicity was Capote's immodest boasting that he had brought forth something new—a nonfiction novel.

Many critics focused, even feasted, on Capote's claim and condemned the book for it. Others showed more latitude, roasting Capote for his claim but generally approving of his work.

One critic who would not ignore Capote's claim was Sol Yurick. He said it was impossible to dissociate *Blood* from the claim that it was a new art form and, "as such, represents a higher objectivity." Yurick said those critics who liked the book demonstrated "a deplorable lack of homework in the history of literature and psychology."[35] The historian Barbara Tuchman, in an essay on how historians used story-telling techniques to good effect, wrote condescendingly in the last paragraph: "New to these techniques, Mr. Capote is perhaps naïvely impressed by them."[36] She condemned Capote not only for thinking that he had done something new, but for doing badly what he did.

One critic questioned the positive reception *Blood* was receiving. "Are we so bankrupt," Stanley Kauffmann asked, "so avid for novelty that, merely because a famous writer produces an amplified magazine crime-feature, the result is automatically elevated to serious literature?[37] Kauffmann also suggested that the book could have been condensed by a third and thus improved threefold. In a play on Capote's dig at Jack Kerouac ("That isn't writing, it's typing."), he suggested that *Blood* wasn't writing, but research.[38]

Other reviewers challenged Capote's claim that *Blood* was literature. Hilton Kramer, while seeing in the book "the prose rhythm of a superior reporter," said, "It is not what the language of fiction, the medium of significant art, always is: the refraction of a serious moral imagination."[39] Diana Trilling made the point that *Blood* was not a work of imagination,[40] which would qualify it as fiction, although she said in language dripping in sarcasm that it was "a work of journalism of an exceptionally compelling kind."[41]

Not everyone was negative. Among those who praised the book was F. W. Dupee, who said, "*In Cold Blood* is the best documentary account of an American crime ever written, partly because the crime here in question is not yet a part of the heritage."[42] George Garrett saw the book as a bold and praiseworthy step for the technically conservative Capote, saying Capote "has always been known as a distinguished stylist and as an imaginative storyteller, but he has not previously shown a great deal of interest in the possibilities of innovative arrangement."[43] The novelist Rebecca West feared that *Blood* "may be regarded simply as a literary *tour de force* instead of the formidable statement about reality which it is."[44] William Phillips said the book "reads like high-class journalism, the kind of journalism one expects of a novelist."[45] William Meacham saw Capote matching "the art of the novelist with a consummate skill of reportage. Tension and suspense are sustained throughout the book as though it were a novel."[46] Three decades later Edmund White praised "the dramatic efficiency of the writing."[47]

Capote said one of his objectives in writing *Blood* was to stay out of the book. There would be no first person passing judgment.[48] But, of course, the way a writer arranges material does make a statement, does pass judgment, as Capote admitted to George Plimpton. Meacham wrote that Capote was "always objective and completely in the background, has no thesis, but makes shrewd use of paradox and antithesis everywhere in his book."[49] Conrad Knickerbocker said the book evidenced a "moral judgment without the author's presence."[50]

Capote's writing technique has been compared to film, short story, and journalism techniques. "The sound of the book creates the illusion of tape. Its taut cross-cutting is cinematic," Knickerbocker wrote.[51] Kauffmann also noted Capote's use of cinematic techniques to develop his story.[52] And while Bernard McCabe referred to the writing as "familiar *New Yorker* documentary style—apparently deadpan, with a laconic piling up of objective detail," he also praised Capote (and the excerpts give a flavor of this) for the cinematic technique of cutting among the worlds of the various people caught in the story—the victims, the killers, the investigators.[53] (Joseph Wambaugh imitated this technique with great success in *The Onion Field.*) "Actually," Phillip K. Tompkins wrote, "the chapters are more like short stories; many of them could stand by themselves with little or no additional context."[54] Another critic said *Blood* was written like a breaking news story, with some chapters standing as features or sidebars— which in part reflects the fact that Capote was involved in reporting the story within weeks of the murders and before the murderers were caught. He was not reconstructing; he was reporting. "The style is much more like journalism than anything else Capote had written before or would write later,"[55] Gary L. Whitby said.

The factuality of the book came under fire. Capote did not provide line-by-line, quote-by-quote attribution, and some critics used that omission to challenge what he wrote. Capote was, after all, a novelist, someone who made up stories, and his immodesty and boastfulness rankled some. Tompkins visited Kansas and interviewed many of the same people. His story in *Esquire* reported several factual errors, including a pat ending Capote had supposedly made up—"supposedly" because it really came down to one person's words against another's. Tompkins attributed the discrepancies not to malice, but to the subconscious personal bias all writers bring to a topic. Tompkins concluded that the book's shortcomings and flaws would eventually be put in perspective and readers would enjoy the book "for its own sake."[56]

In Cold Blood continues to engender mild controversy, focusing mostly on its factuality and to a lesser extent on whether Capote, open about his homosexuality, might have been in love with Perry Smith and softened his part in the story. Capote would say a decade later that Smith was in love with him,[57] but with Smith and Capote both dead, it's difficult to examine what could very well have been a subconscious filter on Capote's part.

Blood does represent a Herculean reporting effort and an artful writing result. Capote deserves credit for helping elevate the place of nonfiction in the world of literature. Four years before he died he said in an interview, which was replayed on the MacNeil-Lehrer NewsHour on public television after his death,

"That's the whole art of it. The whole reason that I ever started doing this is that nobody has ever done anything with factual writing as an art form in itself." He was immodest to the end, but that should not detract from *In Cold Blood*.

ENDNOTES

1. United Press International, "Wealthy Farmer, Three of Family Slain," *New York Times*, 16 November 1959, 39.
2. Gerald Clarke, *Capote: A Biography* (London: Hamish Hamilton, 1988), 320.
3. Charles McGrath, "Remembering Mr. Shawn," *New Yorker*, 28 December 1992–4 January 1993, 134. In response to a letter from me, McGrath said he could not recall the precise nature of Shawn's reservation, although he suspected it had to do with taste. Letter to author, 8 January 1993.
4. Eric Pace, "William Shawn, 85, Is Dead; New Yorker's Gentle Despot," *New York Times*, 9 December 1992, p. B13.
5. George Plimpton, "The Story behind a Nonfiction Novel," *New York Times Book Review*, 16 January 1966, 43.
6. "'In Cold Blood' . . . An American Tragedy," *Newsweek*, 24 January 1966, 59.
7. Antone Gonsalves, "25 years later, 'In Cold Blood' murders still haunt," United Press International, 11 November 1984. Years later, Capote walked up to the agent Swifty Lazar and Michael Korda in a restaurant in New York City. Korda later reported that Capote was wearing a purple velvet jumpsuit and a matching purple hat and looked "like nothing so much as an aging pixie." Michael Korda, "The King of the Deal," *New Yorker*, 29 March 1993, 44.
8. Truman Capote, "The Duke in His Domain," *New Yorker*, 9 November 1957.
9. Truman Capote, *The Muses Are Heard* (New York: Random House, 1956).
10. Eric Norden, "Playboy Interview: Truman Capote," *Playboy*, March 1968, 53.
11. Donna Olendorf, *Contemporary Authors*, New Revision Series, vol. 18 (Detroit: Gale Research, 1986), 85.
12. Tom Wolfe, *The New Journalism*, with an anthology edited by Tom Wolfe and E. W. Johnson (New York: Harper & Row, 1973), 26.
13. Quoted in Pati Hill, "Truman Capote," in *Writers at Work*, ed. Malcolm Cowley, (New York: Viking, 1957, 1958), 291.
14. Lillian Ross, *Here but Not Here* (New York: Random House, 1998), 114.

15. Plimpton, "The Story Behind," 3.
16. Haskel Frankel, "The Author," *Saturday Review,* 22 January 1966, 37.
17. Plimpton, "The Story Behind," 38.
18. Ibid.
19. "'In Cold Blood' . . . An American Tragedy," 61.
20. Jane Howard, "How the 'Smart Rascal' Brought It Off" and "Horror Spawns a Masterpiece," *Life,* 7 January 1966, 71. Howard's name appears only on the first article. I suspect that the second, which is more photo essay than article, was written in house.
21. Quoted in Clarke, *Biography,* 302.
22. Quoted in Ibid.
23. Plimpton, "Story Behind," 38.
24. Ibid., 39.
25. Ibid., 3.
26. John Hersey, "The Legend on the License," *Yale Review,* Autumn 1980, 1.
27. Norden, "Playboy Interview," 56.
28. Plimpton, "Story Behind," 2.
29. Clarke, *Biography,* 362.
30. "The Country Below the Surface," *Time,* 21 January 1966, 83.
31. Howard, "How the 'Smart Rascal,'" 58.
32. Harry Gilroy, "A Book in a New Form Earns $2 Million for Truman Capote," *New York Times,* 31 December 1965.
33. Eliot Fremont-Smith, "Literature-by-Consensus," *New York Times,* 26 January 1996, p. 35.
34. Norden, "Playboy Interview," 51.
35. Sol Yurick, "Sob-Sister Gothic," *Nation,* 7 February 1996, 158.
36. Barbara W. Tuchman, "The Historian as Artist," *The New York Herald Tribune Book Week,* 6 March 1966, 9.
37. Stanley Kauffmann, "Capote in Kansas," *New Republic,* 22 January 1966, 20.
38. Ibid., 21.
39. Hilton Kramer, "Real Gardens with Real Toads," *New Leader,* 31 January 1966, 19.
40. Diana Trilling, "Capote's Crime and Punishment," *Partisan Review,* Spring 1966, 253.
41. Ibid., 252.
42. F. W. Dupee, "Truman Capote's Score," *New York Review of Books,* 3 February 1966, 3.
43. George Garrett, "Crime and Punishment in Kansas: Truman Capote's *In Cold Blood,*" *Hollins Critic,* February 1966, 3.
44. Rebecca West, "A Grave and Reverend Book," *Harper's,* February 1966, 108.
45. William Phillips, "But Is It Good for Literature?" *Commentary,* May 1966, 77.

46. William Shands Meacham, "A Non-Fiction Study in Scarlet," *Virginia Quarterly Review*, Spring 1966, 316.
47. Edmund White, "The Mérimée of Monroeville," *Times Literary Supplement*, 20 February 1998, 14.
48. Plimpton, "Story Behind," 38.
49. Meacham, "New Fiction Study," 319.
50. Conrad Knickerbocker, "One Night on a Kansas Farm," *New York Times Book Review*, 16 January 1966, 37.
51. Knickerbocker, "One Night," 37.
52. Kauffmann, "Capote in Kansas," 19.
53. Bernard McCabe, "Elementary, my dear man," *Commonweal*, 11 February 1966, 561.
54. Phillip K. Tompkins, "In Cold Fact," *Esquire*, June 1966, 125.
55. Gary L. Whitby, "Truman Capote," in *A Sourcebook of American Literary Journalism: Representative Writers in an Emerging Genre*," ed. Thomas B. Connery (New York: Greenwood, 1992), 247.
56. Tompkins, "In Cold Fact," 171.
57. Anne Taylor Fleming, "The Descent from the Heights," *New York Times Magazine*, 16 July 1978, 12.

Chapter 10

❖

Hell's Angels

The series of events that eventually led to *Hell's Angels* began with a news report of the rape of two teenage girls by the Hell's Angels, a motorcycle gang in California. That report was followed by another, compiled by the attorney general of California, that declared the Hell's Angels a menace to society. The attendant publicity in the national news media created more interest in and anxiety over the Hell's Angels.[1] Carey McWilliams, the editor of *The Nation* and something of an iconoclast, asked Hunter Thompson to write a story that separated fact from fancy.[2]

In the resulting story, Thompson challenged the attorney general's view and news media accounts. He pointed out discrepancies between descriptions of the Hell's Angels in news accounts and the real Hell's Angels, and argued that the differences raised "a question as to who are the real hell's angels."[3] That remark was an early shot at the press; throughout his career, Thompson never let up. Timothy Crouse reported Thompson's feelings on the press after the 1968 presidential election: "He told me they had been a bunch of swine, a collection of suspicious reactionary old hacks who cared only about protecting their leads . . . ."[4] Thompson, who was living in San Francisco and had already met some Angels when the assignment came along, wrote that the publicity had obscured the real issues, leading people to feel that once the Angels were subsumed, all would be right with the world.[5]

Within a few weeks, six publishers had asked Thompson to write a book.[6] He eventually accepted a $6,000 advance from Ian Ballantine, the president of Bantam Books, who visited

Thompson at his home to conduct negotiations.[7] Reaching sales of forty thousand copies in 1967, the hardcover edition was a modest bestseller. The paperback went on to sell approximately two million copies between 1968 and 1988.[8]

The following excerpt comes from the beginning of Chapter 12 and begins the story of an outing at Bass Lake. Thompson ends the previous chapter by telling of the Angels arriving in the town riding four abreast and attempting to create "civic trauma." Chapter 11's last sentence: "If I had been a citizen of Bass Lake at the time I would have gone home and loaded every gun I owned."

⚜ ⚜ ⚜

Bass Lake is not really a town, but a resort area—a string of small settlements around a narrow, picture-postcard lake that is seven miles long and less than a mile wide at any point. The post office is on the north side of the lake in a cluster of stores and buildings all owned by a man named Williams. This was the Angels' rendezvous point . . . but the local sheriff, a giant of a man named Tiny Baxter, had decided to keep them out of his area by means of a second roadblock about a half mile from the center of downtown. It was Baxter's decision and he backed it with his three-man force and a half dozen local forest rangers.

By the time I got there the outlaws were stopped along both sides of the highway, and Barger was striding forth to meet Baxter. The sheriff explained to the Angel chieftain and his Praetorian Guard that a spacious campsite had been carefully reserved for them up on the mountain above town, where they wouldn't "be bothered." Baxter is six-foot-six and built like a defensive end for the Baltimore Colts. Barger is barely six feet, but not one of his followers had the slightest doubt that he would swing on the sheriff if things suddenly came down to the hard nub. I don't think the sheriff doubted it either, and certainly I didn't. There is a steely, thoughtful quality about Barger, an instinctive restraint that leads outsiders to feel they can reason with him. But there is also a quiet menace, an egocentric fanaticism tempered by eight years at the helm of a legion of outcasts who, on that sweaty afternoon, were measuring the sheriff purely by his size, his weapon and the handful of young rangers who backed him up. There was no question about who would win the initial encounter, but it was up to Barger to decide just what that victory would be worth.

He decided to go up the mountain, and his legion followed without question or bitterness. The ranger who pointed out the route made it sound like a ten-minute drive up a nearby dirt road. I watched the outlaw horde boom off in that direction, then talked for a while with two of the rangers who stayed to man the roadblock. They seemed a little tense but smiled when I asked if they were afraid the Hell's Angels might take over the town. They had shotguns in the cab of their truck, but during the confrontation the guns had remained out of sight. Both were in their early twenties, and they seemed very cool, considering the much-publicized threat they had just met and sidetracked. I chalked it up later to the influence of Tiny Baxter, the only cop I've ever seen put Sonny Barger on the defensive.

It was about 3:30 P.M. when I started up the dirt road to the designated Angel campground. Thirty minutes later I was still following motorcycle tracks up a fresh bulldozer cut that looked like something hacked out of a Philippine jungle. The angle was low gear all the way, it zigzagged like a deer trail and the campsite itself was so high that when I finally arrived it seemed that only a heavy ground fog lay between us and a clear view of Manhattan Island, at the other end of the continent. There was no trace of water, and by this time the Angels had worked up a serious thirst. They had been shunted off to a parched meadow nine or ten thousand feet up in the Sierras and it was obviously a bum trip. They hadn't minded the climb but now they felt deceived and they wanted to retaliate. The prevailing ugly mood was shared by Barger, who felt the sheriff had duped him. The campsite was fit only for camels and mountain goats. The view was excellent but a camp without water on a California Fourth of July is as useless as an empty beer can.

I listened to the war talk and shouting for a while, then hustled down the mountain to call a Washington newspaper I was writing for at the time, to say I was ready to send one of the great riot stories of the decade. On the way down the road I passed outlaw bikes coming the other way. They'd been stopped at the Bass Lake roadblock and pointed up to the campsite. The Frisco swastika truck came by in first gear, with two bikes in the back and a third trailing twenty feet behind at the end of a long rope in a cloud of dust. Its rider was hanging on grimly behind green goggles and a hand-kerchief tied over his nose and mouth. Following the truck was a red Plymouth that erupted with shouts and horn blasts as I passed. I stopped, not recognizing the car, and backed up. It was Larry, Pete and Puff, the new president of the Frisco chapter. I hadn't seen them since the night of the meeting at the DePau. Pete, the drag racer, was working as a messenger in the city, and Larry was carving totem poles out of tree stumps in other Angels' front yards. They had broken down on the freeway near Modesto and been picked up by three pretty young girls who stopped to offer help. This was the Plymouth, and now the girls were part of the act. One was sitting on Pete's lap in the back seat, half undressed and smiling distract-edly, while I explained the problem of the campsite. They decided to push on, and I said I'd see them later in town . . . or somewhere, and at that point I thought it would probably be in jail. A very bad scene was building up. Soon the Angels would be coming down the mountain en masse, and in no mood for reasonable talk.

In the Carolinas they say "hill people" are different from "flatlands people," and as a native Kentuckian with more mountain than flat-lands blood, I'm inclined to agree. This was one of the theories I'd been nursing all the way from San Francisco. Unlike Porterville or Hollister, Bass Lake was a mountain community . . . and if the old Appalachian pattern held, the people would be much slower to anger or panic, but absolutely without reason or mercy once the fat was in the fire. Like the Angels they would tend to fall back in an emergency on their own native sense of justice—which bears only a primitive resemblance to anything written in law books. I thought the mountain types would be far more tolerant of the Angels' noisy showboating, but—compared to their flat-lands cousins—much quicker to retaliate in kind at the first evidence of physical insult or abuse.

On the way down the mountain I heard another Monitor newscast, saying the Hell's Angels were heading for Bass Lake and big trouble. There was also mention of a Los Angeles detective who had shot one of the suspects rounded up for questioning about the rape of his daughter the day before. The sight of the suspect being led through the hall of the police station was too much for the detective, who suddenly lost control and began firing point blank. The victim was said to be a Hell's Angel, and newspapers on sale in Bass Lake that afternoon were headlined: HELL'S ANGEL SHOT IN RAPE CASE. (The suspect, who survived, was a twenty-one-year-old drifter. He was later absolved of any connection with either the Angels or the rape of the detective's daughter . . . who had been selling cookbooks, door to door, when she was lured into a house known to be frequented by dragsters and hot-rod types. The detective admitted losing his head and shooting the wrong man; he later pleaded temporary insanity and was acquitted of all charges by a Los Angeles grand jury.) It took several days, however, for the press to separate the rape-shooting from the Hell's Angels, and in the meantime the headlines added fuel to the fire. On top of the Laconia stories, including the one in *Life*, the radio bulletins and all the frightening predictions in the daily press—now this, a Hell's Angels rape in Los Angeles, and just in time for the July 3 papers.

Given all these fiery ingredients, I didn't feel a trace of alarmist guilt when I finally got a Bass Lake–Washington connection and began out-lining what was about to happen. I was standing in a glass phone booth in downtown Bass Lake—which consists of a small post office, a big grocery, a bar and cocktail lounge, and several other picturesque redwood establishments that look very combustible. While I was talking, Don Mohr pulled up on his bike—having breached the roadblock with his press credentials—and indicated that he was in a hurry to call the *Tribune*. My editor in Washington was telling me how and when to file, but I was not to do so until the riot was running under its own power with significant hurt to both flesh and property . . . and then I was to send no more than an arty variation of the standard wire-service news blurb: Who, What, When, Where and Why.

I was still on the phone when I saw a big burr-haired lad with a pistol on his belt walk over to Mohr and tell him to get out of town. I couldn't hear much of what was going on, but I saw Mohr produce a packet of credentials, stringing them out like a card shark with a funny deck. I could see that he needed the phone, so I agreed with my man in Washington that first things would always come first, and hung up. Mohr immediately occupied the booth, leaving me to deal with the crowd that had gathered.

Luckily, my garb was too bastard for definition. I was wearing Levis, Wellington boots from L. L. Bean in Maine, and a Montana sheepherder's jacket over a white tennis shirt. The burr-haired honcho asked me who I was. I gave him my card and asked why he had that big pistol on his belt. "You know why," he said. "The first one of these sonsofbitches that gives me any lip I'm gonna shoot right in the belly. That's the only language they understand." He nodded toward Mohr in the phone booth, and there was nothing in his tone to make me think I was exempted. I could see that his pistol was a short-barreled Smith & Wesson .357 Magnum—powerful enough to blow holes in Mohr's BSA cylinder head, if necessary—but at arm's length it hardly mattered. The gun was a killer at any range up to a hundred yards, and far beyond that in the hands of a man who worked at it. He was wearing it in a police-type holster on the belt that held up his khaki pants, high on his right hip and in an awkward position for getting at it quickly. But he was very conscious of having the gun and I knew he was capable of raising bloody hell if he started waving it around.

I asked him if he was a deputy sheriff.

"No I'm workin for Mr. Williams," he said, still studying my card. Then he looked up. "What are you doin with this motorcycle crowd?"

I explained that I was only a journalist trying to do an honest day's work. He nodded, still fondling my card. I said he could keep it, which seemed to please him. He dropped it in the pocket of his khaki shirt, then tucked his thumbs in his belt and asked me what I wanted to know. The tone of the question implied that I had about sixty seconds to get the story.

I shrugged. "Oh, I don't know. I just thought I'd look around a bit, maybe write a few things."

He chuckled knowingly. "Yeah? Well, you can write that we're ready for em. We'll give em all they want."

⚜ ⚜ ⚜

Hunter S. Thompson, by all accounts, lived his entire life on the edge or close to it.[9] He got in trouble with the law as a teenager in Louisville, Kentucky, and eventually chose what he saw as the lesser of two evils, the United States Air Force. In line for electronics school, which he did not want, Thompson found a way to obtain a journalism billet at Eglin Air Force Base in Florida near the beach. He also wrote under an assumed name, Thorne Stockton (Stockton is his middle name), for the Fort Walton Beach, Florida, *Playground News*. Eventually, he ran afoul of Air Force authorities and was dishonorably discharged, ending up as the sports editor at the *Jersey Shore* (Pa.) *Herald*. The morning after he ripped the door off the editor's car while on a date with the editor's daughter, Thompson moved on, first to *Time* magazine and then to the *Middletown Daily News*, north of New York City. He moved on from there after kicking a candy machine to death, but he continued to land on his feet. By age twenty-three, he was the South American correspondent for *The National Observer*, a Dow Jones weekly newspaper that, despite its conservative pedigree, valued offbeat reporting and writing: an echo, perhaps, of Henry Luce's attitude at *Fortune*, where James Agee developed *Let Us Now Praise Famous Men*. The paper's editors liked him and he prospered. Eventually, he moved to San Francisco. He severed his relationship with the *Observer* when its editors refused to publish his enthusiastic review of Tom Wolfe's *Kandy-Kolored Tangerine-Flake Streamline Baby*. He learned later that Wolfe had been fired from the *Observer*, which was why the review had been rejected.

Thompson belongs to a group of writers then known as "new journalists," a term generally attributed to Tom Wolfe. David Eason separated the new journalists into "realist" and "modernist," citing Wolfe and Truman Capote, among others, as realists, and Joan Didion and Thompson as modernists. Realists rely on readers' conventions and prior knowledge, and organize their work to focus on a topic. So Wolfe writes about the space program and Capote writes about a murder, for which the reader has a frame of reference by having, for example, read newspapers or watched television. Modernists, on the other hand, "describe what it feels like to live in a world where there is no consensus about a frame of reference to explain 'what it all means'."[10] In effect, modernists provide the frame of reference—usually themselves. It is clear that the counterculture provides them with rich material.

Thompson respectfully distinguished between himself and Wolfe. He noted that Wolfe re-created stories from events, whereas he got "right in the middle of whatever I'm writing about—as personally involved as possible."[11] For that comment, Wolfe said, Thompson deserved "the all-time free-lance writer's Brass Stud Award."[12] In Thompson's mind, objective journalism is "a pompous contradiction in terms."[13]

In later years, Thompson became known as the inventor of "gonzo journalism." He said "gonzo journalism" was born in 1970 when he was covering the Kentucky Derby. He suffered from writer's block, so he began "jerking pages out of my notebook and numbering them and sending them to the printer." *Scanlan's* magazine published the piece. Thompson said he received calls from people who called it a journalistic breakthrough.[14] (Wolfe had done something similar in 1963 for *Esquire*. After he complained of writer's block, an editor told him to submit his notes and someone would rewrite them. Wolfe did so in the form of a memorandum. The salutation was removed and the piece was published as submitted.) One Thompson biographer, William McKeen, referred to gonzo journalism as "first-draft, written-at-the-moment,"[15] lacking clarity "about what is truth and what is fiction."[16] Put another way, he said, "How they got the story became the subject of the story. Process became art."[17]

Hells Angel's is not gonzo journalism, but a first-person account of life with the Hell's Angels. Thompson rode with the club for a year and then spent six months writing the book. He claimed that he wrote the second half in four days locked in a motel room with four bottles of Wild Turkey and a lot of speed and a hamburger each morning for breakfast—adding, "and that turned out to be the best part of the book."[18]

Some reviewers compared Thompson with George Orwell and Mark Twain. Leo Litwak called Thompson's language brilliant, his eye remarkable and his point of view reminiscent of the Twain character Huck Finn—such that nothing that happens around him affects him.[19] The British illustrator Ralph Steadman, a collaborator with Thompson on some later works, considered Thompson a modern Mark Twain.[20] A *New Yorker* reviewer might have been talking about Twain when he referred to *Hell's Angels*'s "uninhibited tone and its sardonic humor," and pronounced the book "a thoughtful piece of work."[21] Richard Elman made the Orwell comparison, saying that *Hell's Angels* had "the cranky peevishness of Orwell's fine attack in *Wigan Pier* on pseudo-leftists, progressives, and food faddists," but lacked Orwell's "biases toward 'decency'"[22] Indeed, Thompson saw himself as akin to the Angels.[23]

So did some reviewers. Melvin Maddocks described *Hell's Angels* as a "gore-and-gearbox documentary," "horror nonfiction for the middle classes."[24] An *Atlantic* reviewer called Thompson's writing a "lurid narrative."[25] Twenty-five years later, Gerald Nicosia said Thompson sympathized with outsiders and admired "the skills and guts of those who have succeeded in making their mark (in his word, those who have prevailed)."[26] Timothy Crouse, writing of Thompson's appearance as a *Rolling Stone* reporter covering the 1972 presidential election, said: "He had the heroic aura of the veteran war correspondent about him, from having lived among the savages and survived."[27]

One interesting aspect of *Hell's Angels* is that Thompson begins the book by rightfully condemning the press for not finding out for itself the truth about the motorcycle gang— quoting A. J. Liebling on the superficiality of most reporting[28]— but when you finish the book you realize that the cyclists do live up to their clips, if not factually, at least generally. The anonymous *Atlantic* reviewer who mentioned Thompson's "lurid prose" noted in the same sentence that, despite Thompson's sympathy for his subjects, he "reveals the threat they pose." One biographer, William McKeen, felt that, all of Thompson's bravado aside, the book reveals his "real sense of fear about the Angels." And with good reason. A decade removed from the reporting, Thompson described the Hell's Angels as "rejects, losers."[29] One reviewer, S. K. Oberbeck, saw ambivalence: he suggested that the Angels put Thompson on and Thompson may at times try to put the reader on.[30] The ending is no put-on, however. The book ends with some Angels stomping Thompson and he recalls Kurtz's final words in Joseph Conrad's novel, *Heart of Darkness:* "The horror! The horror! . . . Exterminate all the brutes!"

In his prime, Thompson was referred to as "the quintessential outlaw journalist."[31] For *Hell's Angels,* though, he behaved the way a mainstream journalist might. He rode with the Hell's Angels but did not dress like them, and he purchased a different brand of motorcycle.[32] "I told them right away I was a *writer,* I was doing a book and that was it," Thompson said later, noting that had he joined he would not have been able to write about the Angels honestly.[33] To his credit, Thompson kept enough distance to write a compelling story about a band of society's outsiders.

ENDNOTES

1. Peter O. Whitmer, *When the Going Gets Weird: The Twisted Life and Times of Hunter S. Thompson, A Very Unauthorized Biography* (New York: Hyperion, 1993), 142.
2. Ibid., 143. (On the copyright page of *Hell's Angels,* Thompson credits McWilliams for the idea, which he says he used first in an article published in the April 1965 *Nation.* Actually, it was in the May 17, 1965, issue.)
3. Hunter S. Thompson, "The Motor Gangs: Losers and Outsiders," *Nation,* 17 May 1965, 522.
4. Timothy Crouse, *The Boys on the Bus* (New York: Random House, 1973), 312.
5. Thompson, "Motor Gangs," *Nation,* 523.
6. Robert Draper, *Rolling Stone Magazine: The Uncensored History* (New York: Doubleday, 1990), 160.
7. Paul Perry, *Fear and Loathing: The Strange and Terrible Saga of Hunter S. Thompson* (New York: Thunder's Mouth Press, 1992), 100.
8. Ibid., 122.

9. I've relied on Draper's book, *Rolling Stone Magazine*, for this biographical information.

10. David Eason, "The New Journalism and the Image World," in *Literary Journalism in the Twentieth Century*, ed. Norman Sims (New York: Oxford University Press, 1990), 192.

11. Craig Vetter, "Playboy Interview: Hunter Thompson," *Playboy*, November 1974, 88.

12. Tom Wolfe, *The New Journalism*, with an anthology edited by Tom Wolfe and E. W. Johnson (New York: Harper & Row, 1973), 27.

13. Draper, *Rolling Stone Magazine*, 73.

14. Vetter, "Playboy Interview," 88.

15. William McKeen, *Hunter S. Thompson* (Boston: Twayne, 1991), 49.

16. Ibid., 65.

17. Ibid., 11.

18. Vetter, "Playboy Interview," 80.

19. Leo Litwak, "On the Wild Side," *New York Times Book Review*, 29 January 1967, 6, 44.

20. "The Bonds of Friendship," *Daily Telegraph*, 18 April 1990, p. 15.

21. Richard Elman, "Hell's Angels," *New Republic*, 25 February 1967, 34.

22. "General," *New Yorker*, 4 March 1967, 164.

23. Vetter, "Playboy Interview," 78.

24. Melvin Maddocks, "Penny dreadful," *Christian Science Monitor*, 13 April 1967, p. 11.

25. "Books," *Atlantic*, February 1967, 129.

26. Gerald Nicosia, "What a Long, Strange Trip It's Been," *Washington Post Book World*, 18 November 1990, 1.

27. Crouse, *Boys in the Bus*, 311.

28. Hunter Thompson, *Hell's Angels* (New York: Ballantine Books, 1966), 42. "A good reporter, if he chooses the right approach, can understand a cat or an Arab. The choice is the problem, and if he chooses wrong he will come away scratched or baffled." The quotation comes from A. J. Liebling's *The Press* (New York: Pantheon, 1961, 1975), 120, and the rest of the paragraph is: "(There is a different approach to every cat and every Arab.) The best reporters occasionally fail badly, and the fair ones half-fail often."

29. Vetter, "Playboy Interview," 84.

30. S. K. Oberbeck, "Angels With Dirty Faces," *Newsweek*, 6 March 1967, 92.

31. Vetter, "Playboy Interview," 76.

32. Tom Wolfe recounts taking a similar stance when researching *The Electric Kool-Aid Acid Test*. "I arrived in a suit and tie . . . and I never took that necktie off. Never." (Brant Mewborn, "Sixties youth culture broke down the walls between people of different status," *Rolling Stone*, 5 November–10 December 1987, 218.)

33. Vetter, "Playboy Interview," 80.

Chapter 11

❖

Slouching towards Bethlehem

J oan Didion, like several other writers whose work is included in this book, has published in more than one genre. Her novels, short stories, screenplays (which she wrote with her husband, John Gregory Dunne), and essays cover a range of topics. The twenty essays collected in *Slouching towards Bethlehem* originally appeared in *The New York Times Magazine, Holiday, American Scholar, Vogue,* and *The Saturday Evening Post.*

Margaret A. Van Antwerp called Didion a "prominent yet enigmatic literary personality."[1] Barbara Lounsberry compared her favorably in style, physical stature and personality to the poet Emily Dickinson.[2] Donna Olendorf called her "an elegant prose stylist."[3] Leslie Garis said Didion was "famed as an original and insightful reporter of the American scene during the 1960's and early 70's."[4] Yet, in 1977 Didion said it had taken her years to realize that she was a writer, by which she meant "a person whose most absorbed and passionate hours are spent arranging words on pieces of paper."[5]

Slouching, which came out in 1968, was Didion's first published collection. It immediately established her reputation as an essayist. C. H. Simonds described the journalism represented in the book as "a fragmentary chronicle of the breakings-up of society, civilization and her own world; and of her search for a niche in the rubble."[6] Some of the essays have an apocalyptic tone to them, and, in fact, the book's title comes from "The Second Coming," by the great Irish poet William Butler Yeats.

Both excerpts appear in *Slouching towards Bethlehem* under the heading "Life Styles in the Golden Land." The first excerpt comes from "John Wayne: A Love Song," first published in 1965. The second excerpt comes from the essay that gave the collection its title.

❧ ❧ ❧

Almost all the cast of *Katie Elder* had gone home, that last week; only the principals were left, Wayne, and Martin, and Earl Holliman, and Michael Anderson, Jr., and Martha Hyer. Martha Hyer was not around much, but every now and then someone referred to her, usually as "the girl." They had all been together nine weeks, six of them in Durango. Mexico City was not quite Durango; wives like to come along to places like Mexico City, like to shop for handbags, go to parties at Merle Oberon Pagliai's, like to look at her paintings. But Durango. The very name hallucinates. Man's country. Out where the West begins. There had been ahuehuete trees in Durango; a waterfall, rattlesnakes. There had been weather, nights so cold that they had postponed one or two exteriors until they could shoot inside at Churubusco. "It was the girl," they explained. "You couldn't keep the girl out in cold like that." Henry Hathaway had cooked in Durango, *gazpacho* and ribs and the steaks that Dean Martin had ordered flown down from the Sands; he had wanted to cook in Mexico City, but the management of the Hotel Bamer refused to let him set up a brick barbecue in his room. "You really missed something, *Durango*," they would say, sometimes joking and sometimes not, until it became a refrain, Eden lost.

But if Mexico City was not Durango, neither was it Beverly Hills. No one else was using Churubusco that week, and there inside the big sound stage that said LOS HIJOS DE KATIE ELDER on the door, there with the pepper trees and the bright sun outside, they could still, for just so long as the picture lasted, maintain a world peculiar to men who like to make Westerns, a world of loyalties and fond raillery, of sentiment and shared cigars, of interminable desultory recollections; campfire talk, its only point to keep a human voice raised against the night, the wind, the rustlings in the brush.

"Stuntman got hit accidentally on a picture of mine once," Hathaway would say between takes of an elaborately choreographed fight scene. "What was his name, married Estelle Taylor, met her down in Arizona."

The circle would close around him, the cigars would be fingered. The delicate art of the staged fight was to be contemplated.

"I only hit one guy in my life," Wayne would say. "Accidentally, I mean. That was Mike Mazurki."

"Some guy. Hey, Duke says he only hit one guy in his life, Mike Mazurki!"

"Some choice." Murmurings, assent.

"It wasn't a choice, it was an accident."

"I can believe it."

"You bet."

"Oh boy. Mike Mazurki."

And so it would go. There was Web Overlander, Wayne's makeup man for twenty years, hunched in a blue Windbreaker, passing out sticks of Juicy Fruit. "*Insect* spray," he would say. "Don't tell us about insect spray. We saw insect spray in Africa, all right. Remember Africa?" Or, "*Steamer* clams. Don't tell us about steamer clams. We got our fill of steamer clams all right, on the *Hatari!* appearance tour. Remember Bookbinder's?" There was Ralph Volkie, Wayne's trainer for eleven years, wearing a red baseball cap and carrying around a clipping from Hedda Hopper, a tribute to Wayne. "This Hopper's some lady," he would say again and again. "Not like some of these guys, all they write is sick, sick, sick, how can you call that guy sick, when he's got pains, coughs, works all day, *never complains*. That guy's got the best hook since Dempsey, not *sick*."

And there was Wayne himself, fighting through number 165. There was Wayne, in his thirty-three-year-old spurs, his dusty neckerchief, his blue shirt. "You don't have too many worries about what to wear in these things," he said. "You can wear a blue shirt, or, if you're down in Monument Valley, you can wear a yellow shirt." There was Wayne, in a relatively new hat, a hat which made him look curiously like William S. Hart. "I had this old cavalry hat I loved, but I lent it to Sammy Davis. I got it back, it was unwearable. I think they all pushed it down on his head and said O.K., *John Wayne*—you know, a joke."

There was Wayne, working too soon, finishing the picture with a bad cold and a racking cough, so tired by late afternoon that he kept an oxygen inhalator on the set. And still nothing mattered but the Code. "That guy," he muttered of a reporter who had incurred his displeasure. "I admit I'm balding. I admit I got a tire around my middle. What man fifty-seven doesn't? Big news. Anyway, that guy."

He paused, about to expose the heart of the matter, the root of the distaste, the fracture of the rules that bothered him more than the alleged misquotations, more than the intimation that he was no longer the Bingo Kid. "He comes down, uninvited, but I ask him over anyway. So we're sitting around drinking mescal out of a water jug."

He paused again and looked meaningfully at Hathaway, readying him for the unthinkable denouement. "He had to be assisted to his room."

They argued about the virtues of various prizefighters, they argued about the price of J & B in pesos. They argued about dialogue.

"As rough a guy as he is, Henry, I still don't think he'd raffle off his mother's *Bible*."

"I like a shocker, Duke."

They exchanged endless training-table jokes. "You know why they call this memory sauce?" Martin asked, holding up a bowl of chili.

"Why?"

"Because you *remember it in the morning*."

"Hear that, Duke? Hear why they call this memory sauce?"

They delighted one another by blocking out minute variations in the free-for-all fight which is a set piece in Wayne pictures; motivated or totally gratuitous, the fight sequence has to be in the picture, because they so enjoy making it. "Listen—this'll really be funny. Duke picks up the kid, see, and then it takes both Dino and Earl to throw him out the door—how's that?"

They communicated by sharing old jokes; they sealed their camaraderie by making gentle, old-fashioned fun of wives, those civilizers, those tamers. "So Señora Wayne takes it into her head to stay up and have one brandy. So for the rest of the night it's 'Yes, Pilar, you're right, dear. I'm a bully, Pilar, you're right, I'm impossible.'"

"You hear that? Duke says Pilar threw a table at him."

"Hey, Duke, here's something funny. That finger you hurt today, get the Doc to bandage it up, go home tonight, show it to Pilar, tell her she did it when she threw the table. You know, make her think she was really cutting up."

They treated the oldest among them respectfully; they treated the youngest fondly. "You see that kid?" they said of Michael Anderson, Jr. "What a kid."

"He don't act, it's right from the heart," said Hathaway, patting his heart.

"Hey kid," Martin said. "You're gonna be in my next picture. We'll have the whole thing, no beards. The striped shirts, the girls, the hi-fi, the eye lights."

They ordered Michael Anderson his own chair, with "BIG MIKE" tooled on the back. When it arrived on the set, Hathaway hugged him. "You see that?" Anderson asked Wayne, suddenly too shy to look him in the eye. Wayne gave him the smile, the nod, the final accolade. "I saw it, kid."

On the morning of the day they were to finish *Katie Elder*, Web Overlander showed up not in his Windbreaker but in a blue blazer. "Home, Mama," he said, passing out the last of his Juicy Fruit. "I got on my getaway clothes." But he was subdued. At noon, Henry Hathaway's wife dropped by the commissary to tell him that she might fly over to Acapulco. "Go ahead," he told her. "I get through here, all I'm gonna do is take Seconal to a point just this side of suicide." They were all subdued. After Mrs. Hathaway left there were desultory attempts at reminiscing, but man's country was receding fast; they were already halfway home, and all they could call up was the 1961 Bel Air fire, during which Henry Hathaway had ordered the Los Angeles Fire Department off his property and saved the place himself by, among other measures, throwing everything flammable into the swimming pool. "Those fire guys might've just given it up," Wayne said. "Just let it burn." In fact this was a good story, and one incorporating several of their favorite themes, but a Bel Air story was still not a Durango story.

In the early afternoon they began the last scene, and although they spent as much time as possible setting it up, the moment finally came when there was nothing to do but shoot it. "Second team out, first team in, *doors closed*," the assistant director shouted one last time. The stand-ins walked off the set, John Wayne and Martha Hyer walked on. "All right, boys, *silencio*, this is a picture." They took it twice. Twice the girl offered John Wayne the tattered Bible. Twice John Wayne told her that "there's a lot of places I go where that wouldn't fit in." Everyone was very still. And at 2:30 that Friday afternoon Henry Hathaway turned away from the camera, and in the hush that followed he ground out his cigar in a sand bucket. "O.K.," he said. "That's it."

⚜ ⚜ ⚜

The following excerpt comes from "Slouching towards Bethlehem," the essay that gave the collection its title.

⚜ ⚜ ⚜

I am looking for somebody called Deadeye and I hear he is on the Street this afternoon doing a little business, so I keep an eye out for him and pretend to read the signs in the Psychedelic Shop on Haight Street when a kid, sixteen, seventeen, comes in and sits on the floor beside me.

"What are you looking for," he says.

I say nothing much.

"I been out of my mind for three days," he says. He tells me he's been shooting crystal, which I already pretty much know because he does not bother to keep his sleeves rolled down over the needle tracks. He came up from Los Angeles some number of weeks ago, he doesn't remember what number, and now he'll take off for New York, if he can find a ride. I show him a sign offering a ride to Chicago. He wonders where Chicago is. I ask where he comes from. "Here," he says. I mean before here. "San Jose, Chula Vista, I dunno. My mother's in Chula Vista."

A few days later I run into him in Golden Gate Park when the Grateful Dead are playing. I ask if he found a ride to New York. "I hear New York's a bummer," he says.

Deadeye never showed up that day on the Street, and somebody says maybe I can find him at his place. It is three o'clock and Deadeye is in bed. Somebody else is asleep on the living-room couch, and a girl is sleeping on the floor beneath a poster of Allen Ginsberg, and there are a couple of girls in pajamas making instant coffee. One of the girls introduces me to the friend on the couch, who extends one arm but does not get up because he is naked. Deadeye and I have a mutual acquaintance, but he does not mention his name in front of the others. "The man you talked to," he says, or "that man I was referring to earlier." The man is a cop.

The room is overheated and the girl on the floor is sick. Deadeye says she has been sleeping for twenty-four hours now. "Lemme ask you something," he says. "You want some grass?" I say I have to be moving on. "You want it," Deadeye says, "it's yours." Deadeye used to be an Angel around Los Angeles but that was a few years ago. "Right now," he says, "I'm trying to set up this groovy religious group—'Teenage Evangelism.'"

Don and Max want to go out to dinner but Don is only eating macrobiotic so we end up in Japantown again. Max is telling me how he lives free of all the old middle-class Freudian hang-ups. "I've had this old lady for a couple of months now, maybe she makes something special for my dinner and I come in three days late and tell her I've been balling some other chick, well, maybe she shouts a little but then I say 'That's me, baby,' and she laughs and says 'That's you, Max.'" Max says it works both ways. "I mean if she comes in and tells me she wants to ball Don, maybe, I say 'O.K., baby, it's your trip.'"

Max sees his life as a triumph over "don'ts." Among the don'ts he had done before he was twenty-one were peyote, alcohol, mescaline, and Methedrine. He was on a Meth trip for three years in New York and Tangier before he found acid. He first tried peyote when he was in an Arkansas boys' school and got down to the Gulf and met "an Indian kid who was doing a don't. Then every weekend I could get loose I'd hitchhike seven hundred miles to Brownsville, Texas, so I could cop peyote. Peyote went for thirty cents a button down in Brownsville on the street." Max dropped in and out of most of the schools and fashionable clinics in the eastern half of America, his standard technique for dealing with boredom being to leave. Example: Max was in a hospital in New York and "the night nurse was a groovy spade, and in the afternoon for therapy there was a chick from Israel who was interesting, but there was nothing much to do in the morning, so I left."

We drink some more green tea and talk about going up to Malakoff Diggings in Nevada County because some people are starting a commune there and Max thinks it would be a groove to take acid in the diggings. He says maybe we could go next week, or the week after, or anyway sometime before his case comes up. Almost everybody I meet in San Francisco has to go to court at some point in the middle future. I never ask why.

I am still interested in how Max got rid of his middle-class Freudian hang-ups and I ask if he is now completely free.

"Nah," he says. "I got acid."

Max drops a 250- or 350-microgram tab every six or seven days.

Max and Don share a joint in the car and we go over to North Beach to find out if Otto, who has a temporary job there, wants to go to Malakoff Diggings. Otto is pitching some electronics engineers. The engineers view our arrival with some interest, maybe, I think, because Max is wearing bells and an Indian headband. Max has a low tolerance for straight engineers and their Freudian hang-ups. "Look at 'em," he says. "They're always yelling 'queer' and then they come sneaking down to the Haight-Ashbury trying to get the hippie chick because she fucks."

We do not get around to asking Otto about Malakoff Diggings because he wants to tell me about a fourteen-year-old he knows who got busted in the Park the other day. She was just walking through the Park, he says, minding her own, carrying her schoolbooks, when the cops took her in and booked her and gave her a pelvic. "*Fourteen years old,*" Otto says. "*A pelvic.*"

"Coming down from acid," he adds, "that could be a real bad trip."

I call Otto the next afternoon to see if he can reach the fourteen-year-old. It turns out she is tied up with rehearsals for her junior-high-school play, *The Wizard of Oz.* "Yellow-brick-road time," Otto says. Otto was sick all day. He thinks it was some cocaine-and-wheat somebody gave him.

There are always little girls around rock groups—the same little girls who used to hang around saxophone players, girls who live on the celebrity and power and sex a band projects when it plays—and there are three of them out here this afternoon in Sausalito where the Grateful Dead rehearse. They are all pretty and two of them still have baby fat and one of them dances by herself with her eyes closed.

I ask a couple of the girls what they do.

"I just kind of come out here a lot," one of them says.

"I just sort of know the Dead," the other says.

The one who just sort of knows the Dead starts cutting up a loaf of French bread on the piano bench. The boys take a break and one of them talks about playing the Los Angeles Cheetah, which is in the old Aragon Ballroom. "We were up there drinking beer where Lawrence Welk used to sit," Jerry Garcia says.

The little girl who was dancing by herself giggles. "Too much," she says softly. Her eyes are still closed.

⚜ ⚜ ⚜

Like Susan Sheehan, although for different reasons, Didion avoids stories that involve press agents. "If you can't talk to the mayor," Didion once told Susan Stamberg of National Public Radio, "then maybe if you sit around the gas station long enough you can figure out what it's all about."[7]

You can tell from the statement that Didion prefers sitting around the gas station. In the preface to *Slouching,* Didion writes that she was bad at interviewing and did not like to make phone calls. She says that her only advantage as a reporter is that she is so small and unobtrusive that people don't realize her presence is not in their interests. She closes the preface by stating emphatically that "writers are always selling someone out."[8] Twenty years later one anonymous critic suggested that, in fact, Didion had done the reverse of Mencken's advice about getting too close to sources because you might get to like them, and that she actually liked the people she was writing about.[9]

The reporting for "Slouching towards Bethlehem," Didion has said, was extremely frustrating to do, "simply because you couldn't make appointments." As she told Stamberg, the residents didn't get up until noon or 1:00 P.M., "so you lost the morning." And it was difficult to make appointments because anyone who wanted to make an appointment was suspect.[10]

The wait was worth it. Dan Wakefield was effusive in his praise. He compared the essay with *Time's* "hapless cover story on the hippies"—which contained superficial observations such as "They find an almost childish fascination in beads, blossoms and bells, blinding strobe lights and ear-shattering music, exotic clothing and erotic slogans."[11] He praised Didion for going to San Francisco with an open mind, rather than with a predetermined story line, and hanging out to learn what Haight-Ashbury was about. "Miss Didion is not out to expose but to understand," Wakefield wrote. He also praised Didion for being non-intrusive and not self-indulgent but rather informing and illuminating.[12] Late in the 1970s, Stamberg called "Slouching" the "definitive portrait of Haight-Ashbury in the 1960s."[13] Gerald Meyer said that among the young essayists at the time, Didion was "probably the most personal and introspective."[14]

Other reviews were also positive. Simonds noted careful writing "with a perfect eye for detail and an unfoolable ear."[15] MIM noted Didion's modesty in calling herself a reporter—as though all she did was gather information—and said that in fact she was "equally informative and imaginative, and equally relevant and reflective."[16] MIM also suggested Didion was "a little like a feminine Oscar Lewis."[17] (Lewis also influenced Susan Sheehan.) Like Wakefield, Melvin Maddocks noted that Didion avoided condescension and sentimentality so typical of journalists writing about young people and was thorough, exacting and scrupulous.[18] Maybelle Lacey called the book "provocative and rewarding."[19] Alfred Kazin said it was "brilliant journalism," although he offered his highest praise for her first novel, *Run River.*[20]

Janet Coleman's review was also mixed, noting that Didion combined "such superb reportage with such personal and peculiar ax-grinding that at first it is hard not to be wooed by the vision of doom she presents."[21] Citing Didion's affection for John Wayne and "spurious sense of loss" in "John Wayne: A Love Song" and other essays in the book, Coleman complained that Didion created illusions about the past. Writing during the Vietnam War when Wayne was something of a celluloid patriot, Coleman juxtaposed Didion's attitude toward Wayne's machismo with liberal behavior in society. One senses a political disagreement, not a stylistic one, with Didion's view of Wayne.

Didion's essay on Wayne, written as he was making the movie *The Sons of Katie Elder,* echoes qualities of Lillian Ross's portrait of Hemingway and her reportage on the making of *The Red Badge of Courage.* Each story focuses on a single individual, someone viewed as individualistic and rugged. Although Didion's essay is short, parts of it reflect Ross's fly-on-the-wall reporting methods, which result in a story showing the reader what is happening. Of course, the three pieces also differ greatly, primarily in length and scope, but that difference reflects the original assignment, not the talent of either writer.

In a scholarly analysis of Didion's writings, Katherine Usher Henderson praised *Slouching towards Bethlehem.* She was especially high on the title essay, which she called "a major document in social history of the sixties, both a dramatization and an analysis of the hippie movement in the United States."[22] She compared Didion with George Orwell because they "write against stereotyped thinking, received opinion on any subject of importance; they both defined unpleasant truths in areas where pleasant lies prevailed." Henderson also said the two wrote similarly—with "clear, crisp prose that favors short Anglo-Saxon words over long or Latinate ones,"[23] although in writing description Didion is a minimalist and Orwell tends to be rich and evocative. Compare, for example, Didion's minimal description of Deadeye's apartment with Orwell's intricate description of the place he was staying in Wigan.

But not everyone sang Didion's praises. Perhaps the most savage attack came in 1979 from Barbara Grizzuti Harrison. She first condemned Didion's style as nothing but tricks that would jolt readers. She cited as one example the juxtaposition of Al Capone and sweet williams in one sentence. Harrison argued that Didion's style was not used to convey meaning; that Didion was interested in *what* but not *why*.[24] In a parody of Didion's style, she said: "What makes those sentences work? I ask. Cadence, I answer. What do those sentences mean? you may ask. Don't."[25]

Harrison said she would like to see a Didion essay that began "On the morning after the uprising in the Warsaw ghetto . . . ."[26] In other words, she proposed that Didion go to the real front where the center really does not hold. Didion's next book was *Salvador,* a report based on two weeks she and her husband spent in the country during a civil war in which the U.S. government was deeply involved. Linda Hall suggested that, although the connection to Harrison's proposal could be coincidental, she sensed that Didion did "what her harshest critics have said she should do."[27]

Although Didion has written other nonfiction, the collection *Slouching towards Bethlehem* includes her best. Jonathan Yardley said that her reputation rests on it, that her later nonfiction became too self-referential and personal[28] (an observation one could also make about later works by Hunter Thompson after *Hell's Angels*). Interestingly, Didion has said she cannot reread *Slouching,* but Hall added: "She is possibly the only one who can't." What Didion has done is capture a slice of the United States in the 1960s. She has done it with lean prose that gives her subjects room to be themselves.

ENDNOTES

1. Margaret A. Van Antwerp, "Joan Didion," *Dictionary of Literary Biography Yearbook 1981*, ed. Karen L. Rood, Jean W. Ross, and Richard Ziegfeld (Detroit: Gale Research, 1981), 56.
2. Barbara Lounsberry, *The Art of Fact* (New York: Greenwood, 1990), 107.
3. Donna Olendorf, in *Contemporary Authors*, vol. 14, ed. Linda Metzger (Detroit: Gale Research, 1985), 130.

4. Leslie Garis, "Didion & Dunne: The Rewards of a Literary Marriage," *New York Times Magazine*, 8 February 1987, 18.
5. Quoted in Susan Braudy, "A Day in the Life of Joan Didion," *Ms.*, February 1977, 109.
6. C. H. Simonds, "Picking up the Pieces," *National Review*, 4 June 1968, 558.
7. Susan Stamberg, "Cautionary Tales," in "All Things Considered," National Public Radio, 4 April 1977. Reprinted in *Joan Didion: Essays and Conversations*, ed. Ellen G. Friedman (Princeton, N.J.: York: Ontario Review Press, 1984), 26.
8. Joan Didion, *Slouching towards Bethlehem* (New York: Farrar, Straus and Giroux, 1968), xvi.
9. Linda Hall, "The Writer Who Came in from the Cold," *New York*, 2 September 1996, 30.
10. Quoted in Stamberg, "Cautionary Tales," 24.
11. "The Hippies," *Time*, 7 July 1967, 18–22. Didion does mention the piece as a source of some of the information in her article.
12. Dan Wakefield, "Places, People and Personalities," *New York Times Book Review*, 21 July 1968, 8.
13. Stamberg, "Cautionary Tales," 25.
14. Gerald Meyer, "From Hippies to Hawaii," *Des Moines Sunday Register*, 26 May 1968. Reprinted in *The Critical Response to Joan Didion*, ed. Sharon Felton (Westport, Conn.: Greenwood, 1994), 33.
15. Simonds, "Picking Up," 559.
16. MIM, "Slouching Toward Bethlehem," *Commonweal*, 29 November 1968, 324.
17. Ibid.
18. Melvin Maddocks, "Her heart's with the wagon trains," *Christian Science Monitor*, 16 May 1968, p. 11.
19. Maybelle Lacey, "Book Review," *Library Journal*, 15 April 1968, 1646.
20. Alfred Kazin, "Joan Didion: portrait of a professional," *Harper's*, December 1971, 122.
21. Janet Coleman, "Out West: life is gorgeous, cushy, violent and surreal," *Washington Post Book World*, 28 July 1968, 5.
22. Katherine Usher Henderson, *Joan Didion* (New York: Frederick Ungar, 1981), 102.
23. Ibid., p. 92.
24. Barbara Grizzuti Harrison, "Joan Didion: The Courage of Her Afflictions," *Nation*, 29 September 1979, 277.
25. Ibid., 278.
26. Ibid., 284.
27. Hall, "Writer," 32.
28. Jonathan Yardley, "Joan Didion: Up Close and Personal," *Washington Post Book World*, 10 May 1992, 3.

Chapter 12

❖

The Onion Field

L os Angeles police detective sergeant Joseph Wambaugh met Truman Capote on the "Tonight Show with Johnny Carson," a late-night talk and entertainment program. Wambaugh had already published two novels, *The New Centurions* and *The Blue Knight,* and had become a consultant to the television program "Police Story." But he had another story he wanted to write, a true story, a story his editor told him to forget because it could not measure up to Capote's famous "nonfiction novel" *In Cold Blood.*[1]

After the Carson show, Capote invited Wambaugh and his wife to Capote's house in Palm Springs. Over a period of two hours, Wambaugh told Capote about the book he wanted to write. It was the story of how two police officers were kidnapped, one murdered by the kidnappers, and the surviving officer ostracized by his fellow officers; and of how the criminal justice system worked poorly. When he was finished, Wambaugh remembers, Capote said: "My God, that's a story! Would I like to write that story!"

At the time of the conversation, the murder in the onion field was history, and Karl Hettinger, the surviving police officer, had already refused the cooperation Wambaugh would need to write a nonfiction work about it.[2] Since the murder Wambaugh had written two other novels. A year after Capote's endorsement, Wambaugh approached Hettinger again. This time Hettinger consented. "Yeah," Wambaugh recalls him saying, "write that story and get rid of it."[3] Approximately ten years after the murder in the onion field, Wambaugh's book was published.

On the dust jacket was a two-sentence endorsement from Truman Capote.

The excerpt reprinted here begins Chapter 6. It reconstructs the period of time in which the lives of four men—two of them police officers—intersected with tragic results. Shortly after Wambaugh recounts the murder in the onion field, the book picks up a second story, about a gardener, told from the gardener's perspective, and a sub-narrative joins the main narrative. This story is told in short portions at the ends of some chapters and is set off in italic type to distinguish it from the main narrative. Toward the end of the book, the narratives neatly merge the way the final pieces of a puzzle fall into place.

⚜ ⚜ ⚜

"A typical Hollywood Saturday night," said Jimmy Smith, the tension festering in his guts, as he looked at rows of cars jammed up for blocks. "And everybody's too law abidin or too scared of cops or too fuckin lackadaisical to even toot their horns or swear at the guy in front."

Jimmy thought of the Spanish automatic in his belt and what if the miserable thing went off by itself and shot his dick off? And yeah, that was somethin else to worry about. What if I killed myself with my own goddamn gun by squirmin around the wrong way in the seat? Bang! Off goes the cock and there I am, sprawled there dyin in the street. Bleedin to death! And he considered putting the gun in the glove compartment to get it out of his belt.

"Goddamnit," Greg said. "I'm getting out of this traffic. We'll head back toward downtown until we spot a liquor store to knock off."

"But I thought you wanted to take off this market out here in Hollywood?"

"Too goddamn much traffic, Jim. We made the wrong turn off the freeway. We'll find something on the way downtown."

As Ian Campbell drove the Plymouth into the alley near Gower Avenue on this ninth night with Karl, March 9th, 1963, he spotted some mauve-colored flowers in a window box, and rolling up his window against the night chill said, "the sweet peas and azaleas are starting to bloom. That must mean spring is here. I keep warning mine of the Ides of March."

Karl Hettinger grinned in the dark at his big-shouldered improbable partner who talked quaintly of flowers and bagpipes. Then Karl realized he had never heard a set of pipes firsthand.

"I'd like to hear you play those bagpipes sometime, Ian," he said as the little maroon Ford passed by the alley westbound on Carlos.

Gregory Powell was heading north on Gower when he decided to circle the block to the west. He turned on Carlos Avenue, saw the short street called Vista Del Mar straight ahead, and mistakenly thought Carlos Avenue dead-ended there.

"Hearing me play the pipes can definitely be arranged," Ian chuckled. "No one else wants to listen to me. My wife and kids and friends run away screaming when they just see me blow up the bag. I wait for unsuspecting people like you to ask me."

Ian slowed in the alley, flashing his two-cell light toward some shadows in an apartment house doorway, but it was just two bony cats slinking through the alleys, prowling hungrily.

The little maroon Ford made a turn and was coming back their way.

It was now 10:00 P.M. and the unmarked Plymouth police car known as Six-Z-Four was emerging from the alley onto Carlos when the coupe crossed their headlight beam and they saw the two gaunt young men with their leather jackets and snap-brim leather caps in their little car with Nevada plates.

They would have aroused the suspicions of almost any policeman in Hollywood that night. It was patently obvious that they were not ordinary out-of-town tourists cruising the boulevard. The caps were rare enough, but with matching leather jackets, they were almost absurdly suspicious, even contrived. It was as though they'd just driven off the Columbia Pictures lot farther south on Gower; two extras from a Depression era gangster film, caricatures, Katzenjammer Kids.

But still, Ian and Karl had to look for something more tangible, something to tell the court for probable cause in case they came up with an arrest. They could not, or would not, depend upon their own ability to articulate a well grounded suspicion, nor the court's ability to understand the several intangibles which go into the decision to stop and frisk and interrogate. So they looked for and immediately found something else: the tried and true "rear plate illumination."

Even if the Ford's license plate lights had not been out, it is doubtful that Ian Campbell and Karl Hettinger would have let this car go its way. The little Ford looked "too good," which in police jargon means it looked too bad, too suspicious, a "good shake." It had to be stopped and a reason found to search.

The little Ford had but to turn left on Vista Del Mar and it could have proceeded south to Hollywood Boulevard and never have been stopped by Six-Z-Four that night, but Greg decided on a U-turn, and on their ninth night together, the partners made their last wrong turn on Los Angeles streets.

"Fuckin dead ends," Jimmy grumbled when they turned around. "We always seem to be runnin into dead ends."

"We should check these two," said Ian as the little Ford stopped for the red light at Gower.

"All right. When do you wanna take them?"

"Right now," said Ian, who pulled up behind the coupe, turned on his red light, and tooted the horn.

Gregory Powell glanced into the rear view mirror, tightened his grip on the steering wheel, and said: "Cops!"

As the coupe turned the corner onto Gower and stopped, Karl saw the heads move a bit closer.

"Let's be careful," said Karl.

Jimmy *felt* the red light before seeing it, felt the heat from the red light searing the back of his neck, and he was whispering, "I knew it. I knew it," even as he unzipped the brown leather jacket Greg had bought him, removed the .32 automatic Greg had bought him, and gingerly dropped it on the floor, kicking it across the car with his new thirty-five dollar shoes. Greg's eyes were glued to the mirror and the kick was subtle but sharp enough so that the gun ended up very close to Greg's left foot where Jimmy wanted it. It was far enough from Jimmy so that he could swear that Greg had just picked him up hitchhiking and that he knew nothing of the two guns in Greg's possession. Weren't they in Greg's name? And in case that story didn't work he was sure he could come up with others.

"Just take it easy, it may just be a ticket. Just sit tight," Greg said, looking at Jimmy for an instant, and Jimmy tried to answer, wanted to say something sarcastic, but found himself unable to speak.

He could not take it easy, was in fact frantic, wanting as much distance as possible between himself and Gregory Powell when the cops found the gun on the floor at Greg's feet, and the one in Greg's belt. Who knows, this maniac might just try shooting his way out! Jimmy wouldn't put that past him, and he just wanted to show the cops he was only riding along with this guy, a hitch-hiker, that's all.

I got nothin to hide, and I just gotta be cool, gotta be cool, he told himself. But he was all the way to the right, as far as he could sit in the little coupe, and still felt too close to Greg, felt at that moment like they were Siamese twins. And then he leaped out of the car and looked into the eyes of Karl Hettinger, who was flashing his light, advancing slowly on the sidewalk.

Jimmy came forward, fear bursting all over him, and Karl reached inside his sport coat, placed his right hand on the gun butt in the cross-draw holster, and said what he knew was obvious enough despite the unmarked car:

"Police."

Jimmy Smith froze at the sound of the word and threw his hands in the air.

Karl's pulse bucked. He glanced inside the car at Greg and quickly back at Jimmy standing stock still on, the sidewalk, hands high in the air, though Karl had neither drawn his gun nor told Jimmy to raise his hands, and Karl knew for certain. Any policeman would have known. Something. There was something. Narcotics perhaps. They looked like hypes, but Ian was on the street side of the car and couldn't see Jimmy's panic signals.

Jesus, what if he sees the gun? thought Jimmy. What if Greg starts shootin? Christ, I gotta get away from the maniac!

Karl's eyes were not close set, nor did the irises bleed into the pupil, but Jimmy was to forever remember Karl's eyes as being close set and glittering behind his plastic-rimmed glasses. Jimmy bore it as long as he could, about five seconds. Then he said, "What's the trouble, officer?"

"Police officers," said Ian to Greg, coming up on the driver's side, not bothering to show a badge, because it went without saying that these two would certainly know they were police. He wanted one hand free since the other held the flashlight.

"Oh, Lord, I know what I am getting a ticket for this time," said Greg, with only a faint hope that he could bluff the cop, knowing that plain-clothes police don't write traffic tickets. Knowing that when you get stopped by them it's usually a frisk and questioning. He knew it the first instant he looked up at the big policeman, seeing his dark sport shirt buttoned at the throat, and his old gray flannel slacks, and his well worn sport jacket, knowing they were on something other than normal uniform patrol or traffic detail. He *knew* there would be no traffic ticket.

"Would you mind taking your license out of your wallet?" asked Ian.

"Sure."

"How long have you been in town?" asked Ian, glancing at the license.

"We just got in today."

"Would you mind stepping out of the car?" asked Ian, handing back the license.

Greg placed the driver's license in the left front pocket of his leather jacket and lifted and loosened his gun.

"What's this all about?"

"It's just routine."

"Okay. Okay." Greg smiled, shaking his head and sighing, seeing Ian open the door and step back, seeing that Ian held only a flashlight in his hand. Greg turned to his right to back out, then wheeled to his feet.

Ian was looking at the Colt in Greg's hand and stepping backward slowly, unbelieving. Then Greg was behind him, holding him at the back by a handful of jacket, dizzily remembering the things he had learned in the prison yards about police disarming movements. So he clutched the big policeman by the jacket, and if he felt him turn he could push away and step back, and . . .

Karl had been watching Jimmy, who was licking his lips, cotton mouthed, stone still in the flashlight's glare, asking, "What's the trouble, officer?" And then Karl saw Ian coming around the car, with the suspect walking behind *not* in front, and that was wrong, all wrong. And then Greg peeked from behind Ian's back and said, "Take his piece," to Jimmy Smith and fluids jetted through Karl's body and he jerked the six-inch service revolver from the cross-draw holster and pointed it toward the man who was almost completely hidden behind Karl's much larger partner.

"He's got a gun on me," said Ian. "Give him your gun."

And then no one spoke and Karl pointed the gun toward the voice, but the voice had no body. It was like a dream. He was pointing his gun toward Ian, toward a glimpse of black cap and a patch of forehead show-ing around Ian's arm, and there was no sound but the car sounds, tires, cars humming past on Gower, and headlights bathing them in the beams every few seconds. But no cars stopped or even noticed and Karl found himself now pointing the gun at Jimmy Smith, who was like a statue, and then Karl aimed toward the voice again. It was so incredible! It couldn't happen like this. Back and forth went Karl's gun and he was crouched slightly as on the seven yard line at the police combat range. But this wasn't the combat range. There was no sound except from passing cars.

Ian spoke again: "He's got a gun in my back. Give him your gun."

Then Karl looked at Ian, hesitated, and let the gun butt slide until he was holding it only with the thumb and index finger, the custom wooden grips smooth and slippery between his cold wet fingers. Then he held it up and Jimmy, dark eyes shining, walked toward him and took Karl's Colt revolver.

Jimmy Smith held the gun clumsily in both hands at chest level and raised it toward the street light on Gower and squinted with astigmatized vision, like a primitive seeing a gun for the first time. And it *did* seem to him like the first time. This was a cop's gun! It was also unreal to him.

For another moment then they were inert. All four of them. Four brains fully accelerated, four bodies becalmed. Staggered. Inertia for a long moment. Four young men bathed in the purple glow of the street light. Detachment on the faces. Total bewilderment. Two policemen facing that which all policemen firmly believe can never happen to them. Two small-time robbers, fathoms deep, holding the Man at bay. Four minds racing. Tumbling incoherent thoughts.

Perhaps the first one to move was Karl Hettinger. Hands upraised, he began moving the big five-cell flashlight, ever so subtly, in a tiny circle, the beam flashing into the street, striking the windshields of the cars which passed unconcerned every few seconds. Then Ian noticed, and hands upraised, did the same with his little two-cell. Then Greg saw what they were doing and said, "Put those goddamn hands down."

Jimmy Smith stopped holding the gun to the light, stopped staring at it in wonder, and began trying to fit a Colt service revolver with a six-inch barrel into a four-inch pocket. He turned, staring from one to the other until he heard Greg's command, then he shoved the gun into his belt. Perhaps without a command he would have remained there forever.

"Get over there," Greg said, nodding toward the coupe, and hearing the voice, Jimmy wanted to obey. Then he realized Greg was talking to the cops, so he waited for his own orders.

Then it came. His chance. His final opportunity to order fate. Greg said, "Jim, go back to the police car and park it closer to the curb so we won't draw any more heat. And turn out the lights."

Jimmy nodded vacantly and Greg said to the policemen, "Get in the car."

"Where do you want me?" asked Ian, standing at the right side of the little maroon coupe.

"Behind the wheel," said Greg, who was thinking, watching, examining both men, sizing them up. At first it was merely Ian's physical presence which guided Greg. He was a big man. Put the big man behind the wheel where he can be watched more closely. The little man in the back.

"Where do you want me?" asked Karl.

"In the back."

Karl struggled with the seat trying to pull it forward not realizing it was a one-piece backrest and would not move.

"It's stuck," said Karl.

"Goddamnit, get in that car and I mean right now. Climb over the seat!"

Then Karl was inside behind the seat, sitting on the floor of the coupe, knees up to his chin. In the cramped space behind the only seat, on the metal floor of the car, flashlight in hand, pulse banging in his ears so that it was actually hard to hear for a moment.

Jimmy Smith was wrestling with the gears of the police car and with the emergency brake, but most of all with his courage.

"Won't move," he mumbled aloud to himself. "Got it in drive and it won't move!"

He fought with the Plymouth, stepping on the accelerator and killing the engine each time he was caught by the emergency brake. Jimmy Smith didn't know emergency brakes on late model gears were no longer controlled by clumsy levers hanging down. He desperately yanked on the emergency foot brake but didn't know to tug the little chrome lever under the dash. He had been away too long.

"If I'd only knew about late model cars," he was to say later. "I coulda drove off in that police car. I coulda cut him loose right there. But I couldn't get that brake off."

"Hurry up," Greg yelled, and Jimmy gave up, got out of the car, looked toward Hollywood Boulevard, looked toward escape and made his last choice. He walked toward the Ford hopelessly.

"I couldn't get the brake off," Jimmy said to Greg who was seated in the passenger side of the coupe, Colt pointed at Ian's belly, hammer cocked.

"Leave the goddamn thing. Leave it," Greg said, sliding slowly close to Ian to make room for Jimmy in the front.

At that moment a carload of teenagers drove by, talking loudly and laughing. One glanced at Jimmy for a moment and Jimmy became aware of the big revolver under his leather jacket and then the teenagers drove on. Jimmy got in the coupe.

"Did you check the police car for our license number?" asked Greg. "They probably wrote it down when they stopped us."

"Yes," Jimmy lied, wanting to get away, to get away now, to have one more chance to cut Greg loose. If he just had one more chance.

"Where's the other gun?" Greg asked Jimmy, drilling Ian with his eyes, keeping the Colt at his belly, watching Ian's hand on the steering wheel. Already the little car was starting to reek from the smell of fear and sweat from the four of them.

"Where's the other gun?" Greg repeated.

"What other gun?" Jimmy asked, thinking of the automobile, hoping Greg would not notice that Jimmy had kicked it under Greg's side of the seat. And then Jimmy added further confusion to the moment by adding, "You mean the .45 automatic?"

And then Greg, not knowing that Jimmy was referring to the Spanish Star .32 automatic, felt panic, suddenly thinking there was still another cop's gun unaccounted for.

"Was this guy carrying a .45?"

"I dunno," said Jimmy, totally bewildered now, not knowing how many guns there were, or where they were.

"Well look around the floor for the goddamn .45 then," said Greg frantically.

"Gimme that flashlight," Jimmy said to Karl, and with the bright five-cell light he found the .32 automatic on the floor just under the edge of the seat where he'd kicked it. Now he had two guns in his lap: his own automatic, and Karl's Colt service revolver.

"This is all the guns there is," said Jimmy.

"Okay, all the guns are accounted for," Greg said in exasperation. "Now let's get outta here." And to Ian, "Do you know how to get on the freeway to Bakersfield? I want Highway 99."

"Yes," Ian answered. "We can go up the street here on Gower and get on the Hollywood Freeway."

"Well get going," said Greg. "Don't break any laws and don't go fast, because if you get us stopped you're both dead."

Jimmy switched his glance from Karl in the back to his partner Gregory Powell, and rode most of the trip in an uncomfortable twisted position where he could occasionally look at Karl.

Greg's voice had lost its rasp and was coming back normal and confident. "Son of a bitch, we couldn't be any hotter," said Greg, and Jimmy thought he detected a bit of elation in the voice. "I've already killed people. I didn't wanna get in this business, but now that I'm in it, I gotta go all the way."

Oh Jesus, Jimmy thought. Greg was breathing regularly now and saying crazy things, and sounding like some punk Jimmy would expect to see in an old movie and, oh, Jesus.

"Why did you guys stop us?" Greg asked.

"Because you had no lights on your license plate," Ian said as he drove onto the ramp of the Hollywood way.

Greg's gun hit Ian's ribs. "Just a minute. Where're you taking us?"

"This is the way to the Hollywood Freeway. I'm going the right way," said Ian steadily.

"It's the right way," said Karl, peering up over the window ledge from his place on the metal floor, looking over the space back there—finding a hubcap, rags, a jack and handle, cans—nothing that could be of much help against two men and four guns in a tiny car, with one man holding a cocked revolver in the driver's belly.

"We're going on the freeway to the Sepulveda off-ramp. And that'll take us to the Ridge Route," Ian explained.

"Jimmy," said Greg, "your job is to look to and cover that guy. And also to look for a tail."

"Okay," Jimmy mumbled, thinking: Thanks for telling them my name, you dumb . . .

"How often you guys check in on the radio?" asked Greg.

"About every hour," Ian said. "I figure that gives us a fifteen-minute head start," said Greg, who would occasionally glance back at Karl. He and Jimmy were sitting twisted to the left, toward the two policemen. Greg said to Karl, "Don't try anything funny back there, because I got it in your partner's ribs."

"I won't," said Karl. "We've both got families. We just want to go home to our families." And he pulled the corduroy sport jacket up around his chin because he was suddenly very cold.

"Just keep that in mind," Greg said, and now Jimmy sensed that Greg was totally relaxed.

Jimmy hated him more than he ever had because he himself was breathing so hard he was hyperventilating, and his heart was hammering in his throat. From this time on, Jimmy could never think of his friend as Greg. It would be Powell from this moment whenever he thought of him, whenever he would dream about him.

Ian said quietly, "Don't get excited, but there's a radio car up ahead." And everyone in the car went tense as Ian kept up the steady speed in the slower lane, approaching the police car which was stopped in front of them.

"It looks like a roadblock, Jimmy," said Greg, voice razor thin. "Get ready!"

"It looks like they're writing a ticket," said Ian. "That's all. I'm just going to drive by at an even speed."

"Okay," Greg whispered. "Remember. Remember. If we get stopped . . . "

"Yes," Ian said, and they passed the police car at the Sepulveda off-ramp and then they were on Sepulveda Boulevard making good time in the nighttime traffic, catching most lights green, and each man was beginning to think about what all this meant and to make and reject his own plans.

"Can I give you some advice?" asked Ian after several minutes during which time no one had spoken. The wind rushing through the window chilled them all because they were still sweating freely, but the car was filled with the smell of fear on all of them, so the window remained partly open.

"Go ahead," Greg said.

"You should take off those caps. Nobody around here wears them and we're liable to get stopped."

Greg immediately took off his cap, but Jimmy ignored the advice. Fuck it, he thought. I ain't showin them my hair. And I ain't takin no free advice from a cop. At night, in this dark little car, if I just keep my mouth shut or talk like a white man when I have to, they ain't even gonna know my race. And if Powell don't run off with his fat mouth and tell them all he knows about me, well shit, I might get out of this yet. I just might.

And after a few more blocks of driving, Greg reached down on the floor with his free hand and picked up the Schenley's and began drinking.

"If you drink in a moving car the Highway Patrol might stop us," Ian said, and Greg put the bottle down sourly.

Karl peered over the ledge seeing they were passing Van Owen. Already his legs were cramping up, and he longed to stretch out.

Jimmy stopped thinking and listened to the tires hum and the wind rush, and occasionally he blinked when an oncoming driver failed to dim his lights. Then Greg said, "Do you guys have any money?"

"I've got ten dollars," Ian said, characteristically knowing exactly how much money he had.

"I've got eight or nine," said Karl.

"If you take our money it'll get you clear to San Francisco," said Ian, with a faint hope that the gunmen might be tempted by the few dollars. Might drop them off now. Might run for it up the highway in the little Ford. Or might feel that the policemen believed they would run to San Francisco, and then head the other direction. Might do anything, but might just release them. That hope faded quickly as Greg snorted and said, "You know better than that."

They were quiet for a few more miles, and Karl tried to see his watch in the darkness, but could not. His stomach was twisted and he was sweating so badly the watch was sliding down his wrist. But Karl was not idle. He was looking at them, listening to the voices, staring hard whenever one turned. He would have to describe the faces later, and the car, and the voices. He tried to get a better look at the guns, but could not, except occasionally when the darker man pointed one at him over the top of the seat, his eyes like berries. The sight blade looked to Karl like his own gun.

Karl watched the blond one chew his lower lip with a craggy overbite. Then Greg said: "Here's the plan. We're gonna take you guys up on the Ridge Route, drive you out on a side road, drop you off, and make sure you are a long walk back to the highway."

Now Karl felt the tension subside a bit. It was what Gregory Powell said, and partly the friendly tone of his voice. The voice had softened now with the barest trace of hometown middle America in it. "With just a little bit of cornpone twang," as Jimmy Smith was to put it.

So a more relaxed Karl said, "You know, those guns are paid for out of our own pockets. Would you do us a favor and after you drop us off, unload them and heave them into the brush so we can get them after you leave?"

"We don't make that much money," Ian added.

"Sure." Greg smiled. "I think we can do that." And now, even Jimmy's breath was coming at regular intervals.

They were driving through Sepulveda Pass, out of the heavy traffic. The infrequent street lights made it utterly impossible to see what time it was, so Karl gave up. Once in a while he would glance up at Ian, whose hands did not change position on the wheel. Ian looked calm except that there was a trickle coming down the right side of his neck disappearing under the collar.

Greg said, "There's a lake up here."

"It's a reservoir off to the left," Karl said.

"You're damn right there is," snapped Greg, turning, mouth like an iron bar, as though Karl had challenged him. Karl felt himself go tight again. The abrupt change in tone, for no reason, puzzled and upset him.

They could see the reservoir shimmer in the moonlight and then they were near the Mint Canyon turnoff. After that, Sepulveda turned into the Ridge Route.

"Give me your money," Greg said, and Karl removed his wallet carefully, seeing Ian do the same. Karl opened his with both hands and held it up for Greg to see and took out his nine dollars.

"We have a hideout a few hours from here where we'll be safe," Greg said. And this was more than Jimmy Smith could bear. For the very first time he rebuked Gregory Powell.

"Shut up. Don't tell these guys anything." And the moment he said it he stiffened, but Greg didn't seem to notice what he'd said.

The tires hummed on the highway, and Karl looked up and could gauge by the frequency of the stars how far they were getting from the smoggy skies of Los Angeles.

"Where does that road go?" Greg asked suddenly.

Karl raised up and said, "That's the Mint Canyon turnoff. It eventually swings right back into Highway 99 here."

"I know it does. I was just checking," Greg said sharply. Then they were four or five miles up the Ridge and Karl looked out and felt an overwhelming sadness mingle with the fear and he said to no one in particular, "I was fishing out here two days ago. With my wife. She's pregnant with our first."

"Shut up!" Jimmy Smith said. "Shut your mouth!"

"That's all right," Greg said soothingly. "Let him talk." And then Greg leaned over to Jimmy and whispered, "Let them talk. Don't make them nervous."

Jimmy Smith was thinking: Fuck you and fuck the lake and I don't give a fuck if it's covered with fuckin fishes. And you and your knocked-up ol' lady, I don't give a fuck about any of it.

Now as he watched Greg's head turn on its swivel from time to time, he became even more angry, listing everything about Powell, especially that rooster neck. Then Jimmy became aware that Karl was speaking to him.

"Can I change positions if I keep my hands in sight? My legs're going to sleep."

"Stay where you are. I'm cramped too," said Jimmy sticking the gun muzzle an inch or so over the seat once again.

Greg leaned over and whispered something to Jimmy. Then Greg said aloud, "We changed our plan. We're gonna hold you guys until we stop a family car. We need hostages. We're gonna stop a family car and when we get one we'll let you guys go, but let me give you a piece of advice. I know you guys got a job to do, but if you turn us in before we can get away we'll kill every member of the family. Understand?"

"Yes," Karl said, realizing at once the absurdity of it, and feeling once again in danger.

Jimmy Smith was to tell later what had been whispered. "He said to me, 'Jimmy, I told you it was only a matter of time before it would come to this. It's either them or us. Remember the Lindbergh Law?' And I got an awful cold feelin all of a sudden. *'Them or us. Them or us.'* I couldn't get it outta my mind, what he said. But I didn't know for sure what he meant. I never knew of no Lindbergh Law exactly. I mean, I felt like it meant death. And I wondered about the way he said, 'I told you it was only a matter of time.' He *never* told me. He musta told somebody else, because he never told me. And he said, *'Remember* the Lindbergh Law.' Just like we talked about it before. I never heard of no such thing. Like, he was talkin to me about things I never talked to him about. I started gettin a bad bad feelin then."

Karl worried over the whispered conversation and he wished the car muffler wasn't noisy, and that he wasn't down on the metal floor just over the differential of the car with the sounds banging around him, reverberating. He hoped that Ian could hear something. He hated the whispered conversations. But the blond man talked reassuringly. He talked so much he interrupted Karl's thoughts. When Karl was getting very edgy and feeling desperate, the blond one would say something to reassure. It was the other gunman Karl wondered more about, the dark one. What was he thinking? He seemed more volatile. Would he be a threat at the end of their journey? And now the dark one turned and looked at Karl again. He didn't talk enough for Karl to know for sure, but he seemed to be a Mexican. If only he'd talk more, Karl thought.

Then Greg turned and in a quiet voice said to Jimmy: "we oughtta pull a stickup to get some money. Do you think you can handle these guys? If you think so, I'll go into the next likely place and take it off." Then he raised the bottle of Schenley's and took a deep swallow.

"Are you crazy?" Jimmy whispered, caution be damned. And Jimmy was to say later, "Powell's head turned on his big neck like a bird and I knew I shouldn't a said that word. Jesus, not then. The gun in my hand, the automatic, was pointed right toward him. I tried to make it up by humorin him. I said real casual, 'Well, maybe I oughtta pull a job, Greg. You watch the cops and I'll go in someplace in Gorman here and pull a job.' And I held my breath hopin he'd see how fuckin insane it was and he took a little drink and said, 'No.' He shook his bead and said, 'No.' And that was the end of that. Jesus."

Now Karl suspected that Ian was sharing his bad vibrations. The blond one was erratic and the dark one had just said something about pulling a robbery.

Ian said casually, "How're you fixed for gas?" and looked hopefully toward the gas station at Gorman. But the blond one looked at the panel and said, "We got plenty," and smiled. Then Jimmy Smith took a long pull from the bottle, turning nervously as he drank, to keep an eye on Karl.

Now they were past Gorman, almost on that part of the highway known as the Grapevine. They were at the top near old Fort Tejon, with a view of the great, bleak, lonely San Joaquin Valley. The car started the long descent.

But while they were closest to the clouds, Ian Campbell looked up, ducking his head because the roof was low. He looked up and Karl pushed his glasses higher on his nose and followed Ian's eyes. Up. Up. But there was nothing. Only the black sky. Vast in this immense valley. Stars flickering close and familiar, as they do at the top of the Tehachapi Range.

Now Karl felt this was where he belonged. Out here. Where he'd always wanted to be. In cultivated land where things grow. Where the air is so pure and brisk it hurts. And now perhaps, out here in the farmlands, near nightmare earth, he was somehow safe. Perhaps this nightmare was a city dream. He looked at his partner, who was switching his gaze from the road every few seconds as though he had never seen a great sparkling sky before.

The abandoned felony car was not discovered until eleven o'clock. By midnight, several police supervisors were belatedly panic stricken and plans were formulated to search the area. At fifteen minutes past midnight a command post was established at Carlos and Cower. All residences, apartments, buildings in the area were being checked. Many were carefully searched for any sign of the missing officers. Motorcycle units were called in for traffic diversion. Press relations were established and all nightwatch units were held over to assist in the search. No resident of that Hollywood neighborhood slept until later that night when the search was abruptly called off.

❖ ❖ ❖

The Onion Field is first a story about a crime and second a story about the patience of its author. Not only did Joseph Wambaugh need the consent of Karl Hettinger, he also needed the cooperation of the two killers and many other people related to the case. In addition to getting legal releases—modeled after Capote's—from a variety of people, Wambaugh spent "a small fortune" to hire a lawyer to help with the research and picked up travel expenses to return people to Los Angeles to go over the crime scene with him. The payment for legal releases varied according to how much Wambaugh needed someone's cooperation. In all, he paid sixty-two individuals.[4] By Wambaugh's count, he studied fifteen thousand pages of court transcript. He went over the tapes taken during confessions and collected newspaper articles and evidence exhibits.[5]

Despite his care, *The Onion Field* raised some legal eyebrows. A *Los Angeles Times* story reported that one detective quoted in the book said some conversations were attributed to him erroneously and requested a retraction. (Wambaugh said no.)[6] Gregory Powell, seeking a second trial, asked that the book be banned in Los Angeles County so the jury pool would not be prejudiced. The request was denied.[7] But in making the request Powell's attorney referred to *The Onion Field* as a "fictionalized account" and also asked that the distributor add to the book a "disclaimer of accuracy" saying "that the book is not a true and accurate summation of the incidents depicted and contains fictional matter and speculation and conjecture by its author."

Even a reviewer referred to the book as "Mr. Wambaugh's new novel."[8] Perhaps Capote is to be blamed; his cover blurb complimented Wambaugh for making a "distinguished contribution toward the gradually enlarging field of the 'factual novel.'" Others made comparisons to Capote's book *In Cold Blood,* but no one was really censorious in their comments the way some critics were about Capote's "nonfiction novel." No doubt three factors contributed to the differences in reactions: (1) Capote had already taken the heat—and the bows; (2) Wambaugh was not a self-promoter, as Capote was; and (3) Wambaugh was writing from the West Coast at a time when publishing events generally had to occur in New York in order to be considered news.

Several reviewers compared *Onion Field* to Capote's *In Cold Blood*. The most direct comparison considered *Onion Field* the better book. "Wambaugh takes greater liberties with his characters and he lacks Capote's neatness," James Conaway wrote. "But in terms of scope, revealed depth of character, and dramatic coherence, this is the more ambitious book."[9] In a comment that could just as fairly be applied to *Blood*, another reviewer said: "Wambaugh's spare, vivid documentary style draws the marrow out of police, court and psychiatric records while shaping a strong case for the reform of American criminal justice."[10] In the same vein, Christopher Lehman-Haupt viewed *The Onion Field* "as a creative reportorial attempt to present a slice of American life in the decade of the nineteen-sixties."[11]

Other reviewers made implicit comparisons with *Blood*. Millicent Reid wrote: "Wambaugh's style reads almost like fiction but it doesn't let you drift away from the stark reality of the moment."[12] "We are," Robert Kirsch wrote, "there in these pages."[13]

Generally, negative comments focused on the book's length or the amount of detail. Ray Kennedy said "the narrative tends to plod whenever he plays the tireless gumshoe."[14] That remark, echoed a year later in an anonymous *Times Literary Supplement* review that criticized Wambaugh because he could not decide "when to stop taking evidence,"[15] might actually suggest the need for more editing rather than less research. In addition, as Edward Weeks said, "the reading is necessarily slow and dense because of the legal confusion about what actually happened."[16] Another reviewer said that the book was "slow starting" but that "once the action begins it is difficult to put the book down."[17] Dorothy Rabinowitz said Wambaugh was "good on the police and less good on sociology and jurisprudence."[18] Similarly, the *Times Literary Supplement* reviewer suggested that the book would have been more interesting if Wambaugh had ended the book after the trial and summarized subsequent events. "As it is, it moves and excites for half its length while squandering its impetus with the remainder."[19] Even a favorable reviewer said the book was "sprawling," although he meant it as a compliment.[20]

It is difficult to decide whether Wambaugh is a writer who tried police work or a cop who became a writer. His father was at one time a police chief in a small Pennsylvania town. After serving in the Marines, Wambaugh also became a police officer. But even before the Marines, Wambaugh has said he realized that he "was really good at something, and that was literature," and that he dreamed of becoming an English teacher.[21]

Instead he became a cop who wrote novels on the side. Even before *The Onion Field*, with just two novels to his credit—*The New Centurions* and *The Blue Knight*—Wambaugh was becoming famous. His fame eventually affected him on the job. Some criminals requested his autograph.[22] One convinced Wambaugh he had discussed one of Wambaugh's novels with him when in fact the person had been a burglary suspect months before.[23] Another asked him what George C. Scott, an actor who had starred in a movie based one of his novels, was really like.[24] Some, knowing Wambaugh was a consultant on the television show "Police Story," asked for auditions.[25] The audition requests, Wambaugh said later, led him to resign from the force early in 1974 and take up writing full time.

When Joseph Wambaugh was asked which of his first three books he liked the best, he nominated *The Onion Field*. He said, "after writing this book, I'm sure that I'm a writer. I don't know how the book is going to be received, but I know a *writer* wrote this third book."[26] No one has ever contradicted that remark.

ENDNOTES

1. Steven V. Roberts, "Cop of the Year," *Esquire*, December 1973, 151.
2. John Brady, "Joe Wambaugh copes from experience," *Writer's Digest*, December 1973, 20.
3. Ibid., 21.
4. Ibid.
5. Ibid., 18.
6. Bill Hazlett, "Policeman-Writer's Book Stirs Controversy," *Los Angeles Times*, 18 September 1973, sec. 2, p. 1.
7. "Judge Refuses Ban on Officer's Book," *Los Angeles Times*, 7 December 1973, sec. 2, pp. 2, 8.
8. Dorothy Rabinowitz, "The Onion Field," *Saturday Review/World*, 11 September 1973, 47. In the early 1980s, I went looking for a copy for a friend. After much searching and to my surprise, I found the paperback version in a college bookstore's fiction department.
9. James Conaway, "Murder most squalid," *New York Times Book Review*, 2 September 1973, 5.

10. "The Onion Field," *Publishers Weekly*, 23 July 1973, 66.
11. Christopher Lehman-Haupt, "More Than Meets the Eye," *New York Times*, 7 September 1973, 33.
12. Millicent Reid, "The police by a policeman," *Christian Science Monitor*, 17 October 1973, 15.
13. Robert Kirsch, "Joseph Wambaugh Dissects a Cop's Murder in 'Onion Field,'" *Los Angeles Times*, 30 September 1973, "Calendar," 50.
14. Ray Kennedy, "Annals of the Crime," *Time*, 24 September 1973, 128.
15. "The case of the liberal cop," *Times Literary Supplement*, 1 November 1974, 1220.
16. Edward Weeks, "The Peripatetic Reviewer," *Atlantic*, October 1973, 129.
17. Charles M. Sevilla, "Book Review," *Library Journal*, 1 September 1973, 2422.
18. Rabinowitz, "The Onion Field," 47.
19. "The case of the liberal cop," 1220.
20. Kirsch, "Joseph Wambaugh Dissects," 46.
21. Quoted in Roberts, "Cop of the Year," 151.
22. Ibid., 310.
23. Randy Woodbury, "Dilemma of an author-cop: the typewriter or the gun," *Life*, 14 April 1972, 77.
24. "The Beat Goes On," *Newsweek*, 26 March 1973, 113.
25. J. D. Reed, "Those Blues in the Knights," *Time*, 8 June 1981, 78, and Joyce Haber, "For Joseph Wambaugh, the Beat Goes On," *Los Angeles Times*, 4 November 1973, "Calendar," 19.
26. Quoted in Brady, "Joseph Wambaugh copes," 20.

Chapter 13

❧

A Welfare Mother

Susan Sheehan has been a staff writer for *The New Yorker* since November 1960,[1] where she has written several extensively researched articles about people outside the mainstream. She received approval in January 1973 to begin work on what would become *A Welfare Mother*.[2] The article was eventually published as a book, with an introduction by Michael Harrington, a social activist and advocate for the poor, and an afterword in which Sheehan explained her reporting methods.

By her own admission, Susan Sheehan—like Joan Didion—has an aversion toward writing about people who have press officers, "that is, people who want to be written about."[3] Although she has written about such people, she has earned her reputation for her reporting on people of the underclasses—among them, typical Vietnamese dealing with a civil war and western soldiers (*Ten Vietnamese*), people on welfare (*A Welfare Mother*), a prisoner (*A Prison and a Prisoner*), a schizophrenic (*Is There No Place on Earth for Me?*, for which Sheehan received the Pulitzer Prize), a daughter caring for an elderly parent (*Kate Quinton's Days*), and a teenage mother (*Life for Me Ain't Been No Crystal Stair*). As David Haward Bain wrote, Sheehan's subjects "are caught up in problems so pervasive and numbing most other journalists would despair of holding their readers until the end." To her credit, Bain said, Sheehan captures "the humanity of society's victims."[4] Sheehan typically writes about types of people who do not subscribe to or read *The New Yorker,* so her subjects heighten the challenge of getting and maintaining her readers' interest.

The following excerpt comes from midway in *A Welfare Mother*. "Delgado" is Francisco Delgado, Carmen Santana's boyfriend.

❧ ❧ ❧

As soon as Mrs. Santana was back inside her apartment she consulted the fourteen-carat gold Bulova watch Delgado had given her the previous Mother's Day. She seemed relieved that she had returned home in time to watch her favorite Spanish language TV *novela*, which began at noon. She swallowed some cough medicine, turned on the living room television set Delgado had bought some months before from a man on the street for fifty dollars without inquiring into its provenance, and settled into one of her frayed armchairs. She watched the latest episode of the *novela* with her customary enthusiasm.

The *novela* installment was followed by a news program. Mrs. Santana turned off the TV, turned on the phonograph to its top volume, and went into the kitchen. At the dinette table, she brushed away a cluster of cockroaches that sat boldly on half a loaf of Italian bread and two small packages of cheese and ham remaining from breakfast, fixed herself a hero sandwich, poured a glass of Pepsi-Cola, and sang along with the popular Spanish crooner whose latest record she was playing. Local human-interest stories—a subway crime, a rape, a sex murder—sometimes caught Mrs. Santana's fancy; most national and international news stories did not.

Mrs. Santana rarely watches the news on television or buys a newspaper. She didn't vote for Nixon or "the other one" in the 1972 presidential election, didn't favor either side in the Arab-Israeli Yom Kippur War, and didn't watch the Watergate hearings. "The Watergate? I don't know what happened over there," she says. She was opposed to the Vietnam War—although she says she doesn't know what happened over there, either—because she had heard that many Puerto Rican soldiers were killed in the fighting. Five years ago, she had worried that her son Rafael, who spent a few months in the Army before going AWOL, would be sent to Vietnam.

At one, Mrs. Santana's oldest daughter, Casilda, phoned from the lower East Side to discuss the noon *novela* episode and to bring her mother up to date on her own life, which of late had contained enough dramatic incidents for several *novela* installments. At twenty-seven, Casilda looks and acts very much her mother's daughter. She is gravely overweight (she stands five-five and weighs two hundred and fourteen pounds) but very attractive. She, too, married young in order to escape from an unhappy home. In 1953, when Casilda was five, she had flown with her brother Rafael from Puerto Rico to Detroit to live with their father, Rafael Rodríguez; his second wife, Fulgencia; and two children that Fulgencia Rodríguez had had by two different men between the time she went out with Rafael Rodríguez in Cayey in 1946 and the time she met up with him in New York seven years later. Fulgencia Rodríguez lavished clothes, toys, and affection upon her own two children. She bought Casilda and Rafael only the necessities and disciplined them harshly. Casilda was made to help with the cooking, the cleaning, and the laundry. Her stepsister was not required to help with the household chores. Rafael Rodríguez earned a good living as a mechanic in Detroit, but one day in 1963 he decided to move back to Cayey; he reached this decision as abruptly as he had reached the decision to leave Cayey for New York. When Casilda started the tenth grade in Cayey, in September of 1965, she was planning to finish high school and become a beautician. A month later, she met Roberto Figueroa, a trim, eighteen-year-old, seventh-grade dropout, who worked in his parents' small meat business. Fulgencia Rodríguez disapproved of Casilda's going out with young men. She didn't permit Roberto Figueroa, who had the reputation of being a playboy, to come to the house. In mid-December, the seventeen-year-old Casilda eloped with Roberto Figueroa. They spent a week at his parents' house in Cayey. At the end of the week, Rafael Rodríguez forced the young couple to marry. Casilda Rodríguez and Roberto Figueroa were married on November 25, 1965, in a Catholic church, in a double ceremony with Roberto's older brother, Reynaldo Figueroa, who was to get Casilda's then seven-year-old sister Inocencia Castillo pregnant six years later.

"We were married and lived unhappily ever after," says Casilda, who is given to exaggeration and to borrowing the language of true-confessions magazines, which she likes to read. "Ever after" was two and a half years. Casilda and Roberto Figueroa lived unhappily in Cayey, in Dover, New Jersey, and in New York, where Casilda was reunited with her mother after a ten-year separation, and where the Figueroas' daughter, Helen, was born on August 22, 1966, almost exactly nine months after the elopement. Roberto Figueroa had trouble keeping a job in New York, because he knew almost no English, so the Figueroas applied for welfare and received checks to supplement his meager and erratic wages. Wherever they lived, Roberto was unfaithful to Casilda and beat her when she complained about his philandering. In the fall of 1968, the Figueroas separated. Casilda kept Helen and applied for welfare on her own. She has been on welfare ever since. Among the financial resources Casilda has successfully concealed from the Department of Social Services are occasional earnings from selling numbers and holding jobs (packer in a shirt factory, clerk in a discount store) and income provided by Jesús Manrique, a handsome man of thirty-two, with whom she had been living since 1969. Shortly after Jesús Manrique, Jr., was born, in 1972, Casilda decided to report the birth of her baby and the fact that she was living with the baby's father to the Department of Social Services. She told an employee at her local welfare center that Jesús Manrique was earning ninety dollars a week at an electrical appliance factory and was giving her about sixty dollars a week toward the household expenses. Casilda figured that if the welfare paid their rent, one hundred eight dollars a month, she and Jesús could get by without her welfare check. The worker calculated that Casilda and Jesús had a budget deficit of only eighty-four dollars a month, and informed Casilda that she would be receiving thirty-nine dollars every two weeks toward the rent. For two months, the thirty-nine-dollar semimonthly checks failed to arrive. Casilda had to spend two days out of every fifteen at the local welfare center tracking them down. After two months of having to go to the welfare center and of being unable to make ends meet, Casilda came to the conclusion that honesty didn't pay, and reported that Jesús had deserted her. Since then, she has been receiving the grant for a family of three and her entire rent.

For six years, Casilda had been content with her life with Jesús. Although he suffered from an ulcer and she found him an inadequate lover, he was quiet, neat, and handy around the house. He didn't beat her, and he treated Helen kindly. Casilda's contentment had ended a couple of months earlier, when she discovered that Jesús was having an affair. For a while, Casilda tried to pretend that the affair was not taking place. Though Jesús gave her less money on payday than had been his custom, she didn't protest. One of her friends, whose husband worked with Jesús, asked her why she phoned Jesús so often at the factory; she didn't reply that she hadn't been calling him at all, nor did she ask Jesús about the calls. When Jesús started coming home late at night, she didn't challenge his unconvincing alibis. But when an expensive-looking bottle of men's cologne appeared on Jesús's dresser, Casilda couldn't refrain from asking him where he had got it. He said he had bought it at the drugstore for four dollars. The next morning, she priced the cologne at the drugstore; it cost twelve dollars. That afternoon, before she could confront Jesús with the discrepancy, Casilda discovered a pile of love letters under the bedroom linoleum, where Jesús had hidden them. What particularly hurt her feelings, she told her mother, was that the author of the letters was Aida Gonzalez, her next-door neighbor and supposedly a good friend. Aida visited Casilda practically every day while Jesús was at work, and often came by in the evening to see them both. The letters made it clear that Aida and Jesús had gone to elaborate lengths to keep the affair from Aida's husband. In one letter, Aida instructed Jesús to give a thirty-five-dollar ring he had bought for her to one of her trusted girl friends, who could then offer to sell it to Aida's husband at a low price; her husband would be sure to buy it for her and she would thus be able to wear it without arousing his suspicions.

That evening when Jesús came home from work, Casilda threw the letters at him and told him to leave. Later, when Aida came to visit them, Casilda started to beat her up. Jesús stopped her. He was unable to stop her from calling Aida's husband to apprise him of the affair. Jesús tearfully begged Casilda's forgiveness and sought to justify his conduct: Aida had flirted with him, and he had had to prove his manhood by going to bed with her. He had bought her the ring only because she had bought him the cologne. Casilda accepted the rationale. "When a woman bothers a man, he has no alternative but to act like a man," she says. Even her mother considered her partly to blame for the affair: Casilda had seen Aida making eyes at Jesús and hadn't taken action immediately. Jesús agreed to stop seeing Aida and to move with Casilda to another apartment, on East Sixth Street, six blocks away from temptation. Partly at her mother's urging, Casilda agreed to give Jesús a second chance. For two months Jesús was a model husband. He brightened up the crumbling walls of their fifth-floor walkup with gold and green-flocked Con-Tact paper, and he was properly jealous when Casilda stayed out until four in the morning, playing bingo at a friend's house. Jesús hadn't made love to her in several weeks, and when Casilda finally persuaded him to do so, she discovered that the affair had begun again. Jesús didn't want to take off his T-shirt. Casilda took it off for him. She immediately noticed a love bite on his chest. When she tried to put a similar mark of affection on his neck, he wouldn't let her. "Either I do what I want with you, like Aida, or you can go!" Casilda had screamed. Jesús had ignored the ultimatum. For ten days, they had scarcely spoken.

Now, Casilda said, her voice trembling, the climactic moment had arrived. For last night Jesús hadn't come home. Casilda had phoned him that morning at the factory and had been told that he hadn't shown up for work. She was calling to ask what her mother thought she ought to do.

"Get drunk," Mrs. Santana said. In the days since the quarrel over the love bite, Casilda had picked out a prospective new husband, one Alfonso Ortiz. Mrs. Santana hadn't yet met Alfonso, but she didn't like anything Casilda had told her about him: he was three years younger than Casilda, he was unemployed and his last wife had just thrown him out of the house. Mrs. Santana believed that Casilda would be better off staying with Jesús. Casilda didn't care for her mother's advice. "The trouble with you, *Mami*, is that you don't take life seriously," Casilda said. "Getting drunk won't help. I feel so low I could sink in a glass of water."

Mrs. Santana, on whom Casilda's histrionics were wasted, replied, "Casilda, the trouble with you is that you're just like me. You don't have good luck with men. Rafael Rodríguez left me with three children. He's stuck with his second wife for over twenty years. Angel Castillo had no money for me—he was just a field worker when I was with him. Now he's high up in the numbers business in Cayey and lives with his third wife in a fancy house."

This time, Casilda regretfully concurred with her mother. "When I was with Roberto Figueroa, we traveled around like gypsies and we had nothing," she said. "Now Roberto is selling heroin and he's already made twenty thousand dollars. I'm glad I never got around to divorcing him. If something happens to him, I'll be his legal widow."

Mother and daughter turned from Casilda's troubles to family gossip. Casilda had heard that Inés Pérez, Roberto Figueroa's latest wife, was pregnant; Inés claimed that the baby was Roberto's, but Roberto was going around denying it. Casilda had also learned that Fulgencia Rodríguez's son, Martin, a Navy officer, had recently been transferred to Japan, where his wife had "a genuine maid." Mrs. Santana told Casilda that Vincente Santana had given his wife a severe beating; she had been seen on the street with numerous bruises. The latest news about other members of the large Rodríguez, Castillo, Santana, Delgado, Figueroa, and Manrique families kept Casilda and her mother on the phone for fifteen minutes longer.

⚜ ⚜ ⚜

When Sheehan started *Welfare Mother,* she resisted a caseworker's suggestion that she profile several welfare mothers, arguing that by doing so she might "have more facts but not more truth, and I would lose the vividness, the felt truth one gets only when writing about a single person."[5] Eventually the caseworker led her to Carmen Santana, whose name Sheehan changed to protect her from Department of Social Services repercussions.[6]

Sheehan particularly wanted to profile a Puerto Rican, in part because she had written some shorter stories on the subculture for *The New Yorker* and because she admired some books by Oscar Lewis,[7] author of, among other books, *La Vida: A Puerto Rican Family in the Culture of Poverty—San Juan and New York*.

Sheehan and Santana began to meet, talk, and watch television. Eventually Sheehan began asking Santana about her life. Santana and her family, having grown to trust Sheehan, began opening up, even ceasing to use "their Sunday-best language."[8] As the relationship evolved, Santana would sometimes ask Sheehan for advice, but Sheehan would refuse on the anthropological principle that one's presence as an observer should not affect the observed.[9]

In the beginning Sheehan never stayed at Santana's apartment beyond 4:00 P.M. because Santana had not volunteered information on the owner of the men's clothing in the bedroom. But Sheehan was also worried about safety. "I figured it was safer for me to make my way past the dope dealers and junkies in her neighborhood in broad daylight."[10] Eventually Sheehan became part of the neighborhood and felt secure enough that she would stay late into the night.[11] She interviewed many of the people in the neighborhood, among them, Mrs. Santana's doctor and her numbers man. She even brought her husband and two young daughters with her, something she also did when reporting for *Is There No Place on Earth for Me?* and *A Prison and a Prisoner.*[12] Her daughters would play with Mrs. Santana's children and, Sheehan wrote, "I could fade quietly into the background"[13]—a veritable fly on the wall.

What Sheehan, who speaks "adequate Spanish,"[14] did not learn as a firsthand observer, she obtained by reading Santana's file at the welfare office.[15] "I don't do things quickly and don't place a value on doing one piece a year," she once told an interviewer. "I like to do something slowly and well."[16]

Critical evaluations of her subsequent books help illuminate Sheehan's methods. "Massive research and a clear, dry, unsentimental prose style . . . a camera who reports what she learns and observes, neither excoriating or lauding," Peter Gorner said after

Is There No Place on Earth for Me? was published.[17] Referring
to three of her works, including *Welfare Mother,* Samuel G.
Freedman praised Sheehan for resisting interpretation and for a
"detached voice and detailed reporting [that] evoke the flat,
episodic quality of a case history."[18] Megan Rosenfeld described
Sheehan's technique as "a kind of total immersion, observation
and interviews combined with extensive library research" and
said Sheehan "relies on facts" and "equally on the knowledge that
the sum of facts is not always the truth."[19]

Richard Rodriguez faulted Sheehan for not having a point
of view, calling it an "implicit moral failure,"[20] but others have
seen Sheehan's distance from the subject as one of her virtues.
She "construes her chore primly," Mark Kramer wrote. "She
barely dramatizes scenes. She draws life without exploring its
emotion, leaving that part up to us. She just names circumstances, prices, dates, lists, ailments and medicines."[21] Early in
the book, for example, Sheehan presents a table of Santana's
revenue and expenses. Late in the book, she presents a series of
statements of fact, demarcated with bullets, ranging from three
paragraphs at the longest to one paragraph, including a one-
sentence paragraph: "A heroin addict is murdered a block from
Mrs. Santana's apartment."[22]

Such a sentence exemplifies Sheehan's matter-of-fact style.
She opens the book with "Carmen Santana is a welfare mother."
No ruffles, no flourishes. A simple sentence. She ends just as
simply. First, a paragraph explaining that Mrs. Santana had
quarreled with her boyfriend, Francisco Delgado, who had spent
the night on the sofa. The next day she hinted that he should
leave the relationship.

"So that's what you want—for me to leave you," Delgado said.
"Not today," she said.

Sheehan writes in a simple prose that builds on itself by
piling fact upon fact. The terse ending indicates Mrs. Santana's
resignation to her situation, which the reader has just witnessed.

Sheehan's simple style reflects what one reviewer of Truman
Capote's *In Cold Blood* called "the familiar *New Yorker* documentary style—apparently deadpan, with a laconic piling up of
objective detail."[23] It serves Sheehan well. The style indicates

respect for the intelligence of the reader and signals that the writer is not trying to manipulate anyone. You can read *Welfare Mother* and feel sympathy for welfare recipients; you can reasonably conclude from it that the system does not work. Sheehan, because of her style, comes as close to objective writing as a human can get. (George Orwell and James Agee, by contrast, made clear whose side they were on.) It is to her credit that she can maintain such restraint in her writing.

The reviews of *Welfare Mother* were mixed. Those reviewers who were negative faulted Sheehan for keeping a distance from her subject,[24] for not putting in tears and emotions,[25] and for "offering so abbreviated a summary of this woman's history and present situation."[26] Sara Sanborn, however, praised Sheehan for keeping the story tight. "A more self-indulgent writer could have made it twice as long and half as good," she wrote. "Its purity is its impact."[27] Where others saw distance, Sandy Whiteley saw advocacy journalism and said *Welfare Mother* would be useful for social scientists.[28] In some ways, the mixed reaction to *Welfare Mother* echoed the divided reaction to John Hersey's *Hiroshima*, written twenty-five years earlier and also initially published in *The New Yorker*. With both books, some reviewers allowed their political feelings to inform their reviews.

Welfare Mother is wrapped in an authority of fact, thanks to Sheehan's extensive reporting and documentation. Combined with its understated style, it presents a picture of one woman on welfare. It does not claim to be a total picture. It is merely a snapshot, yet it unemotionally evokes a deeper sense of what life is like for Carmen Santana and her family.

ENDNOTES

1. Susan Sheehan, "When Will the Book Be Done?" *New York Times Magazine*, 15 April 1990, 68.
2. Susan Sheehan, *A Welfare Mother* (New York: New American Library, 1977), 130. (Originally published by Houghton Mifflin, 1976.)
3. Ibid., 132.
4. David Haward Bain, "Obstacle Course for the Aged," *New York Times*, 4 November 1984, p. 15.
5. Sheehan, *Welfare Mother*, 133.
6. Ibid., 129.

7. Ibid., 132.
8. Ibid., 141.
9. Ibid., 136.
10. Ibid., 137.
11. Ibid., 138.
12. Glenn Collins, "Susan Sheehan: Chronicler of Psychiatric Pilgrimage," *New York Times,* 2 April 1982, p. B4.
13. Sheehan, *Welfare Mother,* 141.
14. Ibid., 129.
15. Ibid., 129.
16. Quoted in Peter Gorner, "Life on the fringes of sanity: A woman's 14-year ordeal," *Chicago Tribune,* May 17, 1982, sec. 3, p. 1, 3.
17. Ibid., 1.
18. Samuel G. Freedman, "Caught in a Culture of Failure," *New York Times Book Review,* 3 October 1993, 30.
19. Megan Rosenfeld, "The Skewed World of Schizophrenia," *Washington Post,* 1 August 1982, pp. G1, G6.
20. Richard Rodriguez, "Caught in a Cycle of Despair," *Washington Post,* 10 October 1993, p. 2.
21. Mark Kramer, "A Life of One's Own and the Will to Live It," *Washington Post Book World,* 9 September 1984, 1, 6.
22. Sheehan, *Welfare Mother,* 104.
23. Bernard McCabe, "Elementary, my dear man," *Commonweal,* 11 February 1966, 561.
24. Susan Jacoby, "A Welfare Mother," *New York Times Book Review,* 8 August 1976, 6–7.
25. Richard R. Lingeman, "Books of the Times," *New York Times,* 27 August 1976, p. C17.
26. "A Welfare Mother," *America,* 13 November 1976, 330.
27. Sara Sanborn, "A Welfare Mother," *Saturday Review,* 10 July 1976, 56.
28. Sandy Whiteley, "Book Review," *Library Journal,* July 1976, 1545.

Chapter 14

❖

C. D. B. BRYAN

Friendly Fire

When soldiers die not from enemy shelling but because of accidents caused by their own troops, they are listed as victims of "friendly fire." Informed that her son Michael had died in the Vietnam War, a victim of friendly fire, Peg Mullen of La Porte City, Iowa, began a transformation from gung-ho American to a questioning and challenging anti-war, anti-government protestor.

C. D. B. (Courtlandt Dixon Barnes) Bryan learned about the Mullens (Peg and her husband, Gene) while he was visiting a fellow writer at the University of Iowa. Peg Mullen had recently placed an advertisement in the *Des Moines* (Iowa) *Register,* with an illustration of 714 crosses representing the "714 Iowans who have died in Vietnam." (Peg had paid for the advertisement out of the money the Army sent to bury her son.)[1] Bryan decided to do a magazine article and received clearance from William Shawn, then the editor of *The New Yorker.* Bryan expected to write a six-thousand-word article, but instead produced a three-part series for the magazine. Later, he added some history and correspondence and published *Friendly Fire* as a book.[2]

The first excerpt comes from the beginning of Chapter 4, in which the parents learn of the death of their son, which has been described as "the most wrenching scene of this whole book."[3]

❖ ❖ ❖

When the telephone rang in the parish office of the Sacred Heart Catholic Church off Poplar Street in La Porte City a little after nine o'clock on Saturday morning, February 21, 1970, the thin, stooped, late-middle-aged country priest assumed it was just another mother whose child, sick with a midwinter cold, would be unable to attend catechism classes that day. He unhurriedly walked to his desk and, lifting the receiver, was surprised to hear an entirely unfamiliar male voice ask for him by name.

"Father Otto Shimon?"

"Yes-s-s?"

"Father Shimon, this is Master Sergeant Fitzgerald. I'm with Fifth Army Headquarters. . . . Do you have an O. E. Mullen in your parish?"

"O. E. Mullen?" Father Shimon repeated, giving himself time enough to move to the chair behind his desk and ease himself down.

"That's right," Fitzgerald said. "I was just talking to the priest at the Carmel parish and—"

"That would be Father Rahe at St. Mary's," Father Shimon interrupted, then added, "Sergeant," because he had been a captain in the Army during World War II and served now as chaplain for the local American Legion chapter in La Porte.

"Yes, sir, that's the one," Sergeant Fitzgerald said. "Well, the Father, Father Rahe, thinks he has a Ralph Mullen in his parish, but I'm trying to locate an O. E. Mullen and I thought perhaps you—"

"That would be Oscar *Eugene* Mullen," the priest said. "He's listed in the phone book, however, as *Gene* Mullen, hence"—Father Shimon chuckled—"your, ah, confusion."

"Then this O. E. Mullen is in your parish, sir?"

"Yes-s-s, Gene Mullen's in my parish." The priest did not like this sergeant's tone; he was being altogether too businesslike. "As a matter of fact, Sergeant, the Mullens have always been very good members of th—"

"May I see you this morning, sir?"

"Me? This morning, Sergeant? Fitzgerald, you said it was?"

"Fitzgerald, that's right."

"A fine old Irish-Catholic name," Father Shimon said still trying to be congenial, still fighting down the apprehension rising within him. "You are, I presume, Catholic?"

"No, sir, Episcopalian," Fitzgerald said. "Please, Father Shimon, it's important I see you this morning. As soon as possible."

"About Gene Mullen?" Father Shimon asked, his lips suddenly dry. "Is there something, ah-h-h, wrong?"

That morning the sun had finally broken through the flat pearl-gray overcast that had been brooding over the Mullens' farm. Although the temperature hovered near freezing, the week-long Arctic winds had ceased, and at last it again felt warm enough to be outside.

Gene Mullen walked back from the mailbox to the house. As he climbed the stairs into the kitchen, he called out, "Letter from Mikey." He dropped the bills, the Des Moines *Register* and the second-class mail on the kitchen table and tore open the envelope. Peg wiped her hands on a dish towel and put a kettle of water on to boil.

"What's he say?" she asked. "When did he write it?"

Gene glanced at the top of the letter. "Dated the thirteenth," he said. "Let's see now 'Dear Mom and Dad: Went down off the hill to get a haircut and clean up, but ended up hitching a ride to Chu Lai. Went to the MARS station by chance—they were open and not busy—so got a chance to call. Suppose it was midnight at home and guess you were surprised—'"

"Oh," Peg said, "he must have written this the same day he called." Gene had not been home when Michael had telephoned from Vietnam eight days earlier. Peg had written "Mike called" on an envelope and left it on the kitchen table for Gene to read following the late shift at John Deere. It was twelve thirty by the time Gene returned to the farm, and after reading the note, he woke Peg up. She told him that she had spoken with Michael for only about a minute and a half and that before hanging up, Michael had said, "Good-bye, Mom, it's so bad here. . . . " Peg had been so depressed that she hadn't felt like waiting up to tell Gene when he came home and had simply left him a note. She mixed Gene a mug of instant coffee, brought it to him at the kitchen table and sat down. "What else does he say?"

"He says, . . . 'guess you were surprised,' . . . now, here: 'Will be on the bunker line about two more days, then back out into the field.'"

"Ugh!" Peg groaned. "That means more search and destroy."

"No, it doesn't," Gene said. "He's been doing company sweeps like he wrote in the other letter."

"Same thing," Peg said.

"No, it isn't," Gene insisted. "A company sweep is—"

Peg waved her hand impatiently. "Go on with the letter."

"All right, all right. He says, 'Glad that all is well—weather here been rather good. Have decided not to take R&R if I can get a drop. So 'til later, hang loose.'" Gene looked at the letter more closely. "'Hang loose'?"

"Hang loose, you know," Peg said, "take it easy."

Gene shrugged. "'So 'til later, hang loose, Love Michael.'"

"That's it?"

"That's it," Gene said. He passed the letter across the table to his wife.

Peg read through it quickly, "Oh, see," she said, "he's decided for sure to ask for an early drop. You remember the letter before last Michael said he was writing the University of Missouri to get the necessary papers."

Michael hoped to be released early from Vietnam so that he could be readmitted to the Agriculture School. Peg and Gene discussed for a moment what they thought his chances were; Michael himself had written that he felt they were very good. The only part of his letter that bothered them was that he would again be going into the field, that he wouldn't be in the relative safety of the fire base bunker line anymore. Still, in one of his first letters, Michael had written that he was in "probably one of the better places over here," a comparatively quiet part of Vietnam.

"So he might be coming home in June," Gene said.

"Looks that way," Peg said, "knock wood."

Gene finished his coffee and stood up "Well, Mother," he said, "I guess I might as well try to fix the television antenna for you."

"What's it like outside?"

"Fine," Gene said. "Cold, but it's fine. The wind's stopped."

He buttoned up his heavy woolen red and black plaid lumber jacket, turned off his hearing aid, put the earplug into his pocket and went outside.

The windblown television antenna was attached to a post near the east side of the farmhouse. Gene was just coming around that east corner, blowing hot breath on his fingertips and trying to remember where he had last put the light wrench he would need, when, out of the corner of his eye, he noticed two automobiles turning into his driveway. Without his hearing aid he had not heard them approach and he fumbled beneath his lumber jacket for the earpiece, inserted it and thumbed the volume up.

Gene thought he recognized the first car, believed the parish priest, Father Shimon, had one like it, but that second car . . . . Gene read the black letters painted on the Chevrolet's olive-drab door: U.S. ARMY—FOR OFFICIAL USE ONLY. Gene's chest tightened, and he stood still while the priest and the Army sergeant stepped out of their cars and slammed shut the doors.

Gene watched them walking toward him as if in slow motion, their footsteps thundering across the metallic crust of the drifted snow. He tried to see beyond the country priest's black metal-framed glasses to what might show in his eyes. But Father Shimon's downcast lenses reflected only the snow. Not until the priest forced himself to look up did Gene recognize the fright, the despair, the agony within them, then very quietly Gene asked, "Is my boy dead?"

Father Shimon halted so abruptly that the Army sergeant, who was following, bumped into him from behind. "Gene," the priest said, "this is Sergeant Fitzgerald. He's from Fifth Army Headquarters. He . . . ." Shimon was silent.

Gene looked beyond Father Shimon to the sergeant and asked again, "Is . . . my . . . boy . . . dead?"

"Let's go into the house, Gene," Father Shimon said. "I want to talk to you there."

"No!" Gene said, not moving. "I want to know! Tell me, is . . . my . . . boy . . . dead?"

"I can't tell you here," Father Shimon said, his hand fluttering up toward Gene's shoulder. "Come into the house with us . . . please?"

Gene spun away before the priest's pale fingers could touch him.

Peg Mullen heard the back door open, heard Gene rushing up the stairs into the kitchen, heard him shouting, "It's Mikey! It's Mikey!" His voice half a sob, half a scream.

She hurried out of the sewing room in time to glimpse the Army uniform entering the kitchen. Peg found Gene standing with his back to the sink, clutching the counter behind him, the Army sergeant halted just to the side of the doorway. Father Shimon, between them, had removed his glasses to wipe away the steam. Peg started to move toward her husband but had to turn away. Never had she seen such terrible devastation in his face, so raw a wound. She looked next at the sergeant, who avoided her eyes by glancing at the priest whose job it was to tell them. But Father Shimon would not stop wiping his glasses, and Peg, feeling herself wanting to scream, to kick over a chair, to thrash about, to do anything rather than listen to this awful silence a moment longer, saw her husband's lips move as if to say, "It's Mikey," but no sound would come out.

Peg scowled at the Army sergeant and said, "Michael died on Thursday."

Thursday morning, upon waking up, Peg had burst into tears for no apparent reason. Off and on that entire day she had cried, and so that Gene wouldn't know, she had spent the morning by herself down in the sewing room. She decided to make new curtains for the boys' room, and she sewed and sewed but would have to stop because she would begin crying again and couldn't see the material through her tears. She would wait for the tears to pass, pull herself together and sew some more until finally a little after two o'clock, when she heard Gene leave for the John Deere plant in Waterloo, she stopped sewing altogether.

The following day, yesterday, Friday, Peg had awakened not sad, just angry. No matter what Gene said to her she snapped back, contradicting him, defying him. And seeing the hurt and confusion in his face she wanted to apologize but instead became angrier still for feeling that need. At noon Peg felt she simply had to get out of the house. She drove off to spend the day with friends who shared her feelings about the war, with whom she could talk about how worried she was, how frustrated she felt trying to find something meaningful to do.

Before Michael had been drafted, the war had appeared so far away, so purposeless and distant. But when Michael was sent to Vietnam, the war no longer seemed remote. A month after Michael was assigned to the Americal Division, Peg wore a black armband on October 15, Moratorium Day, to indicate her opposition to the war. The same day, in La Porte City, an American Legionnaire backed her up against the post office wall, told her she was a disgrace to the country and ordered her to take the armband off. Peg brushed his arm aside and told him, "You better get with it, you sonuvabitch!"

Still, Peg realized, she had never actively campaigned against the war. She had written letters to Jack Miller, Iowa's hawkish Republican Senator, to express her opposition. Each time the Des Moines *Register* carried an account of an Iowa boy's death in Vietnam, Peg would forward the clipping to the Senator's office in Washington with the note: "Put another notch in your gun, Jack." She had written several letters to President Nixon, pleading with him to end the war. She joined Another Mother for Peace, but really, Peg had to concede, her opposition so far had been limited and ineffective.

Yesterday she had not returned to the farm until dusk and, to keep busy, had begun to clean house. For the next six hours she scrubbed and dusted, waxed and polished, pausing only at ten o'clock for the late evening news on television. There was an account of an accidental shelling at Bien Hoa by South Vietnamese artillery resulting in the deaths of about a dozen American men. The story stuck in Peg's mind when she went back to cleaning, and at midnight she called one of the friends she had seen that afternoon to ask if she had watched the news. They talked about how the accidental shelling seemed to epitomize the stupidity and wastefulness of the Vietnam War. Peg told her friend how busy she had been cleaning, that she had felt this compulsion to polish the house from top to bottom. The friend asked Peg if she were expecting visitors.

"No, none that I know of," Peg had said. "I don't know what's going on with me—I really don't. But whatever it is," she added, "I'm ready."

The Army sergeant did not answer her, so Peg spoke again, "Did Michael die on Thursday?"

"Why do you ask me when he died?" Sergeant Fitzgerald said. "I haven't told you your son is dead."

Peg glared at him with such utter contempt that the sergeant flinched. "You know the Army doesn't come to tell parents that their sons are wounded!" Peg said. "You know the Army comes only when they're dead!"

The sergeant again turned to the priest, waiting for Father Shimon to break the news, to speak. But the priest was incapable of talking.

Very slowly, deliberately, almost threateningly, Gene Mullen pushed himself away from the sink and moved toward the two men. "Now I want to know the truth!" he told them. "Is . . . my . . . boy . . . dead?"

Sergeant Fitzgerald looked at the priest, then back at Gene and said, "Yes."

And, "Yes-s-s-s," Father Shimon said, too, as if he had been holding his breath all this time. "Yes, Gene, yes, Peg, I'm sorry, yes-s-s-s."

⚜ ⚜ ⚜

The following excerpt comes about two-thirds into the book and shows the shift from Bryan the narrator to Bryan as a character in his own book.

⚜ ⚜ ⚜

Snow still covered the Mullens' fields in the middle of that month when a film crew from Another Mother for Peace came to La Porte City to interview and photograph the Mullens. The filmmakers had already completed their work on four other families who they felt best represented the personal anguish caused by the war. The first family's son was killed on Mother's Day. The second family's son had surrendered to federal marshals rather than serve in the Army. The third family's son was a Navy pilot spending his third year as a prisoner of war. The fourth was from a ranching family from Texas; the young father returned from Vietnam without his leg. The film released under the title *Another Family for Peace* was photographed by Joan Churchill and directed by Donald MacDonald. It was edited down to thirty minutes, the final ten minutes of which was the Mullens. To get those ten minutes, the film crew stayed four days at the Mullens' farm.

The film, photographed in black and white, opened with a long shot of the Mullens' farm taken from the field next to the stand of timber which had once held "The Old Eagle Tree." The camera held that shot until the vastness and isolation of that bleak, wintry Iowa landscape seeped in. The only sound was the barking of a neighbor's dog seemingly far away. Perhaps the most extraordinary facet of the film was how unself-conscious the Mullens were. Peg had insisted on being permitted to fix up her hair, but other than that, there was no indication that the Mullen were "acting." There was a great deal of voice-over dubbing, exterior action shots with an imposed sound track: "My reaction to the death of my son was twenty-five years of my life torn out of me," one hears Gene saying as he carries a huge bucket of feed on his shoulder to his hogs. He is calling, "Pig! Pig! Pig!" and is bundled up against the cold. "I was stunned. I couldn't see it because I had great hopes for him. He had a great future. I couldn't see why it had to happen. I felt this very strong bitterness. I couldn't accept it. My boy—it was only when they brought the body back and I was asked to view it, that I could accept it. That it was Mike . . . ." Gene has put the bucket down and is now walking over to the old plum red Farmall Michael had driven his last night. "When I went to the airport," Gene is saying as he climbs into the seat "and I escorted my boy's body back to the funeral parlor"—he presses the ignition and holds it— "I asked to have his dog tags and the military said, 'They still belong to the United States Army.'" The tractor starts, and Gene advances the spark. "I said, 'That's enough! From now on the boy is gone! And I'll bury him as my son and not as a military soldier anymore.'" Gene puts the tractor into gear and drives off. The camera shifts to the Mullens' downstairs recreation room where Peg has set up a table and is writing a letter to Senator Edward M. Kennedy.

Throughout her typing one hears her voice dubbed over saying, "I have to live with this thing. I have to make Michael's death a cause in my household. This is what I'm doing now. Michael has to have died for something! I think it's my duty to see that he did die for something."

The camera pans across the recreation room wall containing photographs of Patrick and Mary Ann Mullen, a photo duplicate of

John Dobshire's original land grant, yearbook photographs of the Mullen daughters; then the camera closes in and holds a tight shot of Michael's photograph as Peg's voice-over continues: "If my protesting of the war is that 'something,' then that's what I'll continue to do. My feeling now is a feeling of guilt. I feel I didn't do enough to enlighten my son. A mother who loses a son simply feels she didn't protect him, I suppose even though he's a man, he's twenty-five years old, you feel you still should have been in there fighting for him. A mother can't let her son go there. It isn't the 'patriotism' thing anymore. This son is yours! He's part of you! They'd have to drag him over my dead body to get him to go now...."

The final sequence was filmed at the Mount Carmel Catholic Cemetery at Eagle Center. The Mullens drive into the cemetery, stop their car and get out. It is a long shot. Gene reaches into the backseat for a snow shovel and then, with Peg wrapped up in a fur coat following slightly behind him, Gene walks up the slight hill to the grave. The wind-drifted snow has blown across Michael's flat headstone and Gene chips away at the ice with the edge of the shovel blade. There is no sound except the harsh grating of the steel shovel across the ice. Peg crosses herself, then kneels in the ice beside Michael's grave to pray. It is an awkward shot, too set-up, and Peg, shivering with cold and discomfort, stands without ever actually having looked at her son's grave. Gene is still chipping away at the ice. He kneels and wipes at the snow with his gloved hand, but a crust diagonally crossing the headstone will not come free. Gene straightens, picks up his shovel again, but before he can use it, he doubles over with grief. His shoulders shake, he buries his face in the back of his gloved hand, and Peg, seeing him weeping, lays a hand across his arm. She touches him for only a moment. Gene pulls himself together and begins shoveling again. The ice will not budge, and Gene crosses himself and prepares to leave. Peg, too, turns away from the grave but pauses and turns back. For the first time she looks at Michael's headstone. The camera is not in tight on her face, and she looks at his stone for only a second but if one stops the projector entirely so that one instant is frozen in a single frame one cannot help recognizing her expression. It is not anguish or sorrow; it is a terrible rage.

The camera follows the Mullens as they cautiously make their way down the glazed hill to their car, then it pans slowly back across the desolate Iowa landscape, back up the hill to the gravesite, and dips down for one last tight focus on the ice-locked stone:

-ael E. Mullen
-n Sept 11, 1944
-illed Feb 18, 1970
Son of Gene & Peg
-ared to ripple my pond"

(In June that year the Another Mother for Peace Committee arranged a showing of the film in an auditorium at the United States Capitol. All the Senators and Congressmen were invited to attend. The only Senators present were Senators Harold Hughes and Jack Miller of Iowa and former Senator Ernest Gruening of Alaska. Miller left before the Mullens' portion of the film was shown.)

[*Chapter 20—excerpt continues*]

On April 12, 1971, a Monday about three weeks after the Another Mother for Peace film crew had departed, I drove up John Dobshire's dirt road to meet Peg and Gene Mullen for the first time.

For two and a half years, from the fall of 1967 through the spring of 1969, my wife and I had lived surrounded by cornfields in a small white frame two-story tenant farmhouse a few miles east of Iowa City. We rented the house from the Reverend and Mrs. Louis Penningroth, whose much grander house and barns stood at the top of the rolling hill about three-quarters of a mile to our southwest. The house and barns of Mr. and Mrs. Flowery Smith, our only other visible neighbors, lay in the opposite direction, across Rural Route 5, our dirt section line road, beyond the little stand of dead timber, atop the rolling hill to our northeast. In the late summer before the corn was cut, our tenant farmhouse seemed to ride like a chip of flotsam between two deep-green giant ocean swells. In the fall, however, when the corn was down, we could climb the pony pasture behind our house to the hilltop from which we flew our kites and, holding our arms straight out from our bodies, be pointing at nothing but sky. With the exception of our two neighbors' barns, there simply wasn't anything in the way. We could see for miles down the dirt road that passed our house, follow it with our eyes over the crest of the first hill, see it reappear as a thinner stripe crossing the hill after that, still thinner crossing the hill after that and the one after that, like the road in a children's book. A children's book, exactly. We were very happy in Iowa. Life on that farm seemed pastoral, almost too good to be true.

In April, 1969, the month before we left Iowa to return East, President Nixon visiting Vietnam told some American ground troops about to go out on patrol, "I think history will record that this may have been one of

America's finest hours because we took a difficult job and we succeeded." How was one to respond to that? Write another angry letter? March in another antiwar parade? To be honest, I didn't do a thing.

Iowa was a respite from that sort of activity; the crises in the rest of the world didn't seem so urgent there. Iowa was a return to the quiet tree-lined town streets of old *Saturday Evening Post* covers, of newspapers cast upon one's lawn, state fairs, soda pops, of being neighborly. The rest of America has always had a bemused, somewhat patronizing attitude toward Iowa. Perhaps this is because the state's ambience suggests the nineteenth century more than the twentieth. The majority of Iowa's 95.5 percent white population still lives in small towns or on farms. There are no large military installations in Iowa; Collins Radio in Cedar Rapids is practically the state's only industry linked with defense. Agriculture continues to be its primary business. Most Iowans depend directly or indirectly on farming for their livelihood, just as their ancestors did at the turn of the century. The eleven o'clock news is broadcast at ten o'clock Central Time so early-rising farmers can get their sleep.

While I was living there, I believed Iowa to be at least ten years behind the tensions, the conflicts, the polarizations of a California or a New York. I was wrong, of course. The 1968 Chicago Democratic Convention with its riots, tear gas, police clubs and sellouts changed all that—changed it for many of the younger generation at any rate.

I was teaching at the University of Iowa's Writers Workshop, and a coed in one of my classes went to the Chicago convention to assist in Senator McCarthy's presidential campaign. She was the daughter of a central Iowa farmer and not an especially promising student; she would write extremely tense and anxious papers filled with "hences" and "thuses," but she was an exceptionally hard worker and terribly nice. Whenever we would throw a Sunday kite-flying party, she would show up with more food than she could possibly afford. And she would arrive later than the others because she would have attended church services and have had to return to her dormitory to change. After our first class following the Chicago convention she said she wanted to talk to me about what had taken place. We walked down to my office, and she took a seat opposite my desk. "Well," she said, taking a deep breath, "we arrived there in the afternoon . . . " and that's all she said. She burst into tears, and each time she would try to speak, her words would emerge as cries instead. She would take another deep breath, swallow hard, shake her head and try again. For at least five minutes she sat across from me gasping for breath, her great shoulders heaving, tears coursing down her cheeks, fingers shredding the Kleenex tissues I had passed. Finally she pulled herself together and in a low, wounded voice said, "Oh, those sons of bitches! Those dirty sons of bitches!" and got up and left. What more could she say? What could any of us say?

During my three years in Iowa, 33,384 Americans had died in Vietnam; another 112,110 had been wounded. What could any of us do?

⚜ ⚜ ⚜

Bryan acknowledged that he used Truman Capote's *In Cold Blood* as a model while writing *Friendly Fire.* Both books begin with descriptions of the countryside and reveal the deaths that inspired the books.[4] One then reads to watch "how" things happen or see "how" they turn out.

But *Fire* is structured differently from *In Cold Blood.* It has three distinct parts, two of which are demarcated only by a change in point of view, from third person to first. The three parts are the story of the Mullens' struggle with the death of their son and the changes his death wrought on them; a smaller segment in which Bryan appears in the first person and tells the Mullens what he learned; and then a final section, which is not presented as a chapter but merely titled "The Mission."

By the end of the opening chapter, two of the major facts of the story have been presented: Michael Eugene Mullen has been killed in Vietnam and a year later his mother was being watched by the FBI. Bryan saw the story as consisting of what happened to Michael Mullen's parents after his death and the impact of the war on the United States. He realized that no one would want to read such a book, but that if he constructed the story in the form of a mystery people would read it. The mystery, then, was finding out how Michael died. But readers don't realize until they have finished about two-thirds of the book that the book is not about how Michael died, but rather about how his death affected his parents. At that point, Bryan told an interviewer, the readers are hooked. "The characters, Peg and Gene, are so strong that you have to find out what happened to them, so you have to keep reading it."[5]

Friendly Fire is part reconstruction, part firsthand reporting—
"a diligently researched and brilliantly reconstructed account of
bereavement and its aftermath," John Breslin wrote.[6] In the
book's first sentence, in an author's note reminiscent of the note
that accompanied *In Cold Blood*, Bryan explains that the book is
based on firsthand observation, historical texts, official records,
correspondence, journals, and tape-recorded interviews, and that
the people interviewed reviewed transcripts of the interviews to
check their accuracy.[7] Bryan explains that he confirmed conversations, and because of that, felt comfortable reconstructing
dialogue. Corroboration came from third parties who reconstructed conversations that Peg and Gene had had. Notes by Peg
Mullen and "the consistency of details as recalled" were also
useful to Bryan.

Various critics rated *Friendly Fire* as one of the best works
of nonfiction published in 1976.[8] *Washington Post* television
critic Tom Shales said: "There have been significant books
about Vietnam—perhaps none more brilliant and troubling than
Bryan's."[9]

By the time ABC-TV's movie version of *Friendly Fire* aired in
1979, drawing a viewing audience of 64 million, the book had
sold only 17,500 copies in cloth. Bryan said years later: "I always
had the hope that it would be a television show. That was how I
knew people would be moved by the story. . . . People would sit
down with their beers and slog through it, and bit by bit they
would see what had happened."[10]

Nearly a decade after *Friendly Fire* was published, Bryan
reflected on Vietnam literature in an essay in *Harper's*. He stated
that Vietnam literature focused on more than form, that while
the topic might be something chaotic or ambiguous, the real aim
was "to make sense of the experience," to make it comprehensible
for the writer, who was then telling the reader, *"This* is for the
record."[11] Bryan said the book grew out of "a sense of frustration
about the war."[12] After seeing the stories *New York Times* reporter
Seymour Hersh had done on the My Lai massacre,[13] Bryan
thought: "Boy, I can really bring the Army to its knees."[14] But it
did not work out quite that way.

"He soon found himself recording not the neat political
morality play he thought he had discovered but a frantic and

unsettling psychodrama," Amanda Heller wrote.[15] She praised Bryan for not softening the melodramatic account and for showing that Peg and Gene Mullen were casualties of the Vietnam War as surely as their son was.

After Bryan tells the Mullens how their son died, he issues this disclaimer: "I never wanted to be in this book. I had intended to be a journalist: unbiased, dispassionate, receptive to all sides." Instead, he admits, he adopted the technique of the novelist, not the journalist, and it led him to participate and include himself. But like others, notably Susan Sheehan, Hunter Thompson and Tom Wolfe, Bryan also had to draw a line. He said that he did resist the Mullens' efforts to have him stay in their house. "I was inundated by the intensity of their emotion; it was exhausting."[16]

A comparison can be made between *Friendly Fire* and Joe McGinniss's *Fatal Vision*, a controversial book in which McGinniss began believing one thing about the murder of an Army doctor's wife and two daughters but ended up deciding that the doctor, who was paying McGinniss to write his story, committed the crime. Bryan himself, who was first paid by *The New Yorker*, made the comparison. "Suddenly you become a character in the story. . . . By the time of the Bryan character's appearance, I think that the reader wants to know what the hell is going on."[17]

In addition to adopting the techniques of the novelist rather than the journalist, Bryan felt the need to render, not the direct quotations typical of journalism, but dialogue and conversations, to show people interacting. For this approach, Bryan saluted the influence of his late stepfather, the novelist John O'Hara, whom he considers a model writer of dialogue."[18]

In showing the Mullens' increasing doubt about how their son died and their growing impatience with what they perceive to be the unresponsiveness of various government officials, Bryan tells how Peg and Gene Mullen refused to be reconciled to the ambiguities of their son's death and how their refusal changed them. Subsequently, Bryan's attitude regarding the circumstances of Michael's death and his feelings toward Peg and Gene changed. Bryan shows the change in the Mullens (from patriots to doubters) and gradually reveals the change in himself (from doubter to believer). Christopher Lehmann-Haupt praised Bryan for carefully interweaving two opposing points of view chronologically and in a way that "gradually weans us from one attitude to the other by showing us how the Mullens grew increasing obsessed with their antiwar mission and how they eventually lost touch with reality."[19] Bryan credited Capote with helping resolve the varying points of view about the same situation. He noted that Capote, rather than blending conflicting accounts, would present them in successive chapters—an approach Bryan followed.[20] Robert Sherrill observed that Bryan "tended himself to be more tolerant, to see both sides,"[21] which, of course enables the reader to see both sides.

Bryan as investigative journalist enters the story when he attempts to resolve the question of how Michael Mullen died. As he says both in the author's note at the book's beginning and in Chapter 25, where he tells the Mullens what he believes is the truth, Bryan interviewed as many of the soldiers in Michael's unit as he could and even read the transcript of a court-martial for one of them. (The court-martial was unrelated to Michael Mullen's death.) He also interviewed Michael's battalion commander, his company commander, the senior medic, the assistant machine gunner (one of Michael's friends), the court-martialed soldier, and a rifleman who lost his leg in the explosion from the same shell that killed Michael. Independently, each corroborated the details of the friendly fire that caused Michael's death, Bryan notes. All of them had been present at the incident. Bryan, after interviewing them, was convinced that the battalion commander, H. Norman Schwarzkopf,* had told the Mullens the truth. At that point, Bryan writes, he had reached the story's end.[22]

Bryan's appearance in *Friendly Fire* comes without warning, with only the turn of a page (see excerpt). He transforms from Bryan the author to Bryan the investigator, or from Bryan the narrator, to Bryan the character as he attempts to learn how Michael Mullen died. The story line changes from the third person and the voices of Peg and Gene Mullen to the first person of Bryan and the mixed voices of Bryan and the Mullens. But

---

*Battalion commander H. Norman Schwarzkopf was later promoted to general. In 1990, he directed the war effort in the Persian Gulf called "Desert Storm." After Schwarzkopf retired, Bryan was among those considered to ghost-write the general's memoirs.

once the shock of the switch ends, the reader begins to appreciate what Bryan has done. He did not let the story rest until he could divine his best notion of the truth.

The reviews of *Friendly Fire* were mixed. Sherrill saw the journalist in Bryan, but also commented about the change that occurred in Bryan's attitude toward the Mullens when they refused to accept his findings. "Suddenly, he became fed up with them."[23] Sherrill generally approved of *Friendly Fire*, but Diane Johnson was less satisfied. Her complaint stemmed from the fact that she had read the book in its original three-part serial in *The New Yorker* and noticed a sharp contrast between the second and third parts. Where Bryan entered the story, she thought the tone shifted from sympathy to condescension as he explained his version of Michael's death.[24] But we should also give Bryan credit for sharing his change.

But was the shift caused only by the content? Sherrill suggested that the serialization and typography of *The New Yorker* diminished the story. "This is one tale," he wrote, "that should not be chopped into pieces separated by week intervals." For Jane Howard, it was the content that created the feeling of change. She wrote that the series took her from weeping to cheering, cheering because *Friendly Fire* "is a work of passionate energy."[25] Other reviewers wrote of the book's "tug of compassion,"[26] "emotional impact,"[27] "visceral power,"[28] and "emotional appeal."[29]

In questioning Bryan's methods, Johnson said she felt readers would find themselves dissatisfied, even though they would accept Bryan's conclusions. She attributed the problem to New Journalism, in which facts are presented like fiction: "The reader experiences such accounts as both truth and fiction, that is, as adequate accounts of the real world, but also as having certain formal qualities we expect in art."[30]

Sherrill and Johnson challenged Bryan's statement that he had done the maximum a human could to learn the truth. Sherrill was appalled that Bryan changed heroes, from the Mullens to Michael Mullen's battalion commander. Johnson questioned whether Bryan had sought out every document he could and pointed out the self-interest of some of those interviewed. Referring to the section titled "The Mission," which Johnson considered fiction,[31] Bryan said he had interviewed various people present the night of Michael's death, and received separate confirmation of the events of that night. Bryan wrote that he sent each of them a copy of "The Mission" section of the book. He said he received responses indicating that each person knew a part of the story but that only Bryan, through his investigation, had the entire story.[32] Perhaps Bryan could be criticized for not seeking yet one more document. But given that Sherrill and Johnson are both skeptical of Bryan's government sources to begin with, one wonders how another official document would assuage their doubts.

The author wanted to write the best possible record of what the government had done. In 1992 he said the book has an underlying sense of outrage. "God damn it! they can't do this to this country," he said. "Somebody's got to do something about it. Writing the book seemed to be the only way I could do anything."[33]

ENDNOTES

1. C. D. B. Bryan, *Friendly Fire* (New York: Putnam, 1976), 276–77.
2. Eric James Schroeder, *Vietnam, We've All Been There: Interviews with American Writers* (Westport, Conn.: Praeger, 1992), 84.
3. Jane Howard, "An American Tragedy," *Washington Post Book World,* 2 May 1976, 5.
4. Schroeder, *Vietnam,* 76.
5. Quoted in Jean W. Ross, in *Contemporary Authors,* New Revision Series vol. 13, ed. Linda Metzger (Detroit, Mich.: Gale Research, 1984), 85.
6. John B. Breslin, "Vietnam Legacy," *America,* 24 September 1976, 173.
7. Bryan, *Friendly Fire,* ix.
8. For example, see Walter Clemons, "Lest We Forget," *Newsweek,* 12 January 1977, 67. Clemons also praises *Born on the Fourth of July* by Ron Kovic and *Winners and Losers* by Gloria Emerson.
9. Tom Shales, "'Friendly Fire' with Power to Penetrate," *Washington Post,* 22 April 1979, p. K1.
10. Quoted in Schroeder, *Vietnam,* 85–86.
11. C. D. B. Bryan, "Barely Suppressed Screams: Getting a bead on Vietnam war literature," *Harper's,* June 1984, 69–70.
12. Schroeder, *Vietnam,* 74.
13. Hersh originally broke the story in the *New York Times.* Two good recapitulations by Hersh are *My Lai 4: A Report on the Massacre and*

its Aftermath (New York: Random House, 1970) and *Cover-Up : The Army's Secret Investigation of the Massacre at My Lai 4* (New York: Random House, 1972).

14. Quoted in Schroeder, *Vietnam,* 75.
15. Amanda Heller, "Short Reviews," *Atlantic,* 1 June 1976, 93.
16. Quoted in Robert Dahlin, "Story Behind the Book," *Publishers Weekly,* 17 May 1976, 40.
17. Quoted in Schroeder, *Vietnam,* 79.
18. Quoted in Ross, *Contemporary Authors,* 83.
19. Christopher Lehmann-Haupt, "Why We're Out of Vietnam," *New York Times,* 12 May 1976, 39.
20. Quoted in Schroeder, *Vietnam,* 76.
21. Robert Sherrill, "Friendly Fire," *New York Times Book Review,* 9 May 1976, 2.
22. Bryan, *Friendly Fire,* 365.
23. Sherrill, "Friendly Fire," 2.
24. Diane Johnson. "True Patriots," *New York Review of Books,* 5 August 1976, 42.
25. Howard, American Tragedy," 5.
26. Peter Gardner, "New Books," *Saturday Review,* 15 May 1976, 34.
27. "Literature," *Booklist,* 1 May 1976, 1236.
28. "Nonfiction," *Publishers Weekly,* 1 March 1976, 93.
29. Mark Stevens, "Paradox of 'Friendly Fire'," *Christian Science Monitor,* 11 June 1976, p. 27.
30. Johnson, "True Patriots," 42.
31. Ibid., 43.
32. Schroeder, *Vietnam,* 86.
33. Schroeder, *Vietnam,* 85, 87.

Chapter 15

❧

Dispatches

I n some ways, it was a journalist's dream assignment: Go to Vietnam and file stories at your leisure. Michael Herr arrived in Vietnam in 1967 on assignment for *Esquire* magazine. The younger soldiers, all conscripted, could not fathom why journalists were there. "You mean you guys *volunteer* to come over here?" one asked.[1] Some of them wanted to know whether the correspondent for *Esquire* was going to write about how the soldiers dressed.[2] And when Herr interviewed the general in charge, William Westmoreland asked whether Herr was going to do "humoristical" pieces.[3]

He did not. Instead he filed dispatches that appeared in *Esquire* and then *New American Review* and *Rolling Stone* as excerpts from the book to come.[4] But the book, announced as forthcoming in 1969, did not come together as quickly as everyone had expected. After two years of reshaping his dispatches, he suffered from writer's block, then went into a five-year funk during which he could not write. "I knew I wasn't the person to bring off that book," he told Joyce Wadler of the *Washington Post*.[5]

But ten years after he left Vietnam, he published *Dispatches*. The book, Maria S. Bonn wrote, has come "to enjoy a privileged place in the Vietnam War canon."[6] Its discursive form has been compared to a poem by Allen Ginsberg.[7] In 1979, it was adapted by Elizabeth Swados as a "rock-war musical."[8] The book has been compared with Joseph Conrad's *Heart of Darkness*, which influenced *Apocalypse Now*, a film for which Herr wrote the narration. Herr was also one of the writers for the screenplay *Full*

Metal Jacket, another film about the Vietnam war, with Stanley Kubrick and Gustav Hasford.

The following excerpt comes from the dispatch titled "Khe Sanh," named for a Marine base. It contains several vulgarities which, surprisingly for *Esquire,* were not printed in full when originally published, but appeared in the print equivalent of a f— bleep in broadcast media.

⚜ ⚜ ⚜

I was walking around by myself in the 1st Battalion area. It was before eight in the morning, and as I walked I could hear someone walking behind me, singing. At first I couldn't hear what it was, only that it was a single short phrase being sung over and over at short intervals, and that every time someone else would laugh and tell the singer to shut up. I slowed down and let them catch up.

"'I'd rather be an Oscar Mayer weiner,'" the voice sang. It sounded very plaintive and lonely.

Of course I turned around. There were two of them, one a big Negro with a full mustache that drooped over the corners of his mouth, a mean, signifying mustache that would have worked if only there had been the smallest trace of meanness anywhere on his face. He was at least six-three and quarterback thick. He was carrying an AK-47. The other Marine was white, and if I'd seen him first from the back I would have said that he was eleven years old. The Marines must have a height requirement; whatever it is, I don't see how he made it. Age is one thing, but how do you lie about your height? He'd been doing the singing, and he was laughing now because he'd made me turn around. His name was Mayhew, it was written out in enormous red letters across the front of his helmet: MAYHEW— *You'd better believe it!* I'd been walking with my flak jacket open, a stupid thing to do even on this morning, and they could see the stitched tag above my left breast pocket with the name of my magazine written on it.

"Correspondent?" the Negro said.

Mayhew just laughed. "'I'd-a rather be—a Oscar Mayer . . . weenieeee,'" he sang. "You can write that, man, tell 'em all I said so."

"Don't pay no attention to him," the Negro said. "That's Mayhew. He's a crazy fucker, ain't you, Mayhew?"

"I sure hope so," Mayhew said. "'I'd rather be a Oscar Mayer weiner. . . .'"

He was young, nineteen, he later told me, and he was trying to grow a mustache. His only luck with it so far was a few sparse, transparent blond clumps set at odd intervals across his upper lip, and you couldn't see that unless the light was right. The Negro was called Day Tripper. It was on his helmet, along with DETROIT CITY. And on the back, where most guys just listed the months of their tours, he had carefully drawn a full calendar where each day served was marked off with a neat X. They were both from Hotel Company of the 2nd Battalion, which was dug in along the northern perimeter, but they were taking advantage of the day to visit a friend of theirs, a mortar man with 1/26.*

"The lieutenant ever hear 'bout this, he know what to do," Day Tripper said.

"Fuck the lieutenant," Mayhew said. "You remember from before he ain't wrapped too tight."

"Well, he wrapped tight enough to tear you a new asshole."

"Now what's he gonna do to me? Send me to Vietnam?"

We walked past the battalion CP, piled five feet high with sandbags, and then we reached a giant ring of sandbagging, the mortar pit, and climbed down. In the center was a large four-oh-deuce mortar piece, and the inside of the pit was stacked completely around with ammunition, piled from the ground to just below the sandbags. A Marine was stretched out in the dust with a war comic spread over his face.

"Hey, where's Evans?" Mayhew said. "You know a guy named Evans?"

The Marine took the comic off of his face and looked up. He'd been asleep.

"Shit," he said. "I thought you was the Old Man for a second. Beg your pardon."

"We're looking for this guy Evans," Mayhew said. "You know him?"

"I—uh—no, I don't guess so. I'm pretty new."

He looked it. He was the kind of kid that would go into the high-school gym alone and shoot baskets for the half-hour before the basketball team took it over for practice, not good enough yet for the team but determined.

"The rest of the crew'll be down here right away. You can wait if you want." He looked at all the rounds. "It's probably not too cool," he said, smiling. "But you can if you want."

---

*1st Battalion, 26th Marines. R.T.B.

Mayhew unbuttoned one of the pockets in the leg of his fatigues and took out a can of crackers and Cheddar-cheese spread. He took the P-38 opener from a band around his helmet and sat down.

"Might as well eat some shit while we wait. You get hungry, it ain't so bad. I'd give my left ball for a can of fruit now."

I always scrounged fruit from rear areas to bring forward, and I had some in my pack. "What kind do you like?" I asked.

"Any kind's good," he said. "Fruit cocktail's really good."

"No, man," Day Tripper said. "Peaches, baby, peaches. All that syrup. Now that's some good shit."

"There you go, Mayhew," I said, tossing him a fruit cocktail. I gave a can of peaches to Day Tripper and kept a can for myself.

We talked while we ate. Mayhew told me about his father, who "got greased in Korea," and about his mother, who worked in a department store in Kansas City. Then he started to tell about Day Tripper, who got his name because he was afraid of the night—not the dark, but the night—and who didn't mind who knew it. There wasn't anything he wouldn't do during daylight, but if there was any way at all to fix it he liked to be deep in his bunker by nightfall. He was always volunteering for the more dangerous daylight patrols, just to make sure he got in by dusk. (This was before daylight patrols, in fact almost all patrols around Khe Sanh, were discontinued.) There were a lot of white guys, especially junior officers trying to be cool, who were always coming on to Day Tripper about his hometown, calling it Dodge City or Motown and laughing. ("Why they think somethin's special about Detroit?" he said. "Ain't nothin' special, ain't nothin' so funny, neither.") He was a big bad spade gone wrong somehow, and no matter how mean he tried to look something constantly gentle showed. He told me he knew guys from Detroit who were taking mortars back, breaking them down so that each one could get a piece into his duffel and then reassembling them when they got together back on the block. "You see that four-oh-deuce?" he said. "Now, that'll take out a police station for you. I don't need all that hassle. But maybe nex' year I gonna need it."

Like every American in Vietnam, he had his obsession with Time. (No one ever talked about When-this-lousy-war-is-over. Only "How much time you got?") The degree of Day Tripper's obsession, compared with most of the others, could be seen in the calendar on his helmet. No metaphysician ever studied Time the way he did, its components and implications, its per-second per seconds, its shadings and movement. The Space-Time continuum, Time-as-Matter, Augustinian Time: all of that would have been a piece of cake to Day Tripper, whose brain cells were arranged like jewels in the finest chronometer. He had assumed that correspondents in Vietnam had to be there. When he learned that I had asked to come here he almost let the peaches drop to the ground.

"Lemmee . . . lemmee jus' hang on that a minute," he said. "You mean you don' have to be here? An' you're here?"

I nodded.

"Well, they gotta be payin' you some tough bread."

"You'd get depressed if I told you."

He shook his head.

"I mean, they ain' got the bread that'd get me here if I didn' have t' be here."

"Horse crap," Mayhew said. "Day Tripper loves it. He's short now, but he's comin' back, ain't you, Day Tripper?"

"Shit, my momma'll come over here and pull a tour before I fuckin' come back."

Four more Marines dropped into the pit.

"Where's Evans?" Mayhew demanded. "Any of you guys know Evans?"

One of the mortar men came over.

"Evans is over in Danang," he said. "He caught a little shit the other night."

"That right?" Mayhew said. "Evans get wounded?"

"He hurt bad?" Day Tripper asked.

"Not bad enough," the mortar man said, laughing. "He'll be back in ten days. Just some stuff in the legs."

"He's real lucky," another one said. "Same round got him killed a guy."

"Yeah," someone said. "Greene got killed." He wasn't talking to us, but to the crew, who knew it already. "Remember Greene?" Everyone nodded.

"Wow, Greene," he said. "Greene was all fixed to get out. He's jerkin' off thirty times a day, that fuckin' guy, and they's all set to give him a medical. And out."

"That's no shit," the other one said. "Thirty times a day. Disgusting, man. That sombitch had come all over his pants, that fuckin' Greene. He was waitin' outside to see the major about gettin' sent home, an' the major comes out to find him an' he's just sittin' there jerkin' off. Then he gets blown away the night before."

"Well," Day Tripper said quietly to Mayhew, "see what happens if you jerk off?"

❧ ❧ ❧

Dispatches, which is a collection of Herr's reportage rather than a single narrative, seems to be a book that reviewers either loved or hated. Then there were the reviewers who imbued it with political meaning weighted toward their view of the Vietnam War. If they supported the war, Herr had written anti-war propaganda; if they opposed the war, Herr had glorified the war.

What Herr wrote was what he saw, which he translated into a prose that reflected the drug and rock-music tone of the period. He did not write the World War II prose of heroic soldiers but rather, as Raymond Sokolov put it, "in the style of the place and the time, cutting his sentences very close to the bone."[9] David Wyatt said that "the distinctive rhythm of Herr's prose is its breathlessness."[10] Thomas Myers said Herr described a Vietnam "that seems the product of the combined imaginative resources of Lewis Carroll, Samuel Coleridge, and the most fearsome, uncontrolled acid dream."[11] In fact, Herr announces early in the book that in Saigon he went to sleep stoned "so I almost always lost my dreams, probably just as well, sock in deep and dim under that information and get whatever rest you could, wake up tapped of all images but the ones remembered from the day or the week before, with only the taste of a bad dream in your mouth like you'd been chewing on a roll of dirty old pennies in your sleep."[12]

No wonder Sokolov said the writing grew "directly out of the souped-up, seemingly offhand, freaked-out writing Tom Wolfe was up to at the same time."[13] John Hellmann added Norman Mailer and Hunter S. Thompson to the list of progenitors.[14] Hellmann recognized that writing about the war called for a different literary strategy and praised Herr for engaging "his subject directly and innovatively."[15] Other reviewers, including William Plummer,[16] an anonymous reviewer in the *Virginia Quarterly Review,*[17] Kenneth F. Kister,[18] and Benjamin DeMott,[19] called *Dispatches* the best or one of the best books about the Vietnam War. DeMott pronounced it "exceptionally authoritative."

But the writing style that some reviewers praised, others criticized. Roger Sale said some of the writing was vivid, "but of a sort that conforms all too closely to our idea of what a very young writer in Vietnam might write."[20] An anonymous *Harper's* reviewer said the book's power and purity were "flawed only when Herr uses the war as an acid-rock background album to a half-mocking, half-aggrandizing study of his own love-hate fascination with the war" and his "macho-correspondent role."[21] Elizabeth Pochoda complained that the book was "built around the wearisome convention of the acid trip," although she also acknowledged in the same sentence that the convention was used carefully "so that the scenes described, the stories told and people encountered" did not come off as the writer's experiences but as the result of the writer "tapping into a general psychosis."[22]

Pochoda's analysis may be the most insightful of all. Even though drugs and rock music were part of the youthful scene in the United States at the time, finding them in a war zone was so unexpected that writing about them was part of the story. Herr recalls in one story that when he was on a patrol and pinned down behind a wall in a rice paddy, he suddenly "heard an electronic guitar shooting right up in my ear."[23] A soldier next to him had pulled out his portable tape player and was listening to Jimi Hendrix. Meanwhile, in the United States, Hunter Thompson reports, members of an antisocial and somewhat lawless motorcycle club called the Hell's Angels were stomping anti-war protestors and offering to serve behind the lines in Vietnam as "a crack group of trained gorrillas [*sic*]."[24] Vietnam was that kind of war.

Pearl Bell said the writing was "drenched in the drug-rock argot of the age." She compared reading the book to "seeing a rock movie with such a deafening sound track" that the audience cannot hear the dialogue, "and maybe you aren't supposed to want to hear it." She went on to acknowledge that Herr did want to be heard and that while his coverage was idiosyncratic journalism, the book was a literary success."[25] Matthew C. Stewart made a similar observation when he observed that reading *Dispatches* was demanding because it wasn't so much a book of facts, opinions and interpretations—which readers could quarrel with—but rather because it required "a reader willing to collaborate in a truth revealed more often than not in pieces, fits and starts, by accumulation and repetition, by variations on themes."[26] Evelyn Cobley praised the book's "documentary dimension," which she said was "squarely located in the narrator's personal honesty and not in the facts speaking for themselves."[27]

And, in fact, "the facts" are part of the problem. Not everyone in the articles and the book really existed. Herr admitted that some of the people were composites—that is, based on several different people. The person whom Herr called Mayhew, for example, "was mostly Mayhew but in real life he wasn't called Mayhew."[28]

Herr sometimes thought of *Dispatches* as a novel and other times as a distillation.[29] In other words, even though some people consider the book journalism, the author rightly does not, and it is probably best described in Cobley's words as "an imaginative recreation of Vietnam's claustrophobic mental and physical landscape."[30] In another context, Dan Wakefield has said imaginative reporting did not mean the author distorted facts but "brought out the sights, sounds, and feel surrounding those facts, and connected them by comparison with other facts of history, society, and literature in an artistic manner" that added depth to the facts.[31] The same point can be made about *Dispatches*.

Political opinion on the book was also divided. Although Paul Gray said that Herr "preaches no sermons, draws no morals, enters no ideological disputes," he also noted that Herr's accounts of United States delusion could anger ex-hawks and that his failure to label the fighting as "war crimes" could anger doves.[32] One hawk, Joseph A. Rehyansky, liked parts of the book but complained about "the endless pages of pointless, dreary intellectualizing, of pompous introspection, of left-wing agit-prop."[33] Rehyansky ended his review by invoking the name of a fabled World War II correspondent, Ernie Pyle, who, he said, went to war because he loved his country and the men he wrote about.[34] That remark overstates Pyle's nobility and misunderstands the difference between World War II and Vietnam, however. *Dispatches* and Herr should not be compared with other wars' books and writers. As Malcolm W. Browne, himself a war correspondent, wrote: "Vietnam was a much longer war than World War II, much smaller in every dimension and much less convincing as a vehicle for journalistic team playing."[35]

As Dale W. Jones put it, the book is "an interpretation of what Herr experienced in Vietnam. It is not exactly history; it is not exactly fiction either."[36] (In later years it was called a memoir.) Wyatt noted that Herr ultimately transformed from journalist to survivor; Herr wrote that he "slid over to the wrong end of the story, propped up behind some sandbags . . . firing cover for a four-man reaction team trying to get back in."[37] Hunter Thompson, the ultimate joiner, the man who rode with the Hell's Angels, to maintain his distance didn't buy a Harley, didn't stomp anyone, didn't participate in a gang-rape. But Herr the journalist became, in Herr's words, "a shooter";* he joined the people he was writing about. James Fenton, citing the shooting incident, condemned Herr because he seemed to enjoy the war.[38] Rehyansky referred to Herr as a bored voyeur.

Apparently, though, life in Vietnam was not black and white, as John Balaban recounts in his memoir *Remembering Heaven's Face*. Balaban, a Quaker and conscientious objector who was doing alternative service in Vietnam about the same time Herr was there, writes that he too carried arms at one time after a non-combatant colleague had been murdered and recalls a feeling of "wonderful relief" at having a weapon.[39] Survival in Vietnam was a grayer area than some cared to admit.

Herr's survival, Wyatt said, led him to "question the value and purpose of journalism as a form."[40] Put another way, Herr found a different form—something other than the "uni-prose"[41] (to use Herr's word) of news magazines and newspapers—to report on the Vietnam War. Herr wrote in a voice, Myers said, "that allows the historian both to approximate in language the internal rhythms of the war and to demonstrate how those rhythms were lost under the increasing volume of the official mythic voices attempting to assert their resounding American epic by sheer force of will."[42] C. D. B. Bryan said the war required not only new techniques of fighting, but also of writing—"an entirely new language, imagery and style were needed so that we could under-stand and feel."[43] Many other reviewers made similar points. *Dispatches* is not the objective journalism, the uni-prose, some would expect to come from a war correspondent. Instead, Herr took advantage of the non-deadline nature of the assignment and reported on the rhythms of Americans at war.

---

*Not to be confused with a photographer.

ENDNOTES

1. Michael Herr, *Dispatches* (New York: Knopf, 1978), 201.
2. Ibid., 193.
3. Ibid., 217.
4. See "Hell Sucks," *Esquire*, August 1968; "Illumination Rounds," *New American Review*, August 1969; "Khesanh," *Esquire*, September 1969; "Conclusion at Khesanh," *Esquire*, October 1969; "The War Correspondent: A Reappraisal," *Esquire*, April 1970; "High on War," *Esquire*, January 1977; and "LZ Loon," *Rolling Stone*, 3 November 1977.
5. Joyce Wadler, "Dispatches: Michael Herr's Stark Account of Terror," *Washington Post*, 4 November 1977, D1.
6. Maria S. Bonn, "The Lust of the Eye: Michael Herr, Glorida Emerson and the Art of Observation," *Papers on Language and Literature* 29:1 (Winter 1993), 29.
7. David R. Jarraway, "'Standing by His Word': The Politics of Allen Ginsberg's Vietnam 'Vortex'," *Journal of American Culture* 16:3 (Fall 1993), 81.
8. James Lardner, "Theatric Cousin of 'Dispatches': Twice Removed," *Washington Post*, 19 April 1979, p. B15.
9. Raymond Sokolov, "Heart of Darkness," *Newsweek*, 14 November 1977, 104.
10. David Wyatt, *Out of the Sixties: Storytelling and the Vietnam Generation* (Cambridge, Mass.: Cambridge University Press, 1993), 186.
11. Thomas Myers, *American Prose Literature: 20th Century* (New York: Oxford University Press, 1988), 152.
12. Herr, *Dispatches*, 33.
13. Sokolov, "Heart of Darkness," 102.
14. John Hellmann, *Fables of Fact: The New Journalism as New Fiction* (Urbana: University of Illinois Press, 1981), 132.
15. Ibid., 127.
16. William Plummer, "Ecstasy and Death," *Saturday Review*, 7 January 1978, 36–38.
17. "Notes on Current Books," *Virginia Quarterly Review* 54:2, Spring 1978, 63.
18. Kenneth F. Kister, "Book Reviews," *Library Journal*, 1 November 1977, 2249–50.
19. Benjamin DeMott, "Two Reporters: At Peace and War," *Atlantic*, January 1978, 91–93.
20. Roger Sale, "Hurled into Vietnam," *New York Review of Books*, 8 December 1977, 34.
21. "Books," *Harper's*, December 1977, 109.

22. Elizabeth Pochoda, "Vietnam, We've All Been There," *Nation*, 25 March 1978, 345.

23. Herr, *Dispatches*, 181.

24. Hunter Thompson, *Hell's Angels*, (New York: Ballantine, 1966), 313–23.

25. Pearl K. Bell, "Writing About Vietnam," *Commentary*, October 1978, 77.

26. Matthew C. Stewart, "Style in *Dispatches:* Heteroglossia and Michael Herr's Break with Conventional Journalism," in *America Rediscovered: Critical Essays on Literature and Film of the Vietnam War*, ed. Owen W. Gilman, Jr., and Lorrie Smith (New York: Garland, 1990), 190.

27. Evelyn Cobley, "Narrating the Facts of War: New Journalism in Herr's *Dispatches* and Documentary Realism in First World War Novels," *Journal of Narrative Technique* 16:2 (Spring 1986), 106.

28. Quoted in Carol Polsgrove, *It Wasn't Pretty, Folks, but Didn't We Have Fun? Esquire in the Sixties* (New York: Norton, 1995), 210.

29. Ibid. (Polsgrove attributes this information to Herr.)

30. Cobley, "Narration," 109.

31. Dan Wakefield, "The Personal Voice and the Impersonal Eye," *Atlantic Monthly*, June 1966, 87.

32. Paul Gray, "Secret History," *Time*, 7 November 1977, 119–20.

33. Joseph A. Rehyansky, "A Mortal S. I. W.," *National Review*, 17 March 1978, 356.

34. Ibid., 357.

35. Malcolm W. Browne, "Notes From the Trenches," *New York Times Book Review*, 8 June 1997, 34.

36. Dale W. Jones, "The Vietnams of Michael Herr and Tim O'Brien: Tales of Disintegration and Integration," *Canadian Review of American Studies* 13:3 (1982), 309.

37. Herr, *Dispatches*, 67.

38. James Fenton, "Nostalgie de la Guerre," *New Statesman*, 7 April 1978, 464.

39. John Balaban, *Remembering Heaven's Face: A Moral Witness in Vietnam* (New York: Poseidon, 1991), 97–98.

40. Wyatt, *Out of the Sixties*," 191.

41. Herr, *Dispatches*, 212.

42. Myers, *American Prose Literature*, 149–50.

43. C. D. B. Bryan, "The Different War," *New York Times Book Review*, 20 November 1977, 1.

Chapter 16

❖

The Right Stuff

om Wolfe has a Ph.D. in American studies from Yale and a few years' experience with metropolitan newspapers. He has been called an anthropologist who writes,[1] "a unique presence in American journalism,"[2] and "a direct descendant of a classic American type—the campfire tale-spinner."[3] The tale he spins in *The Right Stuff* focuses on the original seven United States astronauts and the military aviation program that spawned them.

Wolfe said he was lucky to begin the research when he did. He told Janet Maslin of the *New York Times* that he had arrived at NASA (the National Aeronautics and Space Administration) at a time when the agency was declassifying many of its files and was eager, given the severe budget reductions it was enduring, for publicity. "It was," Wolfe told Maslin, "much easier to find out about this 15 years after the fact than it would have been at the time" because "people involved could look back analytically."[4] Wolfe also cited seven books about military aviation or the space program as helpful.

But the book did not come easily. In addition to doing a tremendous amount of research and solving "a structural problem,"[5] Wolfe was sidetracked by other writing projects. During the gestation period for *The Right Stuff*, he published *The New Journalism*, *The Painted Word*, and *Mauve Gloves and Madmen, Clutter and Vine*. Although *The Electric Kool-Aid Acid Test* had taken him only six months of concentrated writing, plus a few months for rewriting and fact checking,[6] *The Right Stuff* did not come out at Wolfe's usual quota of 1900 words a day.

The book actually appeared six years after the articles that spawned it.

Lacking a central character, Wolfe structured the book so that "each chapter . . . [was] like a short story, with the hope that if that chapter was effective, if the story was effective, then you would go on to the next one."[7] The following excerpt comes from Chapter 2, which, like the book, is titled "The Right Stuff."

❖ ❖ ❖

One fine day, after he had joined a fighter squadron, it would dawn on the young pilot exactly how the losers in the great fraternal competition were now being left behind. Which is to say, not by instructors or other superiors or by failures at prescribed levels of competence, but by death. At this point the essence of the enterprise would begin to dawn on him. Slowly, step by step, the ante had been raised until he was now involved in what was surely the grimmest and grandest gamble of manhood. Being a fighter pilot—for that matter, simply taking off in a single-engine jet fighter of the Century series, such as an F-102, or any of the military's other marvelous bricks with fins on them—presented a man, on a perfectly sunny day, with more ways to get himself killed than his wife and children could imagine in their wildest fears. If he was barreling down the runway at two hundred miles an hour, completing the takeoff run, and the board started lighting up red, should he (a) abort the takeoff (and try to wrestle with the monster, which was gorged with jet fuel, out in the sand beyond the end of the runway) or (b) eject (and hope that the goddamned human cannonball trick works at zero altitude and he doesn't shatter an elbow or a kneecap on the way out) or (c) continue the takeoff and deal with the problem aloft (knowing full well that the ship may be on fire and therefore seconds away from exploding)? He would have one second to sort out the options and act, and this kind of little workaday decision came up all the time. Occasionally a man would look coldly at the binary problem he was now confronting every day—Right Stuff/Death—and decide it wasn't worth it and voluntarily shift over to transports or reconnaissance or whatever. And his comrades would wonder, for a day or so, what evil virus had invaded his soul . . . as they left him behind. More often, however, the reverse would happen. Some college graduate would enter Navy aviation through the Reserves, simply as an alternative to the Army draft, fully intending to return to civilian life, to some waiting profession or family business; would become involved in the obsessive business of ascending the ziggurat pyramid of flying; and, at the end of his enlistment, would astound everyone back home and very likely himself as well by signing up for another one. What on earth got into him? He couldn't explain it. After all, the very words for it had been amputated. A Navy study showed that two-thirds of the fighter pilots who were rated in the top rungs of their groups—i.e., the hottest young pilots—reenlisted when the time came, and practically all were college graduates. By this point, a young fighter jock was like the preacher in *Moby Dick* who climbs up into the pulpit on a rope ladder and then pulls the ladder up behind him; except the pilot could not use the words necessary to express the vital lessons. Civilian life, and even home and hearth, now seemed not only far away but far *below*, back down many levels of the pyramid of the right stuff.

A fighter pilot soon found he wanted to associate only with other fighter pilots. Who else could understand the nature of the little proposition (right stuff/death) they were all dealing with? And what other subject could compare with it? It was riveting! To talk about it in so many words was forbidden, of course. The very words *death, danger, bravery, fear* were not to be uttered except in the occasional specific instance or for ironic effect. Nevertheless, the subject could be adumbrated in *code* or *by example*. Hence the endless evenings of pilots huddled together talking about flying. On these long and drunken evenings (the bane of their family life) certain theorems would be propounded and demonstrated—and all by code and example. One theorem was: There are no *accidents* and no fatal flaws in the machines; there are only pilots with the wrong stuff. (I.e., blind Fate can't kill me.) When Bud Jennings crashed and burned in the swamps at Jacksonville, the other pilots in Pete Conrad's squadron said: *How could he have been so stupid?* It turned out that Jennings had gone up in the SNJ with his cockpit canopy opened in a way that was expressly forbidden in the manual, and carbon monoxide had been sucked in from the exhaust, and he passed out and crashed.

All agreed that Bud Jennings was a good guy and a good pilot, but his epitaph on the ziggurat was: *How could he have been so stupid?* This seemed shocking at first, but by the time Conrad had reached the end of that bad string at Pax River, he was capable of his own corollary to the theorem: viz., no single factor ever killed a pilot; there was always a chain of mistakes. But what about Ted Whelan, who fell like a rock from 8,100 feet when his parachute failed? Well, the parachute was merely part of the chain: first, someone should have caught the structural defect that resulted in the hydraulic leak that triggered the emergency; second, Whelan did not check out his seat-parachute rig, and the drogue failed to separate the main parachute from the seat; but even after those two mistakes, Whelan had fifteen or twenty seconds, as he fell, to disengage himself from the seat and open the parachute manually. Why just stare at the scenery coming up to smack you in the face! And everyone nodded. (He failed—but I wouldn't have!) Once the theorem and the corollary were understood, the Navy's statistics about one in every four Navy aviators dying meant nothing. The figures were averages, and averages applied to those with average stuff.

A riveting subject, especially if it were one's own hide that was on the line. Every evening at bases all over America, there were military pilots huddled in officers clubs eagerly cutting the right stuff up in coded slices so they could talk about it. What more compelling topic of conversation was there in the world? In the Air Force there were even pilots who would ask the tower for priority landing clearance so that they could make the beer call on time, at 4 P.M. sharp, at the Officers Club. They would come right out and state the reason. The drunken rambles began at four and sometimes went on for ten or twelve hours. Such conversations! They diced that righteous stuff up into little bits, bowed ironically to it, stumbled blindfolded around it, groped, lurched, belched, staggered, bawled, sang, roared, and feinted at it with self-deprecating humor. Nevertheless!—they never mentioned it by name. No, they used the approved codes, such as: "Like a jerk I got myself into a hell of a corner today." They told of how they "lucked out of it." To get across the extreme peril of his exploit, one would use certain oblique cues. He would say, "I looked over at Robinson"—who would be known to the listeners as a non-com who sometimes rode backseat to read radar—"and he wasn't talking any more, he was just staring at the radar, like this, giving it that *zombie* look. Then I *knew* I was in trouble!" Beautiful! Just right! For it would also be known to the listeners that the non-coms advised one another:

"*Never* fly with a lieutenant. *Avoid* captains and majors. Hell, man, do yourself a favor: don't fly with anybody below colonel." Which in turn said: "Those young bucks shoot dice with death!" And yet once in the air the non-com had his own standards. He was determined to remain as outwardly cool as the pilot, so that when the pilot did something that truly petrified him, he would say nothing; instead, he would turn silent, catatonic, like a zombie. Perfect! *Zombie.* There you had it, compressed into a single word all of the foregoing. I'm a hell of a pilot! I shoot dice with death! And now all you fellows know it! And I haven't spoken of that unspoken stuff even once!

The talking and drinking began at the beer call, and then the boys would break for dinner and come back afterward and get more wasted and more garrulous or else more quietly fried, drinking good cheap PX booze until 2 A.M. The night was young! Why not get the cars and go out for a little proficiency run? It seemed that every fighter jock thought himself an ace driver, and he would do anything to obtain a hot car, especially a sports car, and the drunker he was, the more convinced he would be about his driving skills, as if the right stuff, being indivisible, carried over into any enterprise whatsoever, under any conditions. A little proficiency run, boys! (There's only one way to find out!) And they would roar off in close formation from, say, Nellis Air Force Base, down Route 15, into Las Vegas, barreling down the highway, rat-racing, sometimes four abreast, jockeying for position, piling into the most listless curve in the desert flats as if they were trying to root each other out of the groove at the Rebel 500—and then bursting into downtown Las Vegas with a rude fraternal roar like the Hell's Angels—and the natives chalked it up to youth and drink and the bad element that the Air Force attracted. They knew nothing about the right stuff, of course.

More fighter pilots died in automobiles than in airplanes. Fortunately, there was always some kindly soul up the chain to certify the papers "line of duty," so that the widow could get a better break on the insurance. That was okay and only proper because somehow the system itself had long ago said *Skol!* and *Quite right!* to the military cycle of Flying & Drinking and Drinking & Driving, as if there were no other way. Every young fighter jock knew the feeling of getting two or three hours' sleep and then waking up at 5:30 A.M. and having a few cups of coffee, a few cigarettes, and then carting his poor quivering liver out to the field for another day of flying. There were those who arrived not merely hungover but still drunk, slapping oxygen tank cones over their faces and trying to burn the alcohol out of their systems, and then going up, remarking later: "I don't *advise* it, you understand, but it *can* be done." (Provided you have the right stuff, you miserable pudknocker.)

Air Force and Navy airfields were usually on barren or marginal stretches of land and would have looked especially bleak and Low Rent to an ordinary individual in the chilly light of dawn. But to a young pilot there was an inexplicable bliss to coming out to the flight line while the sun was just beginning to cook up behind the rim of the horizon, so that the whole field was still in shadow and the ridges in the distance were in silhouette and the flight line was a monochrome of Exhaust Fume Blue, and every little red light on top of the water towers or power stanchions looked dull, shriveled, congealed, and the runway lights, which were still on, looked faded, and even the landing lights on a fighter that had just landed and was taxiing in were no longer dazzling, as they would be at night, and looked instead like shriveled gobs of candlepower out there—and yet it was beautiful, exhilarating!—for he was revved up with adrenalin, anxious to take off before the day broke, to burst up into the sunlight over the ridges before all those thousands of comatose souls down there, still dead to the world, snug in home and hearth, even came to their senses. To take off in an F-100F at dawn and cut on the afterburner and hurtle twenty-five thousand feet up into the sky in thirty seconds, so suddenly that you felt not like a bird but like a trajectory, yet with full control, full control of four tons of thrust, all of which flowed from your will and through your fingertips, with the huge engine right beneath you, so close that it was as if you were riding it bareback, until all at once you were supersonic, an event registered on earth by a tremendous cracking boom that shook windows, but up here only by the fact that you now felt utterly free of the earth—to describe it, even to wife, child, near ones and dear ones, seemed impossible. So the pilot kept it to himself, along with an even more indescribable . . . an even more sinfully inconfessable feeling of superiority, appropriate to him and to his kind, lone bearers of the right stuff.

From up here at dawn the pilot looked down upon poor hopeless Las Vegas (or Yuma, Corpus Christi, Meridian, San Bernardino, or Dayton) and began to wonder: How can all of them down there, those poor souls who will soon be waking up and trudging out of their minute rectangles and inching along their little noodle highways toward whatever slots and grooves make up their everyday lives—how could they live like that, with such earnestness, if they had the faintest idea of what it was like up here in this righteous zone?

But of course! Not only the washed-out, grounded, and dead pilots had been left behind—but also all of those millions of sleepwalking souls who never even attempted the great gamble. The entire world below . . . left behind. Only at this point can one begin to understand just how big, how titanic, the ego of the military pilot could be. The world was used to enormous egos in artists, actors, entertainers of all sorts, in politicians, sports figures, and even journalists, because they had such familiar and convenient ways to show them off. But that slim young man over there in uniform, with the enormous watch on his wrist and the withdrawn look on his face, that young officer who is so shy that he can't even open his mouth unless the subject is flying—that young pilot—well, my friends, his ego is even bigger!—so big, it's breathtaking! Even in the 1950's it was difficult for civilians to comprehend such a thing, but all military officers and many enlisted men tended to feel superior to civilians. It was really quite ironic, given the fact that for a good thirty years the rising business classes in the cities had been steering their sons away from the military, as if from a bad smell, and the officer corps had never been held in lower esteem. Well, career officers returned the contempt in trumps. They looked upon themselves as men who lived by higher standards of behavior than civilians, as men who were the bearers and protectors of the most important values of American life, who maintained a sense of discipline while civilians abandoned themselves to hedonism, who maintained a sense of honor while civilians lived by opportunism and greed. Opportunism and greed: there you had your much-vaunted corporate business world. Khrushchev was right about one thing: when it came time to hang the capitalist West, an American businessman would sell him the rope. When the showdown came—and the showdowns always came—not all the wealth in the world or all the sophisticated nuclear weapons and radar and missile systems it could buy would take the place of those who had the uncritical willingness to face danger, those who, in short, had the right stuff.

In fact, the feeling was so righteous, so exalted, it could become religious. Civilians seldom understood this, either. There was no one to teach them. It was no longer the fashion for serious writers to describe the glories of war. Instead, they dwelt upon its horrors, often with cynicism or disgust. It was left to the occasional pilot with a literary flair to provide a glimpse of the pilot's self-conception in its heavenly or spiritual aspect. When a pilot named Robert Scott flew his P-43 over Mount Everest, quite a feat at the time, he brought his hand up and snapped a salute to his fallen adversary. He thought he had defeated the mountain, surmounting all the forces of nature that had made it formidable. And why not? "God is my co-pilot," he said—that became the title of his book—and he meant it. So did the most gifted of all the pilot authors, the Frenchman Antoine de Saint-Exupéry. As he gazed down upon the world from up there, during transcontinental flights, the good Saint-Ex saw civilization as a series of tiny fragile patches clinging to the otherwise barren rock of Earth. He felt like a lonely sentinel, a protector of those vulnerable little oases, ready to lay down his life in their behalf, if necessary; a saint, in short, true to his name, flying up here at the right hand of God. The good Saint-Ex! And he was not the only one. He was merely the one who put it into words most beautifully and anointed himself before the altar of the right stuff.

There were many pilots in their thirties who, to the consternation of their wives, children, mothers, fathers, and employers, volunteered to go active in the reserves and fly in combat in the Korean War. In godforsaken frozen Chosen! But it was simple enough. Half of them were fliers who had trained during the Second World War and had never seen combat. It was well understood—and never said, of course—that no one could reach the top of the pyramid without going into combat.

The morale of foot soldiers in the Korean War was so bad it actually reached the point where officers were prodding men forward with gun barrels and bayonets. But in the air—it was Fighter Jock Heaven! Using F-86s mainly, the Air Force was producing aces, pilots who had shot down five planes or more, as fast as the Koreans and Chinese could get their Soviet MiG-15s up to fight them. By the time the fighting was stopped, there were thirty-eight Air Force aces, and they had accounted for a total of 299.5 kills. Only fifty-six F-86s were lost. High spirits these lads had. They chronicled their adventures with a good creamy romanticism such as nobody in flying had treated himself to since the days of Lufbery, Frank Luke, and von Richthofen in the First World War. Colonel Harrison R. Thyng, who shot down five MiGs in Korea (and eight German and Japanese planes in the Second World War), glowed like Excalibur when he described his Fourth Fighter-Interceptor Wing: "Like olden knights the F-86 pilots ride up over North Korea to the Yalu River, the sun glinting off silver aircraft, contrails streaming behind, as they challenge the numerically superior enemy to come on up and fight." Lances and plumes! I'm a knight! Come on up and fight! Why hold back! Knights of the Right Stuff!

When a pilot named Gus Grissom (whom Conrad, Schirra, Lovell, and the others would meet later on) first went to Korea, the Air Force used to take the F-86 jocks out to the field before dawn, in the dark, in buses, and the pilots who had not been shot at by a MiG in air-to-air combat had to stand up. At first Grissom couldn't believe it and then he couldn't bear it—those bastards sitting down were the only ones with the right stuff! The next morning, as they rumbled out there in the dark, he was sitting down. He had gone up north toward the Yalu on the first day and had it out with some howling supersonic Chinee just so he could have a seat on the bus. Even at the level of combat, the main thing was not to be left behind.

Combat had its own infinite series of tests, and one of the greatest sins was "chattering" or "jabbering" on the radio. The combat frequency was to be kept clear of all but strategically essential messages, and all unenlightening comments were regarded as evidence of funk, of the wrong stuff. A Navy pilot (in legend, at any rate) began shouting, "I've got a MiG at zero! A MiG at zero!"—meaning that it had maneuvered in behind him and was locked in on his tail. An irritated voice cut in and said, "Shut up and die like an aviator." One had to be a Navy pilot to appreciate the final nuance. A good Navy pilot was a real aviator; in the Air Force they merely had pilots and not precisely the proper stuff.

No, the tests were never-ending. And in the periods between wars a man's past successes in combat did not necessarily keep him at the top of the heavenly pyramid. By the late 1950's there was yet another plateau to strive for. On that plateau were men who had flown in combat in the Second World War or Korea and had then gone on to become test pilots in the new age of jet and rocket engines. Not every combat pilot could make the climb. Two of the great aces of the Second World War, Richard I. Bong and Don Gentile, tried it but didn't have the patience for the job. They only wanted to light the afterburner and poke holes in the sky; and presently they were just part of combat history. Of course, by now, thanks to the accident of age, you began to find young men who had reached the exalted level of test pilot without ever having had a chance to fight in combat.

One was Pete Conrad, who was just graduating, with the survivors of Group 20, to the status of full-fledged test pilot at Pax River. Like every Navy test pilot, Conrad was proud of Pax River and its reputation. Out loud every true Navy aviator insisted that Pax River was the place, and inwardly knew it really wasn't. For every military pilot knew where the apex of the great ziggurat was located. You could point it out on a map. The place was Edwards Air Force Base in the high desert 150 miles northeast of Los Angeles. Everyone knew who resided there, too, although their actual status was never put into words. Not only that, everyone knew the name of the individual who ranked foremost in the Olympus, the ace of all the aces, as it were, among the true brothers of the right stuff.

⚜ ⚜ ⚜

The Right Stuff is a progeny of a four-part series Wolfe wrote for *Rolling Stone* after doing about two months of initial research and attending the Apollo 17 launch, which was the last to the moon. Published under the rubric "Post-Orbital Remorse," the series appeared early in 1973[8] and was originally slotted as a three-parter.[9] Parts of the articles survived in the book. Wolfe also brought into the book part of a later article, "The Truest Sport: Jousting with Sam and Charlie," about two Navy pilots flying into combat over Vietnam from the carrier *USS Coral Sea*.[10] Wolfe once called that article "one of the magazine pieces I'm proudest of."[11]

The voice Wolfe used in the series and the book was that of the astronauts; the series is written as though the astronauts are talking to Wolfe. The first part begins in a style reminiscent of *The Electric Kool-Aid Acid Test:* "Heeeeee-yuh-yuh-yuh-yuh-yuh-yuh-yuh we're not laughing at *you*, Tom. It's just that the question you're asking always used to be such a joke to us. Every time one of us went up, right from the beginning, even before the lunar missions, here would come a bunch of reporters with a look on their faces like the twelve-year-old boy asking the fourteen-year-old boy about . . . *it*."[12] The second part began: "Meanwhile, the inner voice of the astronauts (as revealed to our correspondent) continued,"[13] suggesting that perhaps some readers did not understand what Wolfe was up to and that it had to be explained. Wolfe did not exactly abandon the astronauts' voice, but he did change roles from that of the conveyor of the astronauts' stories to that of the teller of their story, to mixed reviews.

Because some reviewers made the comparison, *The Right Stuff* should be discussed in the context of *The Electric Kool-Aid Acid Test,* a book about Ken Kesey, who was the author of *One Flew Over the Cuckoo's Nest* and the leader of a group of social misfits called the Merry Pranksters. In effect a book about a slice of the 1960s drug culture, with some leftover 1950s beatniks and a visit from the Hell's Angels thrown in, *Test* attempts to capture the mood of the Pranksters and the times. Wolfe likened writing *Test* to method acting. He said he would review his notes for a chapter then try to imagine himself in the scene, "going crazy, for example . . . how it feels and what it's going to sound like if you translate it into words—which was real writing by radar."[14] C. D. B. Bryan said Wolfe was a "wide-angle camera panning back and forth across crowded rooms," then cutting in for closeups and other times piling "elaboration upon elaboration until reality is buried under illusions of evaluation."[15] (The description might also apply to James Agee's *Let Us Now Praise Famous Men.*) Paul Many, who traced the influence of Beats on New Journalism, said *Test* "was recognized as one of the most characteristic manifestations of the New Journalism style and sensibility."[16]

What then was New Journalism? Wolfe proclaimed that New Journalism had four attributes: scene-by-scene construction, real dialogue, status details (clothing and furniture, for example), and point of view (as in showing something through a particular character's point of view).[17] When New Journalism was first promoted by Wolfe and other adherents, mainstream journalists considered it heretical because it did not follow the favored forms of the day. Some critics would analyze a piece of writing that claimed to be New Journalism and pronounce it a piece of fiction, then decree that New Journalism was fiction. Others, such as John Hersey, were more direct, saying Wolfe could not "resist the itch to improve on the material he digs up. The tricks of fiction he uses dissolve now and then into its very essence: fabrication."[18] But Wolfe never advocated making things up, calling that a tremendous mistake and a violation of the rules. He said he derived satisfaction from using facts to create something factual but "engrossing as fiction."[19] What unnerved traditional journalists was that Wolfe's writing came without the usual in-text source notes so typical of a news story. (Where could one go to verify the information?) Wolfe probably also suffered a bit of the Truman Capote syndrome by promoting New Journalism and suggesting that he was on to something new. Although he really did credit others for "inventing" New Journalism, the critics feasted on the "new" in New Journalism: several articles suggested there was nothing new about it, tracing it all the way back to Daniel Defoe, a British novelist and journalist who died in 1731.[20]

For *Test,* Wolfe used one person, Ken Kesey as his central character, but he decided to write *The Right Stuff* as a group portrait.[21] Comparisons were inevitable. Dennis Lynch called *The Right Stuff* a "radical departure" from previous books.[22] In a comment that out of context might sound negative, Chilton Williamson, Jr., called the book Wolfe's "plainest to date," alluding to previous Wolfe books that sizzled with ellipses, italics, and "machine-gun-fire exclamation points."[23] Williamson declared *The Right Stuff* "shrewd, polished, and accomplished." For Wolfe, the style change was intentional. He tried to write in a style that matched the subject, as he had also done in *The Electric Kool-Aid Acid Test*. "I've always insisted," Wolfe said, "that there was no set Tom Wolfe style, that I was trying to make the style fit the event."[24]

Bryan said Wolfe had changed his posture of previous books from that of "the skeptical outsider, the suave, somewhat distant and critical observer, content to move among his subjects with a slightly mocking smile" to an admirer of his subjects that produced a "positive stance."[25] Edmund Fuller and Eric Korn held that positive stance against Wolfe. "If there's one thing more unlovable than the man of letters showing his contempt for physical valour," Korn wrote, "it's the man of letters fawning on physical valour"—which he said Wolfe had done.[26] Fuller called the book a "satirical interpretation, not an objective account," saying that in attempting to balance the over-adulatory and pompous press clips of the past, Wolfe had gone to the other extreme.[27]

Some reviewers saw spiritual or ancient literary dimensions in *The Right Stuff*. An *Economist* reviewer praised Wolfe for producing "an epic poem about courage, about that embarrassing (almost unmentionable) thing called manliness."[28] Ted Morgan pronounced the book "a splendid adventure story, an updating of *The Seven Samurai*."[29] *Publishers Weekly* said Wolfe had "grasped . . . the inner lives of this select group, the gap between the self-created mystique and the all too familiar media-created mystique."[30] Thomas Powers called the book "a work of literature" that shows "the unreflecting competitiveness which drove the original astronauts to the quite extraordinary lengths Wolfe describes so vividly."[31] The *Atlantic* said it was Wolfe's "most ambitious book, and his best";[32] Hersey, although generally censorious, said it was "Wolfe's best so far,"[33] and Christina Kampman concluded her announcement/review by saying: "It's vigorously written and hard to put down. Recommended."[34]

On the downside, Hersey and Laurie Stone faulted Wolfe for interpreting and generalizing. Stone quoted Wolfe describing some women as "moist labial piping little birds," and wondered who was talking—Wolfe or the astronauts[35]—as though one could imagine pilots talking about groupies in anything but the crudest of terms. Hersey complained about Wolfe's description of thirty-six military pilots showing up at the Pentagon to apply for the space program dressed in "Robert Hall clothes that cost about a fourth as much as their watches." Hersey stated that if Wolfe detected a trait in one pilot, they all had it.[36] But both Stone and Hersey refused to allow the writer room to translate what he has observed. Hersey's charge missed the point of the book—that there was a sameness about the men who applied for the space program. They came out of a military environment that did not engender individuals. The suits made a statement about their status and they bought them off the rack at a discount store because they were used to dressing the same. One area in which they could be individuals was in their wristwatches, so they spent more on watches than clothing. Being pilots, they invested more in the mechanical than the sartorial.

As far as Peter Prescott was concerned, Wolfe's ego got in the way of the story. He referred to Wolfe as "America's nerviest journalist" and concluded his review this way: "Wolfe helped invent this kind of smart-ass, exclamatory journalism; his witty prose alone is evidence of what the writer's right stuff is."[37] No doubt Prescott would not see any difference between the original series and the book, although a comparison would show a maturation of Wolfe's style or evidence that he needed time to find the right voice.

Some reviewers wanted a different book. One reviewer, John Romano, said *The Right Stuff* "ended too soon" and that Wolfe "failed to bring out the connections between the world of fighter jocks, the subsequent astronaut period and the broader society of which they are a part."[38] Phyllis Frus also found Wolfe guilty of the sin of omission, pointing out that Wolfe failed to mention the thirteen female pilots who had qualified through the first two phases of astronaut training only to be denied equal opportunity after performing at least as well as the chosen men.[39] In fact, one should note the overall macho tone of the book and the secondary role women play throughout. Parts of the book, one astronaut-reviewer wrote, read "like a NASA press release,"[40] which might suggest the overwhelming amount of NASA material Wolfe had to sift through rather than the lack of critical reporting on Wolfe's part.

Wolfe considered *The Right Stuff* his best book.[41] Most critics would agree. That he did not write the book others wanted should not detract from what he did write. He conducted years of research, overcame a structural problem (the lack of a central character), found a theme, and produced what Michael Sheldrick said was "a couple of years' worth of campfire tales."[42] *The Right Stuff* is a well-told story. It has both literary and historical value. It may well be among those books future historians read when they study the United States space program.

ENDNOTES

1. John Gregory Dunne, "Hog Heaven," *New York Review of Books*, 8 November 1979, 9.
2. "The Grandest Gamble," *Esquire*, August 1979, 5.
3. Michael Sheldrick, "The first astronauts: They had what it took," *Business Week*, 15 October 1979, 11.
4. Quoted in Janet Maslin, "Tom Wolfe," *New York Times Book Review*, 28 October 1979, 54.
5. R. Z. Sheppard, "Skywriting with Gus and Deke," *Time*, 24 September 1979, 82.
6. Joshua Gilder, "Tom Wolfe," *Saturday Review*, April 1981, 43.
7. McLeod, in *Contemporary Authors*, ed. Ann Evory and Linda Metzger (Detroit, Mich.: Gale Research, 1983), 537.
8. Tom Wolfe, "The Brotherhood of The Right Stuff," *Rolling Stone*, 4 January 1973; "How the Astronauts Fell from Cowboy Heaven," 18 January 1973; "The Dark Night of the Ego," 15 February 1973; and "The Last Great Galactic Flash," 1 March 1973. The third part, "The Dark Night of the Ego," appeared in the same issue that included Hunter Thompson's return to *Rolling Stone* as a columnist with "Fear and Loathing at the Superbowl."
9. Jann Wenner, "Editorial Notes," *Rolling Stone*, 4 January 1973, 6.
10. Tom Wolfe, "The Truest Sport: Jousting with Sam and Charlie," *Esquire*, October 1975.
11. Quoted in Gilder, "Tom Wolfe," 43.
12. Wolfe, "Brotherhood," 44.
13. Wolfe, "How the Astronauts," 26.
14. Quoted in Toby Thompson, "The Evolution of Dandy Tom," *Vanity Fair*, October 1987, 127.
15. C. D. B. Bryan, "The SAME Day: HEEEEEEWACK!!!" *New York Times Book Review*, 18 August 1968, 2.
16. Paul Many, "On the Road on the Bus: Beat Influences on the New Journalism," paper presented at the Association for Education in Journalism and Mass Communication, Atlanta, 1994.
17. Tom Wolfe, *The New Journalism*, ed. Tom Wolfe and E. W. Johnson (New York: Harper & Row, 1973), 31–32.

18. John Hersey, "The Legend on the License," *Yale Review*, Autumn 1980, 5.
19. Quoted in Gilder, "Tom Wolfe," 43.
20. Charles H. Brown, "New Art Journalism Revisited," *Quill*, March 1972, 18–23. This article is an even-handed and useful analysis of New Journalism.
21. Herbert Mitgang, "In Wolfe's Clothing," *New York Times Book Review*, 23 September 1979, 47.
22. Dennis Lynch, "The Right Stuff," *New Republic*, 20 October 1979, 38.
23. Chilton Williamson, Jr., "The Good Stuff," *National Review*, 1436.
24. McLeod, in *Contemporary Authors*, 538.
25. C. D. B. Bryan, "The Sky Is Our Domain," *New York Times Book Review*, 23 September 1979, 35.
26. Eric Korn, "Stylishly into space," *Times Literary Supplement*, 30 November 1979, 52.
27. Edmund Fuller, "Into Outer Space With Smirk and Simile," *Wall Street Journal*, 8 October 1979, 24.
28. "Magnificent Seven," *Economist*, 1 December 1979, 113.
29. Ted Morgan, "Orbital Chic," *Saturday Review*, 15 September 1979, 38.
30. "Nonfiction," *Publishers Weekly*, 13 August 1979, 52.
31. Thomas Powers, "Wolfe in Orbit: Our Mercurial Interests," *Commonweal*, 12 October 1979, 552.
32. "Short Reviews," *Atlantic*, October 1979, 107.
33. Hersey, "Legend," 3.
34. Christina Kampman, *Library Journal*, October 15, 1979, p. 2228.
35. Laurie Stone, "Spaced Out," *Village Voice*, September 10, 1979, p. 73.
36. Hersey, "Legend," 9.
37. Peter S. Prescott, "Tom Wolfe in Orbit," *Newsweek*, 17 September 1979, 93, 95.
38. John Romano, "Subculture Chic," *Nation*, 3 November 1979, 440.
39. Phyllis Frus, *The Politics and Poetics of Journalistic Narrative: The Timely and the Timeless* (Cambridge: Cambridge University Press, 1994), 224. Frus is relying on information reported by Joan McCullough in "Thirteen Who Were Left Behind," *Ms.*, June 1973, 41–45.
40. Michael Collins, "So You Want to Be an Astronaut," *Washington Post Book World*, 8.
41. McLeod, in *Contemporary Authors*, 538.
42. Sheldrick, "First Amendment," 11.

Chapter 17

❖

The Soul of a New Machine

Tracy Kidder had one nonfiction book to his credit and was freelancing for *Atlantic Monthly* when an editor suggested he write a book about the computer industry.[1] For the Massachusetts resident, the subject was right in his backyard, but Kidder was not enthusiastic until he realized that other writers he admired—among them George Orwell, A. J. Liebling, and John McPhee—might have taken on the assignment readily. So he settled in at Data General Corporation near Boston and began watching a team of young people design a computer.

The Soul of a New Machine focuses on the events within Data General as two teams, one in Massachusetts and one in North Carolina, compete to create a minicomputer that the company needs to increase its revenues. Kidder writes about the Massachusetts engineers as they work in overtime on overdrive to complete the task.

For his first book, *The Road to Yuba City*, the story about the victims of a mass murderer, Kidder tried to learn how the victims, all homeless men, reached their final destination. So he didn't fly to California, but instead rode the rails with hoboes. When he got to California he got a job as a laborer, the kind of job the victims had when they were killed. The book did not sell well, which Kidder attributed to his inability to get into the mind of Juan Corona, the man convicted of the crimes, as Truman Capote had done in *In Cold Blood* and Norman Mailer had done in *The Executioner's Song*. He did succeed with that approach in *The Soul of a New Machine*.

After *Soul*, Kidder took an interest in the building of a house (*House*), the life of a schoolteacher (*Among Schoolchildren*), and life in a nursing home (*Old Friends*). His later books have also earned critical praise, but *The Soul of a New Machine* won him a Pulitzer Prize and an American Book Award. The title really tells Kidder's "secret" on writing about technology—which is to write about people, as newspaper editors routinely advise beginners.

The following excerpt comes from the end of Chapter 1 and the beginning of Chapter 2. It begins to explain the project and the man behind it, Tom West.

⚜ ⚜ ⚜

At the end of fiscal 1978, after just ten years of existence, Data General's name appeared on the list of the nation's five hundred largest industrial corporations—in that band of giants known as the Fortune 500. It stood in five-hundredth place in total revenues, but much higher in respect to the various indices of profit, and for a while climbed steadily higher on the list. Surely by 1980 such a record entitled Data General to respectability. But some trade journalists still looked askance at the company; one told me Data General was widely known among his colleagues as "the Darth Vader of the computer industry." Investors still seemed jittery about Data General's stock. An article published in *Fortune* in 1979 had labeled Data General "the upstarts," while calling DEC "the gentlemen." The memory of that article, particularly the part that made it sound as if Data General routinely cheated its customers, still rankled Herb Richman.

Building 14A/B is essentially divided into an upstairs and a downstairs, and in one corner of the upstairs the corporate officers reside. A wall of glass separates them from the rest of the company. There is no mahogany here. If there is ostentation in the bosses' quarters, it is ostentation in reverse. The table in their conference room, it was proudly said, was the same that they had used when the company was small. Richman's office was comparatively plush. But saying, "We consider ourselves the Robert Hall of the computer industry," Richman pointed out that he had paid for all his furnishings himself and that what looked like paneling on his walls was really just wallpaper.

Among the founders of the company, only de Castro—the much-talked-about president—and Richman remained engaged in daily operations. Richman had come up through the industry in sales—a supersalesman, some called him—and he had created and run Data General's sales force, which was known if not notorious for its aggressiveness. Curly-haired, trim and in his forties, Richman wore a nicely tailored denim jacket and no tie. "I'm one of the few guys that money made a nice guy out of," he said. "Before, I was just driven, clawing. . . . Success has made me more rational and introspective." He remarked that not long ago he had been playing tennis with a man who had seemed to him just an ordinary fellow, but then he had found out that the man was actually president of an oil company. "And it was one of the largest oil companies in the world, and I was just in awe of him," said Richman. He added, softly, "And yet I bet my net worth greatly exceeded his."

The stock that Richman himself owned in Data General was worth about $13 million then, but, he seemed to say, he was unhappy with the way certain organs of the press depicted his company's achievements. They were, Richman believed, too often depicted as "ruffians," not as merely rough, which they were proud to be. "We agree that a lot of things we've done around here are wild," he said. "But we can't understand why we're tabloid, instead of the *New York Times*."

Some part of Data General's reputation was easy to explain. The company had promoted it themselves, and maybe it had gotten a little out of hand. Richman suggested, "We've done so much so well for so long that everyone seems to think we have to be doing something illegal." A good point, but not a full accounting.

Some years back, in the early seventies, a company called Keronix accused Data General's officers of arranging the burning of a factory. Keronix had been making computers that performed almost identically to Data General machines. The theory was that Data General had taken a shortcut in attempting to get rid of this competitor. In time, the courts found no basis for those charges and dismissed them. Indeed, it seemed preposterous to think that the suddenly wealthy executives of Data General would risk everything, including jail, and resort to arson, just to drive away what was, after all, a small competitor. But Wall Street didn't see it that way, apparently. When Keronix made its accusation, Data General's stock plummeted; there was such a rush to unload it that the New York Exchange had to suspend trading in it for a while. More peculiar was the fact that many years later, some veteran employees, fairly far down in the hierarchy, would say privately that they believed someone connected with the company had something to do with that fire. Not the officers, but some renegade within the organization. They had no basis for saying so, no piece of long-hidden evidence. It seemed to me that this was something that they wanted to believe.

I got this feeling more than once. Turning down the road to Building 14A/B one day, a veteran engineer pointed out the sign that warned against unauthorized parking. "The first sign you see says Don't," he remarked. He imagined another sign by the road; it would say: Use of Excessive Force Has Been Approved. The engineer laughed and laughed at the thought.

In a land of tough and ready companies, theirs, some of Data General's employees seemed to want to think, was the toughest and the readiest around.

Certainly Data General's reputation had other underpinnings besides advertisements and imagination. In an industry where sharp marketing practices were common, Data General's were as sharp as any, and by the late 1970s competitors were challenging some of them in federal court. To the contention, leveled in *Fortune,* that Data General played especially rough with its customers, it was only fair to add that many of Data General's customers knew very well what sort of market they were in, and moreover, it was clear that the company could not have survived if most of its customers had not felt at least fairly satisfied. But Data General was litigious, toward customers as well as others. "Sure," said Richman, "if people don't pay us or breach our contract, we litigate 'em." They did so at least in part to assure Wall Street that they weren't the sort of company that would accumulate a crippling number of bad debts.

The salient feature of Data General, however—what that sharp-eyed, astonished visitor from Wall Street would have pondered—was its growth. This was indeed the industry's salient characteristic. In the main, computer companies that were not dying were growing; they had to do so just to stay alive, it seemed. But no company whose primary business was making computers had grown more rapidly than Data General. Bursts of growth were not uncommon, but Data General had been bursting for a decade, and what's more, it had been maintaining the highest profit margins in the industry next to IBM's. All this would have impressed the analyst from Wall Street, of course, but would also have given him pause.

Building 14A/B and its sparse furnishings, the facts that Data General paid its stockholders no dividends and that its top managers dispensed to themselves and other officers exceptionally small salaries, meting out rewards in the form of stock instead—all were signs of a common purpose. The company had displayed extravagance when it came to financing its tendency to go to court. Otherwise, the management seemed bent on saving all their cash to feed the hungry beast of growth. And, of course, the more this beast gets fed, the bigger it becomes, the more it wants to eat. It is one thing for a company with revenues of a million dollars a year to grow 30 or 40 percent in a year and quite another for a half-a-billion-dollar company to pull off the same trick.

Analysts on Wall Street sometimes become boosters of the companies they follow. Looking for an opinion that was certain to be disinterested, I asked an old friend, a veteran analyst of securities, to take a look at Data General's numbers. He had the advantage of never having followed the company before, and in return for anonymity he agreed to my proposal. A couple of weeks later, he called me back. It seemed to him that Data General was bent on continuing to grow at 30 to 40 percent a year. He pointed out that this meant large growth in everything—in the need for capital, new buildings, new employees. Between 1974 and 1978, for instance, Data General had hired about 7,000 new employees, roughly tripling its numbers; in one year alone the company had increased its ranks by 71 percent. The analyst imagined the difficulties of finding that many qualified people so quickly. And what must it be like, he asked, to work at a place like that? You'd come to work some morning and suddenly find yourself in charge of a dozen new people, or suddenly beneath a new boss to whom you would have to prove yourself all over again. "That sort of growth puts a strain on everything," the analyst concluded. "It's gonna be intriguing to see if they get caught." He thanked me for putting him onto such a marvelous entertainment.

Where did the risks lie? Where could a company go badly wrong? In many cases, a small and daily growing computer company did not fall on hard times because people suddenly stopped wanting to buy its products. On the contrary, a company was more likely to asphyxiate on its own success. Demand for its products would be soaring, and the owners would be drawing up optimistic five-year plans, when all of a sudden something would go wrong with their system of production. They wouldn't be able to produce the machines that they had promised to deliver. Lawsuits might follow. At the least, expensive parts would sit in inventory, revenues would fall, customers would go elsewhere or out of business themselves. Data General got one leg caught in this trap back around 1973. Six years later, a middle-level executive, sitting in an office upstairs at headquarters, remembered that time: "We were missing our commitments to customers. We just grossly fucked over our customers. We actually put some entrepreneurs out of business and I think some of them may have lost their houses. But we recovered from our shipment problems and never repeated them."

Another way of fouling up had less to do with a company's own growth than with the growth occurring all around it. From observers of the industry came such comments as: "Things change fast in the computer business. A year is a hell of a long time. It's like a year in a dog's life." In every segment of the industry, companies announced small new products for sale every day. Companies brought out new lines of computers, much more powerful than the ones they replaced, only every few years or so; but considering all the work that went into them and the fact that they required a redirection of effort throughout a company, the pace at which these major announcements came was very rapid too. Conventional wisdom held that if a company fell very far behind its competitors in producing the latest sorts of machines, it would have a hard time catching up. And failure to stay abreast could have serious consequences, because major new computers played crucial roles in the other business of the companies; they helped them sell all their little products and, often, their older types of machines.

At some companies the task of guarding against this sort of crisis fell mainly to engineers, working below decks, as it were. Executives might make the final decisions about what would be produced, but engineers would provide most of the ideas for new products. After all, engineers were the people who really knew the state of the art and who were therefore best equipped to prophesy changes in it. At Data General, an engineer could play such an important role. It was there for the taking. The president, de Castro, liked "self-starters," it was said. Initiative was welcomed at Data General, and in the late seventies it appeared that the company had need of some initiative from its engineers. For Data General was in a bind. The firm had fallen behind the competition: it hadn't yet produced the latest big thing in minicomputers.

Early in 1979 the businessman who told me about Data General's problems and recovery back in '73 hit upon a heroic metaphor for success in the computer business. "The major thing," he said, "is avoiding the big mistake. It's like downhill ski racing: Can you stay right on that edge beside disaster? At Data General we keep coming up with these things that are basically acts of recovery. What Tom West and his people are doing is a great act of recovery."

[Chapter 2—excerpt continues]

Tom West went to work these days in freshly laundered blue jeans or pressed khakis, in leather moccasins and in solid-colored long-sleeved shirts, with the sleeves rolled up in precise folds, like the pages of a letter, well above his bony elbows. He expostulated with his hands. When dismissing someone or some idea or both, he made a fist and then exploded it, fingers splaying wide. The gesture was well known to the engineers who worked for him. Long index fingers inserted under either side of the bridge of his glasses signified thought, and accompanied by a long "Ummmmmmmmmh" warned that some emphatic statement was near. He kept his car and his office as neat as the folds in his sleeves. He was decisive, and in his manner, exact. For all of that, he was vague. "When I first went to work, he was my boss," an engineer said of West, "and it was amazing! Half the time I couldn't figure out what he was saying." He was not always this way, said one of his oldest colleagues, but sometimes you got the feeling that West expected you to be on his secret wavelength, and if you weren't he'd be disappointed in you. If you weren't, that was your problem. He didn't have time to explain.

Seen at the wheel of his sporty red Saab, driving to work down 495, West made a picture of impatience. His jaw was set, he had a forward lean. Sometimes he briefly wore a mysterious smile. He was a man on a mission.

Into the world of the minicomputer a new thing had been born, a class of computer known as a 32-bit supermini. West said, with characteristic enthusiasm: "Everyone thinks they want one now. It's an emotional issue. In fact, it's kind of a fire storm." As for the present state of affairs, sometimes he called it "a disaster." Sometimes he would say, "We're gonna get schmeared if we don't react to VAX."

A number of Data General's rivals had produced 32-bit super-minis, and the most important from West's point of view was the computer that DEC had recently sent to market, a machine called the VAX 11/780. Data General, meanwhile, had not yet produced a computer of this class. Many people, including West, believed that they must do so, and in fairly short order. Partly it was a matter of keeping up appearances: customers get married to their computer companies in many different ways and they don't usually want to get or stay married to a company that has fallen behind the state of the art. Besides, you had to grab a piece of the new market for the 32-bit supermini because that market was huge and growing fast; most observers agreed that it would be worth several billion dollars by the middle 1980s. You did not have to be the first company to produce the new kind of machine; sometimes, in fact, it was better not to be the first. But you had to produce yours before the new market really opened up and customers had made other marriages. For once they are lost, both old and prospective customers are often gone for good.

It had been painful for West and for a number of engineers working with him at Westborough to watch DEC's VAX go to market, to hear it described as "a breakthrough," and not have a brand-new machine of their own to show off. It had been painful for them to read in the trade press of the VAX's growing success; VAX was beginning to look like one of those best-sellers that come along only once in a while. But by the fall of 1978 West had drawn around him a team of enthusiastic engineers and they were finally working on their own supermini, which they had nick-named Eagle. A new computer, especially one of this class, does not get built in a month. Often it takes years to bring one to life. But it wasn't too late, West was saying. Not if they could build this computer in the record time of something like a year. This was at last "the right machine." This was "the answer to VAX." At times West fancied that this computer would become the source of Data General's continued ascent in the Fortune 500. "This is the second billion," he said. His doubts he did not share widely.

Secretly, West felt afraid of VAX. DEC had published a great deal of technical literature describing VAX, and West had read all of it. Nothing in this material had made him feel that his team's approach was inferior to DEC's. In some engineers, however, reading does not constitute knowing. For them, touch is the first of the senses. And so, one holiday morning in 1978, when his team was already well launched on the building of its own machine, West went away from Westborough to have a look at a VAX for himself.

He traveled to a city, which was located, he would only say, some-where in America. He walked into a building, just as though he belonged there, went down a hallway, and let himself quietly into a windowless room. The floor was torn up; a sort of trench filled with fat power cables traversed it. Along the far wall, at the end of the trench, stood a brand-new example of DEC's VAX, enclosed in several large cabinets that vaguely resembled refrigerators. But to West's surprise, one of the cabinets stood open and a man with tools was standing in front of it. A technician from DEC, still installing the machine, West figured.

Although West's purposes were not illegal, they were sly, and he had no intention of embarrassing the friend who had given him permission to visit this room. If the technician had asked West to identify himself, West would not have lied, and he wouldn't have answered the question either.

But the moment went by. The technician didn't inquire. West stood around and watched him work, and in a little while, the technician packed up his tools and left.

Then West closed the door, went back across the room to the computer, which was now all but fully assembled, and began to take it apart.

The cabinet he opened contained the VAX's Central Processing Unit, known as the CPU—the heart of the physical machine. In the VAX, twenty-seven printed-circuit boards, arranged like books on a shelf, made up this thing of things. West spent most of the rest of the morning pulling out boards; he'd examine each one, then put it back.

Across the surfaces of a typical computer's printed-circuit boards stand columns of small rectangular boxes, with metal legs descending from their sides. They might be some odd strain of caterpillar bred for mathematical ability. In fact, each of these boxes holds inside it another box, as it were—the intricate integrated circuitry known as a chip. Etched into the boards, among the housings of the chips, run many silvery bands; they make patterns like the tracks in large railroad yards.

Some boards are colorful and most finished ones please the eye. A computer's boards seem to show order triumphing in complexity. They look as if they make sense, but not in the way the moving parts of an engine make sense. The form on the surface of a board does not imply its function. It's difficult but possible to get inside the littlest boxes inside the boxes that constitute a modern computer, and bringing back the details, to create a functionally equivalent copy of the machine. Reverse engineering is the name for that art.

West called it "knockoff copy work." He had a cleaner, simpler purpose. He examined the outside of the VAX's chips—some had numbers on them that were like familiar names to him—and he counted the various types and the quantities of each. Later on, he looked at other pieces of the machine. He identified them generally too. He did more counting. And when he was all done, he added everything together and decided that it probably cost $22,500 to manufacture the essential hardware that comprised a VAX (which DEC was selling for somewhat more than $100,000). He left the machine exactly as he had found it.

"I'd been living in fear of VAX for a year," West said afterward, while driving along 495 one evening. "I wasn't really into G-Two. VAX was in the public domain and I wanted to see how bad the damage was. I think I got a high when I looked at it and saw how complex and expensive it was. It made me feel good about some of the decisions we've made."

Looking into the VAX, West had imagined he saw a diagram of DEC's corporate organization. He felt that VAX was too complicated. He did not like, for instance, the system by which various parts of the machine communicated with each other; for his taste, there was too much protocol involved. He decided that VAX embodied flaws in DEC's corporate organization. The machine expressed that phenomenally successful company's cautious, bureaucratic style. Was this true? West said it didn't matter, it was a useful theory. Then he rephrased his opinions. "With VAX, DEC was trying to minimize the risk," he said, as he swerved around another car. Grinning, he went on: "We're trying to maximize the win, and make Eagle go as fast as a raped ape."

⚜ ⚜ ⚜

The Soul of a New Machine, parts of which first appeared in *Atlantic,*[2] went right to the bestsellers' list. It received many positive reviews, in technical publications as well as in mainstream review circles. Kidder was modest about his skills and said he had hit the market at the right time. "I've been the beneficiary of a renewal of interest in technology," he told Edwin McDowell of the *New York Times.*

Indeed, Kidder had turned computer engineers into humans and computers into something non-technical, if not almost human. Susan N. Bjørner said Kidder had endowed the makers of the computer "with almost transcendental qualities."[3] *The New Yorker* said Kidder had given "a full sense of the mind and motivation, the creative genius, of the computer engineer." The magazine also said that, while Kidder did not quite explain the "practically inexplicable workings of a computer," the reader was still able to "come away with a *sense* of such contraptions."[4] Other reviewers echoed that observation. Edward R. Weidlein, for example, liked the way Kidder wove into the story "artful digressions on the history of computers."[5] *The Economist* said the story was written "from the worm's eye view—and a good one at that,"[6] "worm's eye" being the British equivalent of "fly on the wall," the journalism expression in the United States.

Kidder was also praised for his art. Samuel Florman said in the *New York Times Book Review* that Kidder "has endowed the tale with such pace, texture and poetic implication that he has elevated it to a high level of narrative art."[7] Florman compared Kidder to one of Kidder's favorite journalists, John McPhee, and said Kidder's work should also be called literature. The *Christian Science Monitor* had Frederick H. Guidry, a member of the newspaper's computer-system staff, review the book. He spoke of the book's "near-novelistic suspense story drawn from the actual development of a new high-performance computer."[8] The suspense comes from, of course, the competition between the two Data General teams vying to be the first to bring the computer to market, although Kidder does not write about the other team and the tension really arises as the engineers scramble to de-bug their creation.[9]

Some reviewers saw other virtues in the book. Guidry called the book "multipurpose nonfiction" because it provided a lay-man's guide to computers, a factual account of how something was designed and built, and "an informal study of management and professional styles."[10] In fact, the business section of the *New York Times* excerpted part of the book in a column devoted to motivating workers.[11]

High praise also came from Jeremy Bernstein, himself the author of a popular book on computers,[12] who began his review by questioning Kidder's methods, that is, the fly-on-the-wall reporting that results in a book in which the source of some material is not always clear. So Bernstein started checking on Kidder's work, the way others had checked on Capote. He talked to the soul of the project, J. Thomas West, who told Bernstein that Kidder's story was essentially correct and, "except for a few minor misquotes, took place just as Mr. Kidder said it did." (Bernstein did not explain why West, an engineer, was any more reliable on direct quotations than was Kidder, a pro-fessional writer.) "Next time," Bernstein said, "perhaps Tracy Kidder will provide a bibliography and a few references and photographs." (Kidder's next two books do provide several pages of "Acknowledgments and Sources"; only "Acknowledgments" appear in *Soul*.) His concerns about documentation aside, Bernstein ended his review by highly recommending the book and saying that, while the story might seem implausible, it had the feel of truth.[13]

The Soul of a New Machine was also praised by reviewers in technical journals. Philip Morris said in *Scientific American* that the book was informed by Kidder's "sensitive and sharp eye for personality and style" and "the pithy insight into just what a computer is, far from formal or complete but extremely helpful to the tyro."[14] A *Chemical Engineering* reviewer said the book was "lively, easy to read," and "also a book to recommend to non-technical friends who wonder what it is that engineers really do."[15] The president of Data General, Edson D. de Castro, told the *New York Times:* "What's depicted in the book is how projects really get done; it doesn't work differently anywhere else."[16] Jack Patterson, reviewing in *Business Week,* a magazine where one would not expect notice taken of good writing, called the book "a riveting account."[17]

The one totally negative review came from Jack Miles, who, in a *Los Angeles Times* review, cited five problems: changing point of view, collapse of tension, the modesty of the enterprise compared with other computer projects of the time, bad science writing and the lack of human qualities in the engineers.[18]

The Soul of a New Machine is perhaps best compared with Lillian Ross's *Picture,* in which Ross wrote about the making of the movie *The Red Badge of Courage.* Like Ross, Kidder is very much *in* his book—thus the point-of-view problem Miles correctly noted. Like Ross, who was faulted for showing warts and all, Kidder does not hold back in *Soul.* The reader knows how the engineers feel about their leader and about each other. Comments about Data's president reveal how his employees really see him compared with the public persona he has. And in one of the most revealing parts of the book, Kidder draws from West the idea that the race belongs to the swift, not necessarily the best, that the goal is to get an inexpensive working computer on the market quickly and worry about the details later. In West's words: "If you can do a quick and dirty job and it works, do it."[19]

Asked how his fly-on-the-wall reporting might affect the subjects of a book, Kidder replied: "The longer you spend in one of these situations, sort of immersed, sitting there, taking notes, the more people take your presence for granted; generally, I think that's been true."[20] The history of journalism is replete with similar stories in which the subjects of a story forget about the fly on the wall and behave as they would normally. *Picture* and *Soul* are but two examples.

Kidder also provided insight on computers at a time when computers seemed poised to effect a revolution and spread egalitarianism across the workplace, if not the universe. After explaining what many were predicting, Kidder wrote: "But in the main, computers altered techniques and not intentions and in many cases served to increase the power of executives on top and to prop up venerable institutions."[21] Late in the book, decrying those who had predicted a revolution, Kidder said: "And it should not have been surprising to anyone that in many cases the technology had served as a prop to the status quo."[22] In other words, the new technology enabled humans to carry out old tasks. Not surprisingly then, in 1993 the man who had written about building a computer revealed in an interview that he had just recently started using a computer to write, but had not yet tried database software to help him arrange his notes.[23]

A decade and a half after *The Soul of a New Machine* appeared, its staying power showed up in an article about microprocessors being used to make smart sneakers. The article was titled: "Sole of a New Machine."[24] Tracy Kidder produced a successful book on technology by using his powers of patient observation and focusing on people, not machines. The book remains a standard in journalism.

ENDNOTES

1. Edwin McDowell, "Behind the Best Sellers," *New York Times Book Review,* 29 November 1981, 46.
2. Tracy Kidder, "Flying Upside Down," *Atlantic Monthly,* July 1981, 54–64, and "The Ultimate Toy," *Atlantic Monthly,* August 1981, 24–33.
3. Susan N. Bjørner, "Book Review," *Library Journal,* August 1981, 1558.
4. "Briefly Noted," *New Yorker,* 19 October 1981, 206.
5. Edward R. Weidlein, "When the Microchips Are Down: Creating a Computer," *Washington Post Book World,* 6 September 1981, 5.
6. "Order out of Chaos," *Economist,* 20 March 1982, 97.
7. Samuel C. Florman, "The Hardy Boys and the Microkids Make a Computer," *New York Times Book Review,* 23 August 1981, 1.
8. Frederick H. Guidry, "The building of a computer, told with suspense," *Christian Science Monitor,* 23 September 1981, p. 17.
9. Weidlein, "When the Microchips," 6.
10. Guidry, "Building."

11. Tracy Kidder, "The Cathedral Was a Computer," *New York Times*, 6 September 1981, p. 2. This is an excerpt from the book and appears in the business section. For what it's worth, my copy of the book resides on a shelf devoted to technology, not with my journalism collection.
12. Jeremy Bernstein, *The Analytical Engine: Computers, Past, Present, and Future.* (New York: Random House, 1964.)
13. Jeremy Bernstein, "Modern Times," *New York Review of Books*, 8 October 1981, 40.
14. Philip Morris, "Books," *Scientific American*, October 1981, 48.
15. Roy V. Hughson, "The Soul of a New Machine," *Chemical Engineering*, 22 February 1982, 134.
16. Quoted in Stanley Klein, "The Man Behind the Soul of a New Machine," *New York Times*, 20 September 1981, "Business," p. 7.
17. Jack Patterson, *Business Week*, 28 December 1981–4 January 1982, 11.
18. Jack Miles, "Computer Tale That Doesn't Add Up," *Los Angeles Times*, 3 September 1981, p. V25.
19. Quoted in Kidder, *Soul*, 119.
20. Quoted in Mary Carroll, "The Booklist Interview," *Booklist*, 1 November 1993, 489.
21. Kidder, *Soul*, 12.
22. Kidder, *Soul*, 241.
23. Carroll, "Booklist Interview," 488.
24. Richard Stengel, "Sole of a New Machine," *New Yorker*, 20 and 27 October 1997, 80.

Chapter 18

❖

The Great China Earthquake

Nurse
peasant } *characters*

O n the morning of July 28, 1976, at 3:42 A.M., the Chinese city of Tangshan was leveled by an earthquake that killed 242,769 people and injured 164,851. In terms of the number of deaths, it was the second-worst earthquake in the history of the world. (The worst occurred in January 1556, when 830,000 people died in Shensi Province in China.)

Qian Gang arrived in Tangshan within a week as a member of the People's Liberation Army epidemic prevention squad. But he was also there as a journalist and had maneuvered his way to the disaster site. Although he would not write *The Great Tangshan Earthquake*—as the book was titled in China—for another ten years, he realized immediately that he needed to gather material.

Qian Gang was born in 1953 to a military family in Hangzhou. He graduated from the junior middle school in 1968 during the early years—what he calls the "frenzied period"—of the Cultural Revolution. Consequently, he received only one year of middle-school education plus five years of primary schooling. He joined the People's Liberation Army in 1969 at the age of sixteen, no doubt thanks to his father, who was a veteran himself, and became a reporter. According to Thomas Moran, a China scholar, Qian's* only other choice besides the army was to be sent into rural China to learn how peasants lived, a fate many intellectuals endured during this period of upheaval.[1]

---

*A Chinese name appears with the family name first and the given name last. Because I told my students in China that my name is Thomas Berner, some of them called me "Mr. Tom."

245

In 1984, Qian seized the opportunity to study in the Literary Department of the People's Liberation Army Art College. The department was chaired by Xu Huaizhong, who wrote the preface to *Earthquake,* and had been set up to educate distinguished writers who were in the army. Among Qian's classmates were Li Cunbao, who wrote *Bountiful Flowers Under High Mountain,* a book about the China-Vietnam war, and Mo Yan, the author of *Red Sorghum* and *The Garlic Ballads,* which have been published in the United States. Another classmate was his wife, Yu Jin,* who wrote *Bad Luck* and *Shanghai 1949: The Great Collapse.* It was she who ultimately gave the earthquake book its title.

Earthquake received the Fourth National Reportage Award.[2] Parts of the book were read over the radio,[3] much the way *Hiroshima* was. It was translated into English and Japanese. (Qian received a thousand yuan—about $116—for the English version.) Qian has also written *The Blue Commander* and *Surging Tides,* which are about military reform. Neither has been translated. He hopes to revise *The Great China Earthquake,* he said, because "there is really lots of material for me to add."[4]

The following excerpt comes from shortly after the beginning of the book. (The footnotes are the translators'.)

⚜ ⚜ ⚜

In order to leave an accurate historical document for posterity, I have tracked down the eyewitnesses one by one. Those who, on that silent night, saw the entire process of the earthquake's beginning with their own eyes, are extremely rare. The author has only transcribed nine of their taped interviews.

Li Hongyi (originally a nurse in the Infectious Diseases Department of the No. 255 Hospital):

---

*I had the pleasure of hosting Qian Gang and Yu Jin at a luncheon in Beijing at the Chai Jing City Restaurant on August 8, 1996. Our interpreter was Ma Zhan of the Xinhua News Agency, a former student of mine in the China School of Journalism.

I was on the late shift that night. It was hot and muggy, and I had not slept at all. I was exhausted after coming on duty at midnight. I stayed on the ward until three-thirty, when I decided to go outside for some cool air. I remember that I sat beneath a big tree at a small stone table that was often used for playing chess.

Everything around me was still. I thought it strange, since usually at that time of night you could hear insects and frogs everywhere. What was going on? There wasn't a sound; it was abnormally still, so still it was frightening.

Suddenly, I heard a strange whirring rushing over my head. Was it like wind? No. And it wasn't like the call of any animal. I can't say what it was like; I can't compare it to anything, for I'd never heard anything like it before. It was a shrill sound, like a knife cutting through the sky. I shivered; I was covered with goose bumps.

I looked up at the sky; it was overcast, and there was a strange cloud, not red, exactly, and not quite purple either. The sky seemed unusually dark. I thought, "Is it going to rain?" I got up to go inside.

But I became inexplicably terrified. I had never felt like that before, like someone would creep up behind me at any moment and grab me. Usually I'm quite brave; I'm not afraid to stand by myself in a mortuary, for instance, but at that moment I was scared to death. My heart was pounding wildly; I walked, then began running, but I was wearing slippers, so I couldn't run very fast.

I turned my head and saw that the sky to the northwest was unusually bright, as if it were on fire, but I didn't hear anyone shouting. It was as if everything, everywhere had died. I felt more anxious than ever; I ran inside, yanked on a light, and bolted the door.

Then I heard a tremendous roar, like hundreds of trucks all starting at once. "Oh my God!" I'd heard that same sound before when I was in Cangzhou during the Xingtai earthquake. I knew right away: It's an earthquake.

As soon as I said it, the room began to rock violently. The thermos on the table fell off and shattered. I struggled to open the door; I could only open it a little way, but I rushed out, and dashed to that old tree.

I hugged the tree with all my might. In the dark, I just felt the earth shaking from side to side, and then the big tree and I were falling down, down, down a bottomless pit. It was still quiet all around; I didn't hear the buildings collapse at all. I just saw that the shadow of the dormitory building that was still there a moment ago had now disappeared.

I reached out my hand and waved it in front of my face, but I couldn't see anything clearly. I was scared witless; I used every ounce of strength I had to howl, "Ow . . . "

Tian Yu'an (peasant, Daodi Brigade in Fengnan County in Tangshan):
That night was really scary.

At the time of the earthquake, I was still outside threshing. Why was I working so late? Our brigade leader had just been promoted, so of course he was strict. He made us work all night. We had to, though. It had rained for the past several days in a row, and the wheat was about to rot. So we had no choice; we had to put in overtime.

At midnight the electricity went out, so there was no way to use the thresher. Everybody shouted, "Let's go home and get some sleep!" But our team leader was all fired up to work. "No way!" he said, "We'll wait! When the electricity comes back we'll go on threshing!"

We never dreamed that his words would end up saving many lives.

So we sat there cursing and waiting until two o'clock, when the lights came on—the electricity was back. We worked like dogs, and finally finished after three. The others gathered up the tools and headed back to the village; I stayed behind with two others to sweep up.

All of a sudden, like thunder right overhead, BOOM, "the earth moved and the mountains swayed." It was like my legs were pulled out from under me, and I fell to the ground. I swerved to the left, then rolled to the right; I couldn't get up no matter what, and then all the lights in the field went out at once.

I turned around, Mother of God! A great ball of fire was coming up out of the ground, so red it burned your eyes—pow, pow, pow it went, and shot halfway up into the sky before it burned out. When it got light, I saw the place where the ball of fire had come out—there was a big crack in the ground, and the dirt on either side of it was scorched.

Jiang Dianwei (veteran worker, Kailuan Printing Plant):
At the time of the earthquake, I was near the gate of Phoenix Mountain Park practising taijiquan.*

I had high blood pressure, and was on sick leave. I was learning the twenty-four forms from this old guy over seventy. He got up every day at three, and since I was his disciple, I had to do the same. On the morning

---

*A kind of traditional Chinese shadow-boxing.

of July 28, we met at the park gate a little after three-thirty. There was another guy with us by the last name of Tang.

We exchanged a few words, and were just getting set up to begin our exercise when we heard a loud roar, like a big wind, or like the "warning air" in the mines of the old society. Then I faced southwest and the old man northeast; I just heard him yell, "Bad! Fire!" I turned around and saw that the whole northeast was fire-red!

I really hadn't had time to react when the earth jolted. At first it was bumping like crazy, and then it started shaking. Tang grabbed tight onto an iron railing, and the old man and I just stood with our legs braced and hung onto each other for dear life. At first we still spoke. I said, "When the earth moves and mountains sway, and flowers shed their petals, there's sure to be a good harvest next year." He said, "No, it's a fire." I said, "No it's not, it's an earthquake!"

The argument was only a few sentences long, but I felt like I was being shaken apart, or like I'd been put on a giant sifter and was being endlessly sifted to death. Crash! The park walls fell. A second later, the big building across the street fell too, in the blink of an eye! I could just hear the roar of bricks and tiles. The whole sky was filled with dirt. "It's awful!" I said, "we should hurry home and dig people out!"

My home wasn't far away; it was just by the railroad tracks. But when I ran down the tracks, I was dumbfounded; I couldn't find my house—the whole stretch of houses around where we lived had been flattened!

Zhang Yixi (commune member, Qianli Village near Bogezhuang Farm):

On the night of the 27th, I loaded a wheelbarrow with hay to carry to the purchasing station.

At the time of the quake, I was halfway down the asphalt road between the army farm and Xiaoji Town. All of a sudden thunder roared in the northeast sky, and lightning, and it sounded like a thunderstorm was coming. The wheelbarrow became so heavy and my feet so light, that, clinging to the handles, I actually floated in the air. A second later I touched ground again.

At that moment I saw the young trees lining the road bend so low their tops touched the ground. I saw it clearly!

I collected myself and thought, "Is it an earthquake?" But I couldn't move; my feet just didn't belong to me. About a minute later I was able to move, but the road became too bumpy for the wheelbarrow. I left it there and ran home for dear life. More and more people appeared on the road, all scared out of their wits, asking one another,

"Has your *kang** spurted water?"

"Has sand oozed from your yard?"

In some houses near the road, water gushing from underground flooded the yards; oozing sand rose like small burial mounds. Some were so panic-stricken that they scrambled up trees.

Yang Songting (cadre, Capital Construction Department, Gas Company):

Before the earthquake, it was hot and muggy. It felt like a dank fog was rolling in. That year I was sixteen; I had just graduated from middle school and didn't have a job yet, but I was helping out at the Lubei District Public Security Branch Office, catching thieves and "vagabond criminals." On the night of the 27th, we were patrolling the bus station because it was so crowded and chaotic. After three, there wasn't much to do, so we were sitting in front of the bus station hotel chatting when suddenly I felt furious vibrations beneath where I was sitting and what sounded like a bull bellowing, or what a person riding a great wind would hear. We were so scared we jumped up and ran into the street. It was quite narrow, and we were afraid the buildings or the street lights would fall and crush us. Then, all at once, the street lights went out.

A guy named Wang Guoqing and I clung together, but we couldn't stay up; it was like a pair of hands was yanking us apart. We both fell. I pulled myself up, and someone else came, and the three of us leaned together, but we couldn't stay up either. It was like standing on the deck of a ship on the crest of a wave—you rock, I sway. . . . Finally we squatted on our heels and hung onto each other for dear life. The ground was bumping so hard my feet were numb.

Then I heard the roar of buildings falling and collapsing, and was choked by the stench of dirt and ash. Crowds of people poured into the street, but no one was running very fast, just rocking and swaying, a step here, a somersault there. I saw the three women who sold tobacco, liquor and candy run out of their stand, but the woman who was making jellied bean curd in the station restaurant didn't come out. Something, I don't know what, hit her and her head plunged into a boiling pot.

---

*A heatable brick bed.

Song Baogen (switchman, Tangshan Train Station):

I nearly fell to my death from the top of a railway car in the earthquake.

I'm a switchman. I was on a special trailer car, right, it was a car full of bamboo, piled really high. I was sitting high atop the bamboo, swinging the light. The engine was already connected, so I gave the engineer the green light. He pulled the whistle and was just about to go when there was a tremendous groan, and the car started rocking violently. My first thought was, "Damn! We've lost a wheel!" I immediately gave the red light, but before the light had swung out, I fell. It was rocking like crazy! I was flung off the bamboo and rolled to the side of the car. "Done for!" Without a thought for anything else, I grabbed onto a bamboo bundling wire. Who cared that it was cutting my hands? If I didn't hold on I'd be thrown to my death.

Then there was more rocking; fortunately it wasn't from side to side, but from front to back. My hair was standing on end—if it had been from side to side, the car would have toppled for sure.

As soon as that rocking stopped, I slid down from the car. At that time, the headlight was still on, and up ahead, my God! The track was twisted as a cruller, winding like a giant snake. It was then that I realized that it was an earthquake, I heard somebody shout, "The ground's going to open up, quick, grab onto the track!" I threw myself to the ground, and clung onto a rail for dear life. Everybody was scared out of his wits. . . .

Zhang Keying (attendant, Tangshan Train Station):

I'll never forget the roar of the earthquake for as long as I live. It scared me half to death.

That day, I got up around two to go to work, selling platform tickets at the information counter. A little after three I heard somebody say it was going to rain. I hurried outside to move my new bicycle and the sky was dark red, like there was lightning somewhere in the distance. Out in front of the station, everybody was rushing to get in before the rain.

At that time, there were over two hundred people in the waiting room, meeting trains, or taking them, or waiting for the morning buses to start running after coming in on a night train. It was utter chaos.

I remember a young man and woman who wanted to buy platform tickets to meet the Beijing train. I told them, "There is no Beijing train now; come back after five." But they didn't leave; they just stood there waiting at the window. Who could have guessed that an earthquake would happen while they were waiting there?

Before the earthquake hit, I was talking to Chen on the other side of the window about getting a midnight snack; I wanted him to bring me back two steamed buns. But we hadn't even finished talking when boom! That sound! It scared everybody to death. I thought two high-speed engines had crashed head-on! Before there was even time to shout, all the lights in the waiting room went out. It was pitch-black. The building started rocking; the waiting room was a madhouse. People were yelling Mom, Dad, trampling each other, things were bumping into each other; there was every sound in the world. First there was the crash of chandeliers and ceiling fans falling on people's heads, and then grownups, children moaning and screaming. A few minutes later, there was a great rumbling, and the frame of the whole station building fell in. At least two hundred people smashed inside!

Fortunately, the door tilted over onto a small baggage check rack and I had slid inside, so I was relatively safe. Close by, I heard two cries: "Ai" "Mom—" I recognized them. It was the man and woman who had been waiting to buy platform tickets. But that was all they said, nothing more. . . .

Liu Xun (vice-head, Medical Affairs Office, Tangshan No. 1 Hospital):

On July 28 at 3:30 A.M., I was at home, sound asleep, when I heard someone knocking at the door, yelling, "Dr. Liu, Dr. Liu!" He sounded particularly anxious. I opened the door; it was Wang Kaizhi of the suburbs hospital. He said, "That patient we operated on together a few days ago is in terrible condition; can I trouble you to come and have a look at him? There's a car waiting."

It was really quite a coincidence to get a night call then. I got dressed, but no sooner were Wang and I out the door than the earthquake began! It felt like the earth was spinning, and it rocked so hard we couldn't stand up, let alone get away. And the ground was bumping; the soles of my feet felt like they were being electrocuted. A second later, the bricks and tiles of the house started flying, and it's strange, they were raining down upon me, but it didn't even hurt, I was so frightened. The roar of the earth was horrifying.

I had seen a documentary on a volcanic eruption once; the mouth of the volcano was like a cauldron of bubbling molten iron. But I felt that the earthquake at that moment was even more terrifying than standing at the mouth of a volcano would be. There was absolutely no way to control oneself; my heart was palpitating wildly. It was pitch-black everywhere, the air was filled with smoke, houses were collapsing.

After a moment, I was suddenly able to turn. Even I don't know how I did it. But I'd only run three or four steps before I realized something wasn't quite right beneath my feet, and I looked—I was on a rooftop!

Zhang Junqing (worker, Tangshan Power Plant):

At the time of the earthquake, I was working in the boiler control room. Suddenly the room began to sway and all the meter readings went wacko. All of a sudden, the switches on all the equipment went off automatically, and the whole plant was pitch-dark.

I fell on my butt. Chairs turned over, thermoses shattered, and the safety helmets, tool bags and flashlights hanging on the walls clattered to the floor of the control room. I grabbed a flashlight and immediately cut off the steam. No one knew what was going on, we just knew that a terrible accident had happened in the network and that we had to fix it fast.

I rushed out of the control room; the building groaned and bricks and tiles flew, but all I could see was that the fires in boilers 8 and 9 had been put out, and smoke was curling out from beneath them. We were all enveloped in billowing smoke and dust.

And then somebody yelled through the darkness, "It's an earthquake! But the duty chief has ordered no one to leave his post. If you do, you'll have to reckon with the law!"

Nerves in the whole plant were strained to the limit; rooms were collapsing; the ground was shaking. Alarm buzzers were sounding, and bells, and horns; everything was going off like crazy. But the most frightening sound of all was the exhaust escaping from the boilers. The safety valves had kicked open, and steam, at a hundred kilos of pressure per square centimetre, spewed forth with a piercing scream. Everyone was stupefied. It was louder than the hiss of steam from a thousand train engines; it was shrill enough to rip your heart out.

⚜ ⚜ ⚜

The Great China Earthquake began as Qian's graduation thesis, then became a magazine piece. Tao Taizhong, editor of the *PLA Art Magazine*, wanted Qian to write about the changes that had occurred in Tangshan since the earthquake. The proposed work was given the title "The Death and Revival of a City." Qian took on the assignment, but chose to focus on the death of the city because he said, he "believed that 'death' would carry deeper meanings than 'revival'."[5] He also said he wanted to write a book that portrayed the earthquake as an event having significance for the entire human race.[6] *Earthquake* was turned into a book at the request of the Liberation Army Literature and Art Publishing House.

Qian has told scholars that he was informed by several western authors, including Jack London and John Toland. But the book he said informed his writing the most is *Hiroshima*, by John Hersey. Qian and Hersey used similar techniques to tell the stories of two major disasters of the twentieth century. Both writers relied on eyewitness accounts and allowed the victims to tell their stories. Both conducted interviews at the disaster sites rather than relying solely on government reports, thus providing a human perspective. And both covered not just the disaster, but a longer span of time, enabling readers to follow the lives of the victims since the disaster. Both also attempted to draw a larger meaning from the events.

There are differences between the two books, such as the nature of the disasters (natural versus human), the life experiences of the victims, and the cultural contexts, as well as in the structures of the books. And there are major differences between the reporting methods (virtual first person versus interviews after the fact) and in point of view (constant versus variety).

Structurally, Qian borrowed from Hersey's approach in *Hiroshima* in that he found survivors to report what they were doing before the earthquake and how they survived. Like Hersey, Qian interwove the survivors' stories with stories he developed through other interviews, stories about people who did not survive and about the heroics of coal miners, other residents, and soldiers who participated in the rescue operation. Unlike Hersey's survivors, however, Qian's come from all walks of life. He quotes at least thirty eyewitnesses by name, nine of them at great length: a nurse, a peasant, a worker in a printing plant, a commune member, a cadre (government bureaucrat), a railroader, a train station attendant, the vice head of a medical affairs office, and a worker at the power plant. Even prisoners were interviewed.

Unlike Hersey, Qian was able to write from an inside view. Because Qian is Chinese, unlike Hersey he did not need translators. Qian was part of the rescue team that arrived in Tangshan shortly after the earthquake, so he had firsthand experiences that enabled him to ask questions. Furthermore, he returned to Tangshan years later and continued interviewing select survivors, which Hersey did not do in writing the original *Hiroshima*.

Qian did a tremendous amount of research, starting with his arrival in Tangshan, which enabled him to see firsthand the death and destruction. He left Tangshan with three full notebooks. He used the information he had acquired to his advantage when he returned nearly a decade later to interview a select number of survivors. Qian not only mentions the details of the earthquake, he draws on records to report the number and types of goods shipped to Tangshan between the earthquake and the end of the year, the daily number of people evacuated by air between July 30 and August 5, and their destinations.[7]

Given the decade lapse between the earthquake and publication of the book, Qian made good use of his time so he could read relevant documents and provide background on the survivors. Qian said it was difficult collecting source material right after the earthquake because some people did not want to talk for fear of political consequences.[8] The English language version of *Earthquake* also contains an article first published in *Beijing Review* a decade after the disaster. The article focuses on the redevelopment of Tangshan's economy and infrastructure, and tells how the handicapped survivors are doing in general. (Hersey also did a follow-up to *Hiroshima*, but because he published his book a year after the bomb was dropped, it would be thirty-nine years before another edition of the book was published with an afterword providing an update on the characters in the original.)

Qian's images are strong. "Only a few hours before Tangshan had been like a leaf fluttering in a wild wind. Now it was mangled and maimed, at its last gasp," he wrote.[9] Even the subhead on this section is graphic: "Dawn on the brink of death." When the soldiers arrived, he wrote: "Tangshan had already been groaning in pain for a whole day."[10] And when he wrote about his own arrival: "Ten years ago, when I, a callow youth [he was twenty-three], took the step from a tranquil life onto ruins piled high with corpses, I experienced the meaning of the word catastrophe firsthand."[11]

Despite his firsthand observation, Qian changes point of view. Sometimes he writes as a member of the epidemic prevention squad, sometimes as a reporter interviewing people years later. Other times, he tells the story from the point of view of the survivors. A very good example is a story that follows the excerpt included here, a story of five miners who spent fifteen days wandering through tunnels until they reached safety.

Qian closes the first section of *Earthquake* with this: "I want to leave a true account of a great natural disaster and its victims. I want to leave a historical fact upon which definitive comment has not yet been made. And I want to leave my own thoughts and doubts."[12] Qian investigated what happened and wrote the equivalent of a feature story. He provides facts not generally known and then comments on them. In seeking to understand larger issues, he also functioned as an investigative reporter. He interviewed officials in the Bureau of Seismology and gained access to records that revealed a horrible truth: political paralysis stymied those who might have predicted the disaster and saved lives.

The earthquake occurred at the tail-end of the Cultural Revolution, the cause of the political paralysis. The Cultural Revolution was in effect a purge of anyone Mao Zedong, the founding leader of modern China, didn't like. Students turned on teachers and other people suspected of being enemies. Many people were beaten to death; others committed suicide. It was a decade of lawlessness. Nobody knows how many victims there were. Estimates run from one million[13] to several hundred times that,[14] but a social historian told Harrison Salisbury that it did not matter how many there were. "The greatest damage," he said, "was to human character."[15]

Mao had sown the seeds for the Cultural Revolution in 1964 with the Four Cleansings movement (that is, a general reform of economics, ideology, politics, and organization).[16] The revolution became more serious in 1965 and was driven by Mao's wife, Jiang Qing, and the Central Cultural Revolution Group—which Mao nicknamed "the Gang of Four."[17] (Today in China, when some people talk about the Gang of Four, they hold up five fingers to indicate Mao's culpability.)

The Great China Earthquake appeared ten years after the Cultural Revolution had ended. Mao had been dead for nearly a decade and the Gang of Four was dead or dying. Thus, it was safe to publish a book that pointed a finger of blame at Mao and his cronies.

Consequently, *Earthquake,* as it tells what was not done correctly at Tangshan, is a political document as well as one writer's account of the suffering and the aftermath of a earthquake. (In that regard, it is similar to Gabriel García Márquez's *Story of a Shipwrecked Sailor.*) Qian's philosophy on reporting is to write the truth and study the past to know the present. He insists on making an honest attempt to uncover the factual truth. And one truth he learned was that if the Cultural Revolution had not cast so much fear into the lives and minds of many people, the people of Tangshan might have been spared. Why? Because seismic experts knew an earthquake of some magnitude was about to occur near Beijing, but feared what would happen to them if they predicted it and were wrong.

Qian presented several examples of the shortsightedness that impaired the Chinese during this period. The government even refused offers of aid from other nations, preferring to show that a Socialist country could take care of itself. In this regard, *Earthquake* is an analysis of the failure of Mao's leadership as well as a story of a natural disaster.[18]

In China, *Earthquake* is credited with starting the movement for the genre that the Chinese call "literary reportage" or "reportage literature."[19] Liu Binyan, who is considered the leading practitioner of Chinese literary reportage, has written that the Central Committee of the Communist Party, in fact the entire party and the nation, are re-evaluating history. He wrote that "reportage has been able to reflect life more fully and realistically than at any time before in the past 35 years," as *Earthquake* demonstrates. Liu wondered about the difference between reportage literature and journalism, noting that the distinction between them is not very clear. He also noted an "increasing indifference toward fiction, while the market for works about real people and real problems grows larger and larger."[20]

Hersey recognized why the market was growing. He noted that people read journalism because they want to learn about the larger world in which they have to exist. They expect their information to be trustworthy. Hersey also said that "in reporting, the writer's authority matters."[21] Reporting, Qian wrote, encompasses "a process of thinking" that "should be full of imagination and association." A reporter needs to bring events back to life. "Only if you make full use of your thinking process," he said, "can you discard imagination in writing and turn out a down-to-earth book."[22] *The Great China Earthquake* is such an achievement.[23]

ENDNOTES

1. Thomas Elton Moran, *True Stories: Contemporary Chinese Reportage and Its Ideology and Aesthetic.* Ph.D. diss., Cornell University, 1994. Biographical information comes from Moran and a personal letter to me from Qian, 26 August 1994, which was translated by my then–graduate student, Sun Tao.
2. Personal letter.
3. Shi Anbin, a graduate student at the Pennsylvania State University in 1998, recalled listening to the broadcast during a month-long period. Shi says that many works of writing were serialized and broadcast.
4. Personal letter.
5. Ibid.
6. Moran, *True Stories*, 321.
7. Ibid., 96.
8. Personal letter.
9. Qian Gang, *The Great China Earthquake*, trans. Nicola Ellis and Cathy Silber (Beijing: Foreign Languages Press, 1989), 39.
10. Ibid., 81.
11. Ibid., 12.
12. Qian, *Earthquake*, 14.
13. John King Fairbank, *China: A New History* (Cambridge, Mass.: Harvard University Press, Belknap Press, 1992), 402.
14. Harrison E. Salisbury, *The New Emperors: China in the Era of Mao and Deng* (New York: Avon, 1992), 249.
15. Ibid.
16. Salisbury, *The New Emperors*, 227.
17. Fairbank, *China*, passim.
18. Zhang Yingjin, "Narrative, Ideology, Subjectivity: Defining a Subversive Discourse in Chinese Reportage," in *Politics, Ideology, and Literary Discourse in Modern China*, ed. Liu Kang and Xiaobing Tang (Durham, N.C.: Duke University Press, 1993). Passim.
19. Wei Liming, "Reportage—China's New Journalism," *Beijing Review*, 17 and 23 October 1988. Passim.

20. Liu Binyan, "Is Reportage to Be Excluded from the Realm of Literature? The Function of Warning Bells," *Modern Chinese Writers*, ed. Helmut Martin and Jeffrey Kinkley (Armonk, N.Y.: M. E. Sharps, 1992), 131. Liu's essay is identified as having been originally published as "Reportage literature and social life" in *Contemporary Writers*, edited by the Chinese Department of the Central Broadcasting and Television University, Beijing, 1984.
21. John Hersey, "The Legend on the License," *Yale Review*, Autumn 1980, 20.
22. Personal letter.
23. Update on Qian Gang: In 1989, Qian Gang headed the news gathering department of the *Liberation Army Daily*, a newspaper in Beijing. That was the year of the Tiananmen Square incident in which an estimated three hundred to one thousand protesters—mostly students—were killed by PLA troops on government orders. Shortly after, Qian was forced out of the army because of his political attitudes. He had visited the protesting students in Tiananmen Square and sent protesting students in Shanghai a telegram of support. After a year "of twists and turns," as he put it, "I was finally accepted by the National Earthquake Bureau [State Bureau of Seismology]." He now writes for the *China Disaster Relief News*, which is a publication of the very bureau he criticized in *The Great China Earthquake*.

Index

About the Author

R. THOMAS BERNER is a professor of journalism and American studies at the Pennsylvania State University. He has written several textbooks on contemporary newspaper editing and writing, including an examination of how journalists use rhetorical devices in writing literary feature stories. Berner has worked on newspapers in Pennsylvania and has degrees in English and journalism. His essays on various contributors to the literature of journalism have appeared in *A Sourcebook of American Literary Journalism,* the *Dictionary of Literary Biography,* and *American Journalism.*